LIFE OF THE MARLOWS

The surviving Marlow brothers, George (left) and Charles, as they appeared in Rathmell's *Life of the Marlows.*

LIFE OF THE MARLOWS

A TRUE STORY OF FRONTIER LIFE OF EARLY DAYS

Revised by William Rathmell

Edited, with an Introduction and Annotations by Robert K. DeArment

Number 3 in the A. C. Greene Series

University of North Texas Press
Denton, Texas

10 9 8 7 6 5 4 3

Permissions:
University of North Texas Press
P.O. Box 311336
Denton, TX 76203-1336

The paper used in this book meets the minimum requirements of the American National Standard for Permanence of Paper for Printed Library Materials, z39.48.1984. Binding materials have been chosen for durability.

Library of Congress Cataloging-in-Publication Data

Rathmell, William, 1862-1943.
Life of the Marlows : a true story of frontier life of early days / revised by William Rathmell ; edited, with an introduction and annotations by Robert K. DeArment.
p. cm. — (A.C. Greene series ; no. 3)
Includes bibliographical references and index.
ISBN-10: 1-57441-179-9 (cloth : alk. paper)
ISBN-13: 978-1-57441-179-9 (cloth : alk. paper)
ISBN-10: 1-57441-253-1 (pbk. : alk. paper)
ISBN-13: 978-1-57441-253-6 (pbk. : alk. paper)
1. Marlow family. 2. Murder—Texas—Young County—History—19th century. 3. Frontier and pioneer life—Texas—Young County. 4. Young County (Tex.)—History. I. DeArment, Robert K., 1925- II. Title. III. Series.
F392.Y7R38 2004
976.4'545061'0922—dc22

2004010512

Life of the Marlows is Number 3 in the A. C. Greene Series.

The photo on the cover is of the five Marlow brothers on horseback, circa 1887. Left to right: George, Boone, Alfred, Llewellyn, Charles. Photo from the personal collection of the author.

Design by Angela Schmitt

CONTENTS

Dramatis Personae

Marlow Family:

Wilburn Williamson, Sr., father of the boys.
Martha Jane Keaton, mother of the boys.
The fighting brothers:
Alfred "Alf."
Boone.
Charles "Charley."
George H.
Llewellyn "Ep," "Ellie."
Wilburn Wiliamson, Jr. "Willie," another brother.
Charlotte Murphy, a sister.
Elizabeth "Eliza," Gilmore, a sister.
Nancy Jane "Nannie" Murphy, a sister.
Emma Coppenbarger, wife of Charley Marlow.
Lillian May "Lilly" Berry, wife of George Marlow.
Venie Davis, wife of Alfred Marlow.
Anna Jane (Mrs. C. V. Hallenbeck), George's daughter.

Marlow brothers supporters:

Robert Frederick Arnold, attorney.
William Shelby Delaney, attorney.
Oscar G. Denson.
James Denty.
Bill Gilmore.
Jim Gilmore.
John Gilmore.
Frank Herron.
Jerome Claiborne Kearby, attorney.
Marion L. Lasater.
Bill Ribble.

Mob Members in Dry Creek Fight:
David "Dink" Allen.
William R. Benedict.
Lewis Pinkney "Pink" Brooks.
Dick Cook.
Columbus Frank Harmonson.
Robert Hill.
Will Hollis.
Robert Holman.
Clinton Rutherford.
Bruce Wheeler.
Verner Wilkinson.
Jack Wilkins.
William "Bee" Williams.

Municipal Officers:
J. Squire Starrett, Graham justice of the peace.
Samuel V. Waggoner, Graham constable, member of Dry Creek mob.

County Law Officers:
J. H. Bradley, sheriff, Ouray County, Colorado.
William T. "Doc" Burns, sheriff Las Animas County, Colorado.
Thomas B. Collier, Young County deputy sheriff, became sheriff with murder of Wallace.
Maurice Corbett, sheriff, Ouray County, Colorado.
Samuel H. Criswell, Young County deputy sheriff, member of Dry Creek mob.
G. T. Douglas, sheriff, Wilbarger County, Texas.
John J. Douglass, sheriff, Stephens County, Texas.
Arthur Thomas Gay, Young County clerk.
John Y. Leavell, Young County deputy sheriff, member of Dry Creek mob.
Eugene Logan, Young County jail guard, member of Dry Creek mob.
Phlete A. Martin, Young County jail guard, member of Dry Creek mob.

George W. Moore, sheriff, Jack County, Texas.
Cyrus Wells "Doc" Shores, sheriff, Gunnison County, Colorado.
Marion DeKalb Wallace, sheriff, Young County, killed by Boone Marlow.
Marion A. "Little Marion" Wallace, nephew of M. D. Wallace, later sheriff, Young County.

State Law Officers:
J. M. Britton, Texas Ranger.
William Jesse McDonald, captain, Texas Rangers.

Federal Law Officers:
William L. Crawford, special U. S. prosecutor.
Augustus Hill Garland, United States attorney general.
Francis Washington Girand, clerk of federal court at Graham.
John Barton Girand, deputy U. S. marshal.
John Goodman, deputy U. S. marshal.
Lon Burrison, deputy U. S. marshal.
Ben F. Cabell, deputy U. S. marshal.
William Lewis Cabell, U. S. marshal for Northern District of Texas.
H. H. Dickey, deputy U. S. marshal.
Edward W. Johnson, deputy U. S. marshal, the villain of the piece in Rathmell's account.
George A. Knight, U. S. marshal for Northern District of Texas.
Andrew Phelps McCormick, federal court judge.
Eugene Marshall, U. S. attorney.
John Miller, deputy U. S. marshal.
W. H. Morton, deputy U. S. marshal.

Bounty Hunters:
Jim Beavers
John Derrickson.

Doctors:
W. R. Dunham.
R. N. Price.

Accused Outlaws:
Pete Berry.
"Curley Charley," Kansas tough.
William D. Burkhart, Marlow cellmate, in Dry Creek fight.
William Harbolt, Marlow cellmate.
Louis Clift, Marlow cellmate, in Dry Creek fight.
Marion Cummings.
Bill Murphy.
John Frank Spears, Marlow cellmate.

Indians:
Bar-Sin-da-Bar, Caddo.
Black Crow, Comanche.
Sun Boy (Sunday Boy), Kiowa chieftain.
Washington, Caddo.

Illustrations

All photos are from the personal collection of Robert K. DeArment.

Maps were prepared by Rosemary DeArment Walter.

Frontispiece: George and Charles Marlow as they appeared in *Life of the Marlows* by William Rathmell

Appearing after page 86:

Editor's Introduction

The story of the five Marlow brothers and their tribulations in late nineteenth century Texas is the stuff of Old West legend. Violent, full of intrigue, with characters of amazing heroism and deplorable cowardice, it was first related in a little book published in 1892, shortly after the events it described. It told how Boone, the most reckless of the brothers, shot and killed a popular sheriff and escaped, only to be murdered by bounty hunters later; how the other four brothers, arrested and jailed, made a daring break from confinement and were recaptured; how, while in their cells, they fought off a lynch mob; how, shackled together, they were placed on wagons by officers late at night and started for another town, but were ambushed by angry citizens and in the resulting battle two of the brothers were killed, the other two severely wounded, and several citizens died; how the surviving brothers were eventually exonerated, but members of the mob that had attacked them were prosecuted in cases that went all the way to the United States Supreme Court.

Ramon F. Adams, Texas bibliophile, writer and collector, after examining nearly 3,000 books dealing with Western outlaws, lawmen and gunfighters, included *Life of the Marlows, As Related by Themselves,* in his compilation of the 150 most important works in this field. A book's importance, he said, was determined by the historical significance of the work or its rarity. *Life of the Marlows* rated highly in both respects.[1]

The edition, which was published in 1892 at Ouray, Colorado, by "Plaindealer Print, Kelly & Hulanski, Publishers," in pictorial wrappers

[1] Adams, *Adams One-Fifty,* 10.

with illustrations, was rated by Adams as "exceedingly rare." In about 1931, "Ouray Herald Print, W. S. Olexa, publisher, Ouray, Colorado" brought out a new edition with additions and revisions. The title page indicated that it had been revised by William Rathmell. Adjudged as "quite scarce" by Adams,[2] it is this edition that is here presented.

As the title suggests, the surviving Marlow brothers related their story, but it was William Rathmell, a man of many talents, who authored both volumes.[3] Arriving in Colorado as a young man in 1880, Rathmell prospected unsuccessfully and worked for day wages on farms and in the mines and sawmills of the Western Slope. He became a teacher and in 1886 was elected Ouray County judge, an office he held only two terms, but the title "Judge" stuck with him the rest of his life. He engaged in a successful abstract business until his death at the age of eighty.[4]

The story of the Marlows was evidently his only literary effort, but we are indebted to him and to surviving brothers George and Charley Marlow for making that story known. Without the publication of *Life of the Marlows,* the dramatic and exciting events that shook Young County, Texas, in the winter of 1888–89 and the bitter legal battle that followed might have been forgotten and lost in the dust of history.

Although neither edition of the Marlow book enjoyed great circulation or readership, later writers have drawn on the Rathmell work to retell the story and keep alive the memory of the fighting brothers. The first presentation of the Marlow saga for a national audience appeared while the court wars were still being fought and was headlined in the June 1891 edition of *The National Police Gazette:*

HUNTED IN THE LAW'S NAME,
FOUR MEN IN SHACKLES AGAINST A HUNDRED,
BORDER LIFE IN TEXAS,
THE FAMOUS MARLOW MOB CASE.

[2] Ibid., 55.

[3] "Wm. Rathmell was employed by the Marlow family to write a history of their doings," wrote Rathmell's daughter-in-law (*Of Record and Reminiscence,* 77). It has been suggested that Mattie Marlow, a niece of the surviving brothers, authored the original manuscript depicting the Marlow story, and that Rathmell wrote only the later edition (Ledbetter, *Ordeal,* 175). Most of the two books are identical, however, and it appears from the style that the same person authored both. Rathmell may well have had the benefit of a manuscript composed by Mattie Marlow from which he worked.

[4] Rathmell, *Of Record and Reminiscence,* 41–44.

The article is quoted in its entirety in this volume. Although no author is credited, certain familiar literary mannerisms and turns of phrase lead to the suspicion that William Rathmell wrote this account also.

The first edition of *Life of the Marlows* appeared the following year to its limited readership and for the next three decades no one stirred up the embers of the fading Marlow saga. Then, in the mid-1920s, Charles A. Siringo, former Texas cowboy, long-time Pinkerton detective and recurrent autobiographer, became interested in the Marlows. Siringo was gathering material for a manuscript entitled "Bad Man Cowboys of the West," and wanted to include the Marlow story. He contacted C. W. "Doc" Shores, a friend of the surviving Marlow brothers and a Colorado lawman with whom Siringo had worked during his years with the Pinkertons. From Shores he learned, apparently for the first time, of the 1892 book.[5] Siringo obtained a copy and also located Charley Marlow with whom he corresponded.[6] Following the Rathmell book closely, he added the story of the Marlows to his "Bad Man Cowboys" manuscript. He was careful to point out, however, that the brothers did not belong in the "bad man cowboys class" but in the "daredevil class."[7]

Siringo's manuscript was never published as planned, but when the latest rewrite of his own experiences, *Riata and Spurs,* ran into a threatened lawsuit by Pinkerton's National Detective Agency in 1927, his publisher hastily withdrew the second half of the book dealing with the author's detective years and substituted material from the "Bad Man Cowboys" manuscript. In this expurgated edition of *Riata and Spurs,* the Marlow tale, drawn almost entirely from the 1892 *Life*, was told again.[8]

William MacLeod Raine, a prolific writer of Western fiction, picked up on the *Life* account, adding details culled from contemporary newspapers and information received from George Marlow, whom he had met twenty years before,[9] to write a magazine article entitled "Texas

[5] Siringo to Lamborn, April 12, 1924. Lamborn was a lifelong collector of stories and information on criminals, particularly of the frontier West.

[6] Letter, Siringo to Lamborn, February 28, 1925.

[7] Siringo, *Riata and Spurs,* 206.

[8] Ibid., 206–13. Siringo's problems with the Pinkerton Agency over publication of *Riata and Spurs* are recounted in *Siringo,* by Ben E. Pingenot, 127–33.

[9] George Marlow, "a tanned, weather-beaten little Westerner with faded blue eyes and long drooping mustache," was driving a stagecoach when Raine met him. "Certainly this gentle, apologetic little fellow in dusty jeans and pinched-in Stetson did not look the part of hero (or villain if you take that point of view) of a drama so stark and bloody. But I remembered that the

as Was" in 1928. The next year he incorporated the story as a chapter in his book *Famous Sheriffs and Western Outlaws,* an effort at a factual depiction of some of the dramatic events of the Old West, and included it again in *Cattle,* a collaborative effort with Will C. Barnes in 1930.[10]

Perhaps prompted by the renewed interest in the Marlow story by the appearance of these books, William Rathmell republished *Life of the Marlows* about this time, adding new material in the latter pages to the history of George and Charley after 1892.[11]

In 1943 Glenn Shirley drew on the book for a Western dime novel story he called "Hell Riders of the Brazos." A decade later he would include the story as a chapter in his first book, *Toughest of Them All.*

Southwestern historian C. L. Sonnichsen in 1951 published his *I'll Die Before I'll Run,* a recounting of a number of bloody Texas feuds, and included the Marlow story, supplementing the basic Rathmell account with details gleaned from old newspapers and discussions with Young County old-timers. He also had the benefit of information received from Mrs. C. V. Hallenbeck of Grand Junction, Colorado, a daughter of George Marlow.[12]

In 1956 Carrie J. Crouch, a local historian, published *A History of Young County,* which necessarily contained an account of the Marlow tragedy, unquestionably the most dramatic event to take place there. To tell the story, she drew on the fading memories of Young County old-timers, but found this a difficult task, as the issue of the Marlows was still a very touchy topic in the region. As early as 1927 Mrs. Crouch had confided in a letter: "The story of the Marlow boys is one of the

---

fighting men of the old West rarely filled the eye satisfactorily" (Raine, *Famous Sheriffs and Western Outlaws,* 24–25).

[10] In 1953 Raine would reprise the story again in "The Fighting Marlows" for the *Empire Magazine* of the *Denver Post.*

[11] The book published by W. S. Olexa did not carry a date. In 1967 Ruth Rathmell, daughter-in-law of the author, in response to an inquiry from Mrs. Alys Freeze of the Western History Department, Denver Public Library, wrote that she did not know and could not determine exactly when the book was published. "Mr. Olexa bought a house in Ouray in Dec. of 1928 and sold it in January of 1933," she said, "so it had to be published during the four years."

[12] In his "Sources and Notes" to this 1951 edition published by Harper & Brothers, Sonnichsen, forgetting *Life of the Marlows,* which he had obviously used, stated that Raine's account was the only previous appearance in print of the Marlow feud (page 285). When Adams pointed out this oversight to him, Sonnichsen corrected the error in a later expanded edition published by Devin-Adair Company in 1962 (Adams, *Six-Guns and Saddle Leather,* 598). Strangely, both writers completely ignored the contribution of Charlie Siringo.

unpleasant bits of our county history, and still a very delicate subject. . . . Several of the mob are well respected citizens now, but of course cannot be approached, for any respectable person is ashamed [of] having been a member of such a mob."[13]

Rehashes of these previously published Marlow accounts appeared over the years with little or no new information added. When interest in the Old West peaked in the late 1950s and '60s and "westerns" dominated the television screen, the Marlow tale was told and retold in the proliferating "true Western" magazines.[14] Colorado historian Robert L. Brown was so struck by the drama of the Marlow story that he included it in detail in his 1965 book, *An Empire of Silver: A History of the San Juan Silver Rush,* although its only connection to the San Juan Mountain country was the residence there of the two surviving Marlows in their later years.

That year elements of the Marlow story were used in a motion picture, *The Sons of Katie Elder,* starring John Wayne and Dean Martin. About 1953 screenwriter William H. Wright had picked up a copy of *Life of the Marlows* in a Los Angeles bookstore and thought it would make the basis for a good western. He contacted members of the Marlow family and paid them $1,000 each for permission to turn the tale into a screenplay. In a typical Hollywood makeover, the movie that was produced twelve years later bore little resemblance to the historical record other than the inclusion of a battle at a river crossing between a mob and four brothers chained together. Wright, Allan Weiss and Harry Essex were credited with the screenplay, said to be based on a story by Talbot Jennings.[15]

The historical account was resurrected again in 1986 in yet another Western magazine article[16] and as a lengthy footnote in *Colorado*

[13] Crouch to Lamborn, October 31, 1927. With her letter, Mrs. Crouch included a greatly flawed sketch of the Marlow troubles. She had corrected most of these errors by the time she published her history twenty-one years later.

[14] Hartley, "The Men Who Wouldn't Be Lynched," appeared in 1959; Taylor, "Story of the Marlow Boys," in 1962; Patten, "He Killed a Heap of Men" in 1966.

[15] *Montrose Daily Press,* September 15, 1965. Fictional names were used in the film, including "Katie Elder," the mother of the boys. Curiously, this name was borrowed from an historical figure, "Kate Elder" having been one of the names used by Mary Katherine Horony, consort of the celebrated western gunman, "Doc" Holliday, during her days as a sporting girl (Bork and Boyer, "The O.K. Corral Fight at Tombstone: A Footnote to Kate Elder," 65–84). Of course, neither she nor Holliday was historically connected to the Marlows.

[16] Stanley, "A Desperate Escape."

Gunsmoke: True Stories of Outlaws and Lawmen on the Colorado Frontier, by Colorado writer Kenneth Jessen. Neither author enhanced the familiar narrative by drawing on an article appearing six years earlier that, for the first time since Rathmell's original book in 1892, attacked the favorable representation of the Marlow brothers.

The article, entitled "Deputy Marshal Johnson Breaks a Long Silence," had been written in 1932–33, probably in response to the reappearance of *Life of the Marlows* and the national success of the Siringo and Raine publications. It was authored by Ted Johnson, son of Deputy U. S. Marshal Edward W. Johnson, a central figure in the Marlow story, and a man who had been painted as a villain in the Rathmell account and those that followed. Ted Johnson, who wrote the piece with the obvious intention of vindicating his father, whom he saw as a brave man unjustly condemned, was about fifteen years old and living in Graham when the Marlow drama unfolded. Some of the events he described from personal memory and others he reported as told to him by his father. Ted Johnson's grandson, Dennis Glasgow, submitted the unedited article to *True West* magazine in 1979, remarking that he thought it historically significant and "it is the only account of the incident from a point of view other than the Marlows'."[17] The article provided some badly needed balance to the Marlow saga and has been used extensively in the notes to this edition as a counterweight to the open bias of the Rathmell account.

For the first time since the second publication of Rathmell's *Life,* an author came out with a book devoted to the Marlow story in 1991. Barbara A. Neal Ledbetter, a resident of Graham, Texas, the scene of the Marlow tragedy, researched the story for many years and in 1991 privately published the results of her study. Entitled *Marlow Brothers Ordeal 1882–1892: 138 Days of Hell in Graham on the Texas Frontier,* this volume benefits from Mrs. Ledbetter's exhaustive research and previously unpublished photographs and information obtained from descendents of the Marlow brothers, but makes no pretense of objectivity as it follows the Rathmell lead in whitewashing the brothers and castigating their enemies.

[17] Johnson, "Deputy Marshal Johnson Breaks a Long Silence," 6.

In 1994, fifty-one years after his original recounting of the brothers' story for a pulp magazine, Glenn Shirley, that indefatigable chronicler of violence on the Texas and Oklahoma frontier, retold the Marlow story again in a volume entitled *The Fighting Marlows, Men Who Wouldn't Be Lynched*. Relying to a great extent on Rathmell's seminal *Life*, the book presented the Marlow brothers as heroes and ignored or minimized their anti-social and at times criminal behavior.

In 2001 novelist Alan C. Huffines related the Marlow saga in fictional form in his *A Pilgrim Shadow*. In his acknowledgments and suggestions for further reading he lists the Ledbetter and Shirley books and, of course, William Rathmell's seminal work, *Life of the Marlows*.

Ramon Adams, who throughout his life was highly critical of books on Western outlaws and lawmen in which he detected careless or deliberate misrepresentation and historical distortion, devoted two of his own volumes to exposing these factual errors.[18] In *Burs Under the Saddle* (1964) he chastised Carroll C. Holloway for referring to the Marlows as "Texas outlaws" in his 1951 book *Texas Gun Lore*. Adams insisted that the brothers "were not outlaws in the true sense of the word, only victims of some shady frame-ups."[19] And in *More Burs Under the Saddle* (1979), he took to task E. Buford Morgan, author of *The Wichita Mountains* (1973) for the same offense, asserting that Morgan was "also mistaken in calling the Marlow brothers outlaws. They were victims of false charges."[20] It would seem that Mr. Adams was unduly influenced by the Rathmell account and his admiration for the undisputed bravery of the Marlows overcame his good judgment. One of the brothers shot and killed two men on separate occasions and fled, aided and abetted by family members, rather than face a court. Officers in two states and a territory, armed with felony arrest warrants for livestock theft, hunted the Marlows. The constant peregrination of the brothers could not be attributed entirely to wanderlust passed down from the gypsy-like lifestyle of their father. If an outlaw is defined as

[18] Adams himself made a serious blunder when he wrote: "Of the five brothers only the two authors of [*Life of the Marlows*] escaped the ambush which killed the other three" (*Adams One-Fifty*, 55). Actually, two brothers died in that ambush, the third was killed later, miles away. It was the kind of error for which the historical perfectionist had castigated many another writer.

[19] Adams, *Burs Under the Saddle*, 256.

[20] Adams, *More Burs Under the Saddle*, 106.

someone who disregards and defies the law, then the Marlows were indeed outlaws.[21]

Aside from its undoubted historical significance and attraction for the collector of rare books, *Life of the Marlows* as written by William Rathmell is a classic example of why editors are indispensable in the publishing business. Peppered with punctuation, grammatical, and spelling errors, most of which I have corrected in this edition, the book is poorly constructed and at times repetitious. It is replete with overblown descriptive passages laced with strained alliterative phrases, i.e. "spread out like a sheet of shimmering silver,"[22] and "wrong and riot ran rampant."[23] Saccharine nineteenth-century romanticism ("the depths of her dark liquid eyes")[24] is cheek by jowl with unabashed nineteenth-century bigotry ("It will not do to trust a Mexican.").[25]

But despite its weaknesses, the book still remains the primary source for the remarkable saga of the Marlow brothers, extraordinary men in an extraordinary time.

Robert K. DeArment
Sylvania, Ohio

[21] Even the son of the deputy U. S. marshal whose arrest of the brothers led to the violence and controversy of the Marlow drama hesitated to call them outlaws. "Whether the Marlow brothers were outlaws I am not going to say," wrote Ted Johnson, "[but] twelve federal grand jurors and about fifteen witnesses said they were" ("Deputy Marshal Johnson Breaks a Long Silence, 6-7).

[22] Page 17.

[23] Page 12.

[24] Page 13.

[25] Page 17.

Chapter 1

PIONEER DAYS—AN INDIAN SCARE

In Nashville, Tennessee, in 1822, there lived in happiness and comparative prosperity, a very youthful married couple, the husband being scarce eighteen years of age. This was the handsome and ever good-natured Williamson Marlow Sr. and his child wife.[1]

After the birth of their first child[2] they moved to Missouri, and a few years later, when three little pledges of love had gathered about the family fireside, the grim King of Terrors came in the still hours of the night and robbed that peaceful little home of its dearest treasure—a mother's love and watchful care. A tiny spark of humanity was placed in the young widower's arms, making four little ones[3] for the grief-stricken Williamson to be both father and mother to, and on that memorable day life lost for him its charm. Grief for the loss of a dutiful wife and loving mother knocked at his heart with a knell and he became for a time a wanderer, a brother and sister caring for the children. But time heals all wounds, so after the keen edge of his sorrow had worn

[1] The father's name is given variously as Wilson Williamson and Wilburn Williamson in *Marlow Brothers Ordeal* and his year of birth as 1800 (Ledbetter, 1). He is listed in the 1850 U.S. Census records taken at St. Clair County, Missouri, as Wilson W. Marlow, born in Tennessee in 1816. The name appears as W. W. Marlow with the same place and date of birth in the 1860 U. S. census taken at Carthage, Missouri.

[2] The firstborn, a daughter, was named Acenthy (Ledbetter, *Ordeal*, 1). The U.S. census records identify her only as A. L., born in Tennessee in 1835 (1850 U. S. Census).

[3] The four children born to Marlow's first wife were Acenthy L. in 1835, James Robert in 1837, Pleasant M. in 1843, and Bithel A. in 1845 (Ibid.)

away to some extent and it became possible to apply himself to any kind of work he took up the study of human ills and their cures.[4]

About two years later, while on his way across the hills and prairies between Pike county and Jefferson City, on the green banks of a little stream that gurgled noisily on its hurried way towards the great Missouri, he met pretty little Martha and sturdy John Keton, who were preparing fish for their evening repast. It was a handsome picture. The red summer sun sinking to rest in its bed of crimson just beyond the tree tops, the bright foliage bending over the busy little brook, the shrilling of the insects in the grass, and the chirp of the birds among the tall sumac bushes, the honest face of the lad who was helping his sister prepare the supper, and the beautiful little maid herself, all formed an entrancing panorama, pleasing alike to the sight and senses. No wonder, then, that he tarried here to rest, and no wonder, either, that the sweet smile and winning ways of the gentle Martha were the cause of prolonging his stay from hours to days and days to weeks. 'Twas the same old story that is forever new—you know how it always ends. In a short time the once gay Williamson, though now the grave and dignified Dr. Marlow, took pretty Martha Keton for a wife, and hand in hand they started down life's pathway. This second child-wife was a direct descendent of that famous man and honest pioneer, Daniel Boone.[5]

After a number of peaceful and prosperous years had passed, during which two little daughters were sent by a kind providence to brighten their home,[6] the great gold excitement of '49 attracted the Doctor's attention to California, and, like thousands of others, he wended his way to that land where the shining treasure lies hidden within the rugged mountains and fortunes were made and lost in a day. It was during these

[4] There is no mention of an established school attended by Williamson Marlow for his medical education. Like many other self-proclaimed "doctors" on the frontier, he probably had little or no formal education in medicine. The narrative suggests that he was much more inclined to a life of peregrination and adventure than to a commitment to healing.

[5] According to the U.S. census records (1860, 1900), Martha Jane was born in Missouri in May 1826. Family records indicate she was one of the nine children of William Edmund Keaton and Nancy D. (Cole) Keaton and was born in 1823 (Ledbetter, *Ordeal*, 1).

[6] Barbara Ledbetter, relying on information in the Marlow family Bible, records that Nancy Jane was born February 29, 1845, and Charlotte was born four years to the day later, on February 29, 1849. However, these dates cannot be accurate as 1845 and 1849 were not leap years and contained no February 29 (Ledbetter, *Ordeal*, 1, 34). Census records show the birth of Nancy J. in 1847 and Charlotte in 1849 (1860 U.S. Census).

trying times that Martha showed her sterling worth, and for two years although yet in her teens she filled the place of father and mother to six little children, four of them not her own. The mad rush for the Golden Gate country continued, and many men left their families and spent their last dollar to get there only to return broken financially and in health. Others, more fortunate, came home with bright hopes and well-filled purses, and Dr. Marlow was among the latter, for while scores and hundreds around him failed he succeeded beyond his brightest hopes.

Shortly after Dr. Marlow's return his oldest child, a daughter, was married, and about the same time his first son, James Robert, in his fourteenth year, set out to view the wonders of the Pacific coast. The following spring the family moved to Sherman, Texas, where they resided in a log cabin that stood where now the finest business block of that city is erected.[7] But the memory of old Missouri was bright in the mind of Martha, and accordingly back they went, and two months after again arriving there Williamson Marlow, Jr., was born.[8] Years of domestic tranquility passed, and another daughter and another son arrived to cheer the home,[9] and shortly after the birth of George they again made their way to Texas and back. Then came the birth of Charles, Alfred and Boone[10] and an emigration to the great mountains of Colorado.

It was the balmy season of spring when a train of one hundred wagons set out to cross the plains of Kansas and penetrate the gulches, glens and valleys of Colorado and did space and time permit, a description of the vicissitudes of the journey would be given. Their first Indian scare happened one lovely evening after supper. The wagons had been corraled,

[7] Sherman was named seat of Grayson County when that county was established in 1846. Originally located a few miles west of its present site, it was moved in 1848 due to a scarcity of wood and water (Tyler, *New Handbook of Texas,* 5:1021–22). The Marlows evidently first came to this section about three years later. Grayson was one of the northern tier of counties lying just south of the Red River, which divided Texas from the Indian Territory to the north. It would be to Grayson, its neighboring Texas counties, and the wild country to the north in the Chickasaw Nation that in the coming years the Marlows would return from their periodic wanderings and become well known.

[8] Wilburn Williamson Marlow, Jr., was born July 4, 1852 (Ledbetter, *Ordeal*, 2).

[9] Daughter Elizabeth, called "Eliza," was born May 27, 1854, and George H. on August 11, 1855 (Ibid.; 1860 U.S. Census).

[10] Again relying on family information, Ledbetter writes that Charles was born October 17, 1857, Alfred L. on June 1, 1862, and Boone on June 20, 1864. She says that Anthony, another son, not mentioned by Rathmell, was born January 23, 1860 (Ledbetter, *Ordeal*, 2–3). The 1900 U. S. Census records show the birth of Charles in November 1859. His gravestone, pictured in *Marlow Brothers Ordeal*, shows an 1860 date of birth.

the evening meal cooked over the blazing camp fires and devoured with the keen relish of hardy pioneers, and then as first one and then another of the men knocked the ashes out of their pipes and settled themselves comfortably around the cheerful fires, the alarm of Indians was noised through the camp. Instantly everyone was alert for they knew what that meant. The women and children huddled together with fear depicted upon their blanched faces, and every man reached for his gun. Only those who have experienced such a situation can appreciate its horrors. Hist! What is that? Indians, sure, crossing the creek above and below. Another moment and they will be in their midst, and with stern looks and set teeth each man stood ready to die if need be for his wife and little ones that crouched in the wagons, expecting the horrible war whoop every second. The determined look upon their faces boded no good for the unlucky redskin that fell into their hands, One, two, three and not there yet—what did it mean? Were they to be taken by surprise? The seconds ticked into minutes and the minutes into an hour and still that never ceasing splash, splash, in the creek below was continued. Were all the Indians in North America crossing there to-night? Heavens! Thc strain of this suspense can be borne no longer. Someone must reconnoitre. Who will volunteer? All felt that it meant death to venture outside the corral, yet the danger must be met. One man came forward into the firelight, rifle in hand, and while the night breezes lift the dark hair from the white forehead the clear voice of Dr. Marlow speaks from the height that towers over other men, and says: "My friends, I will make this investigation." At the time a slight boyish form arising by the grave doctor's side announces an intention of going, too. It was young Williamson, and as his father nodded his assent the two turned and disappeared in the darkness among the trees that fringe the banks of the little stream.

All held their breath in the silence of dread, while the brave doctor and his son moved cautiously toward the sound in the waters of the creek. After crawling along stealthily for a few hundred yards they arose to a standing position where they commanded a view of the water below. A smile flitted across the doctor's face, and a merry ripple of laughter came from Willie, for there in plain sight was the cause of all their anxiety.

The supposed Indians proved to be a band of beavers, very busily engaged in erecting their mansions.

After enjoying the sight for a few minutes they made their way back to camp, and among the men, who stood in amazement to see them return with whole scalps. Willie crept slyly under his blanket to keep from being questioned, while the doctor proceeded very unconcernedly to fill and light his pipe. Then he told them the cause of all the scare, a big laugh went up as they all stacked their arms and once more gathered around the camp fire. The darkness deepened, the fires flickered low, and silence settled down over the camp once more as each one prepared for rest and sleep, silently breathing a prayer of thankfulness that the bloodthirsty Indians had turned out to be nothing more formidable than a band of busy little beavers.

Chapter II

ADVENTURES IN THE SOUTHWEST—A LOVE AFFAIR

The Marlow family located near Denver in 1865, and at that place the two oldest daughters of Martha, Nannie and Charlotte, were married to two worthy brothers, John and William Murphy. The girls were young to leave a mother's care, being about 13 and 17,[1] but love triumphed over reason, as usual, and the weddings took place on the same day, amid the ringing of bells, feasting, and much enjoyment.

Next year found Dr. Marlow and his family again back in Missouri, the spirit of travel and a disposition to see the world preventing him from being contented more than a year or two in one place, and near Carthage, on the 14th of October, the youngest of the five brothers, who have in late years become so famous for dangers overcome and adventures encountered, was born.[2]

About this time, P. M. Marlow and Bithel came in from Texas to visit their father for the first time in a number of years. They had been

[1] Nancy was twenty years old and Charlotte was sixteen in 1865, according to the birth dates provided by the family.

[2] Born on October 14, 1866, the youngest brother was named Llewellyn, sometimes spelled "Lewellyn" (Ledbetter, *Ordeal*, 3). The baby of the family, he was called "Ellie," "Epp," "Ep," and "Eph." Ted Johnson recalled that he was generally known as "Lep" (Johnson, "Deputy Marshal Johnson," 7). Brothers Pleasant and Bithel both served in the Confederate Army, enlisting on the same day. After the war, they worked cattle in Texas and drove herds to Kansas. Pleasant Monroe Marlow married Mary Caroline "Carrie" Whitaker on December 26, 1865, in Red River County, Texas. He died in 1878 at the age of thirty-six. Bithel Alexander Marlow married Mary Susan Howe in Cooper Couny, Missouri, on October 14, 1868. Just three weeks before the birth of his last child, he died at the age of thirty-three on Christmas Day, 1876 (Vicki Walberg to RKD, January 14, 15, 2004).

separated during the war, as the former was in the Confederate service, and while conveying important documents from one post to another was taken prisoner and confined in a Northern prison. Both were married, the former to a daughter of J. W. Whiteaker [*sic*], a wealthy planter of Austin, Texas, and the latter to a Miss Howe, of Booneville, Missouri. When the elder son returned to his far away Texas home, Williamson, Jr., accompanied him,[3] and shortly after Dr. Marlow himself journeyed thither to visit and see the country. Father and son then purchased a large herd of cattle and drove them to a northern market and after selling off the stock and getting a supply of mules, wagons and provisions the entire family returned to the Lone Star State. A few years later both P. M. and Bithel died and were laid to rest near their Texas homes. These two, as was James, were the sons of Dr. Marlow's first wife.

Not long after this Eliza, the fourth and only single daughter, was married to a Gainesville[4] gentleman named Gilmore, and the doctor, with the balance of the family, removed to the Indian Territory where he settled down to the practice of his profession.

This section of the country was wild and lawless in those days, and dangers beset the few inhabitants on every hand. Wild and hostile bands of Indians made life full of constant terror, outlaws and gangs of desperate men roamed the country at will, and dark deeds that will never be told were daily and hourly committed. Disputes were more often settled with the ever-ready six-shooter than by process of law, and crime and wrong-doing ran riot through the land.

One morning in the next July, while four of the Marlows and two Poe boys, neighbors, were plowing corn, a clear ringing pistol shot was heard close by, followed by five more in quick succession, and while the smaller boys climbed upon the horses and plowbeams in an endeavor to look out over the towering corn, the older ones hastened toward the spot where the tiny puffs of smoke slowly ascended on the summer air. What was it? Only a misunderstanding between a couple of men over a

[3] The young son, Anthony, also reportedly was taken to Texas with Willie (Ledbetter, *Ordeal*, 3). Nothing further is heard of young Anthony, and he presumably died in childhood.

[4] Eliza Louisa Marlow married R. H. "Raz" Gilmore. Family members believe this man's name was Rufus (Vicki Walberg to RKD, January 14, 2004). Gainesville, county seat of Cooke County, Texas, lay only a few miles south of the Red River and the Chickasaw Nation to the north.

trivial matter, and one lies weltering in his blood upon the ground, pierced by five leaden bullets, while the other strolled unconcernedly away. The wounded man, one Jack Stimer, was hastily conveyed to the residence of Dr. Marlow, where by careful nursing and the doctor's remarkable skill as a surgeon, he finally recovered after months of lingering suffering. No arrests were ever made and no questions asked. Such were the customs of the day, and such scenes were nothing unusual or to be wondered at.

From hunting and trapping so continually these boys at a very early age found themselves possessed of quite an amount of money, and the question arose as to what they had better do with it. Their worldly possessions, like their joys and sorrows, were shared jointly, and so whatever was the fortune or misfortune of one was likewise that of six. They finally decided to invest in horses and cattle, take them out of the Chickasaw Nation and pasture near the Comanche reservation where there were no settlers and where there was always a ready market for trail cattle at the Indian agency.[5]

[5] The Marlows had settled on Wild Horse Creek in the Chickasaw Nation, some forty miles east of Fort Sill. Their dugout home was located near what is now the site of Marlow, a community of several thousand in the northwest corner of present-day Stephens County, Oklahoma. On March 13, 1891, a post office was established at the town that took its name from what was called the Marlow Brothers Ranch (Shirk, *Oklahoma Place Names*, 136).

In the early 1870s, however, this was wild, sparsely populated country, a strange choice of home for a doctor to establish a medical practice. But the Marlow homestead was located directly on the Chisholm Trail. During these years, hundreds of thousands of longhorn cattle passed by, driven from their ranges in south Texas to Kansas markets, and the site was an ideal base for recovery of cattle lost in the dense woods and thickets of the area. For the Marlows it was a small step from taking possession of normally strayed cattle to deliberate stampeding and scattering of herds in order to increase the bounty, and it was here that the brothers developed the reputation for stock theft and outlawry that would plague the family and bring tragedy and death to several of them. James Marion Garner, boss of a crew that took a herd of 2,000 head up the trail from Nueces County, Texas, in the spring of 1873, recalled having "a little trouble with the Marlow boys, on Wild Horse Creek, in the Indian Territory. These fellows were a lot of bandits and stampeded our cattle and ran twenty head of them off. We followed them twenty miles and got our cattle back" (Hunter, *Trail Drivers of Texas*, 586).

The Marlows must have been precocious outlaws indeed. In the spring of 1873 George was seventeen years old and Charley was fifteen. Alfred, Boone and Ellie were only ten, eight, and six respectively.

Reportedly, the Marlows soon branched out into horse thievery and "foraged deep into eastern Oklahoma on horse-stealing expeditions. They built a stone corral near the head of Mission creek, in the slick hills, and kept their captured ponies there until they could be driven to the Texas or Kansas markets." Remains of the old corral were still visible a century later, according to Everett Cook, a longtime resident and local historian (Morgan, *Wichita Mountains*, 141).

There were a great many hostile Indians at this time and the white man who braved the dangers of settlement among them did so at the daily and hourly peril of his life. Often were these boys forced to flee for their lives or make a desperate fight to save their scalps from the clutches of the red devils, and many is the hairbreadth escape and thrilling danger they experienced. A peculiar characteristic was noticed in Charley, which this wild life brought out and which gained for him the nickname of "The Fawn." Whenever the cry of Indians was given he would always run in exactly the direction he happened to be turned at the time, and very often fleeing in the opposite direction from camp. One morning while he and a small party of cowboys were out with their cattle, a band of about fifty hostiles dashed in among them, uttering the most unearthly yells and war whoops, brandishing guns and tomahawks and stampeding the cattle in all directions. A lively skirmish ensued and a brisk rattle of firearms was heard from the fearless little group of herders, who slowly retreated toward camp and kept a shower of lead from their Winchesters pouring into the painted and yelling devils who were circling around them and scattering the cattle away over the prairies. All succeeded in reaching the camp safely with the exception of a few flesh wounds which were minded very little, but upon roll call Charley was nowhere to be seen. Search was immediately instituted and the brush over the prairies and along the draws carefully examined, no one doubting but what his mangled body would be found, stripped of its clothes, arms and scalp. But not a trace of him was seen, and after two days of search they concluded that he must have been taken away by the Indians into captivity. On the evening of the second day, while all were mourning him as lost, perhaps forever, in walked Charley, weary, footsore and hungry. When the Indians dashed in among them he had run, as usual, in the direction he happened to be facing, and that being directly opposite to where he ought to have fled, he lost himself on the open prairie in consequence and wandered around for two days and a night before finding his way back to the camp. The Indians kept on their mad ride across the country, leaving death, destruction, ruin and disaster in the wake. The families of over twenty settlers were murdered and mutilated by them on that same raid, the houses burned to the ground, the stock run off and the women carried into captivity to meet a fate far worse than death.[6]

After a year of this dangerous existence they moved nearer to civilization and settled at Blue Grove,[7] having at that time four hundred cattle and fifty head of horses. While here a serious misfortune overtook them, entailing much loss. Many will remember the disastrous fires which swept the country between Kansas and Texas in '75—it was a sight and an experience of a life time. For the Marlows this great conflagration destroyed sixty head of cattle and hundreds of tons of hay and bushels of corn, and in fact swept away the bulk of all they had on earth save the house they lived in, which was only saved from the flames by the most tireless efforts in fighting fire for several days.

A fire in a prairie country is an awful spectacle. For days before that raging sea of flames reached their humble log cabin it could be seen far away on the horizon like a wave of crimson fire upon the sky. Traveling with the velocity of the wind, it came rolling and sweeping on like a roaring avalanche of hell; a seething, scorching, devastating and death-dealing scourge that left naught in its blackened track but ruin and wreck. On and on it came, snarling, crackling and roaring through the forest of tall blue joint grass that covered the prairies and grew rank through the draws and valleys, throwing angry sparks and dense volumes of smoke upwards to the very heavens, and passing over and around the little unprotected cabin, nearly suffocating and roasting the inhabitants and left it a charred and blackened smouldering in its own ashes and embers.

Homeless and adrift on the world, they left this place and located near Burlington, on the Indian Territory side.[8] This was some better, but at that time there was no place in that barren and desolate region where

[6] 1874 was the year of the Red River War when Kiowas and Comanches, enraged over the slaughter of the buffalo herds on their hunting grounds in the Texas panhandle, broke out of their reservation and attacked Whites throughout the area. Most of the depredation took place west of Fort Sill, but the concern of the Marlows, situated so close to the embattled tribes, is understandable. If, as was later alleged, the Marlows were in the business of stealing Indian ponies, they were doubly jeopardized.

[7] Apparently Rathmell meant Bluegrass, a small village in what is now Beaver County in the Oklahoma panhandle. In the 1870s this was in the Neutral Strip, or No Man's Land (see Chapter 5, n. 5). There was a post office at Bluegrass between the years 1886 and 1898 but the town has since disappeared (Shirk, *Oklahoma Place Names*, 25).

[8] Burlington was about one hundred miles east of Bluegrass in what was then referred to as the Unknown Nation. Later this section was called the Cherokee Strip of Indian Territory (Ibid., 32).

one could move to escape the sickening sights, the hardships and dangers of a pioneer life on the frontier. There was no law to fear and consequently none to respect, wrong and riot ran rampant; wild Indians and lawless white men held full sway, and the wild, free life of the cowboy, the hunter and the ranger prevailed. The grinning skulls and whitened skeletons often found by these boys while out on their hunting trips, told a tale of murder and robbery that neither book nor paper has ever told, and spoke louder and more than volumes could, of the customs and horrors of the country. Another instance which may be cited in this line was the finding one bright Sunday morning by Mrs. Marlow and youngest son, Ep, who went out to get water for breakfast from a sparkling spring nearby. Three unknown men had been hanged by unknown parties to a tree hard by and buried during the night.

About this time there moved into the neighborhood with her family a beautiful young half-breed Indian maiden, and Charley, being young and susceptible to female charms, fell desperately in love with her. She was a lovely young creature, with just enough of the Indian blood in her to make her picturesque and romantic in her ways, and Charley could hardly be blamed for seeing a world of love and a life time of joy in the depths of her dark, liquid eyes. But such a union would be a mesalliance, and must not be considered for a moment. How to break off his infatuation, then, was the question, and not a very easy problem to solve, either. She was as graceful as an antelope, as enchanting as a wood nymph and as wild and free as the air she breathed. She could ride and hunt and fish with an ease and success characteristic of her tribe, and could love with an ardor that only the sun-kissed nations can. Her beaded and fringed wahotoya hung in graceful folds about a form divine in perfect mould, concealing yet half-revealing only dreamed of charms it hid. Poor Charley! No wonder his boyish heart fluttered wildly in its human cage.

George, the rascal, was the one who finally hit upon the plan that dashed poor Charley's high hopes of wedded bliss to atoms and prevented a mixture of Marlow and half-breed blood. The new mustache he was growing probably suggested the diabolical plot which he carried into effect, but be that as it may, it certainly worked to a charm. He dressed up in his best, visited the maiden many times and made such hot and persistent love to her that, if the expression may be allowed, soon threw Charley's nose entirely out of joint. Then he gradually cooled his own ardor and in "two moons" the dangers of young love's impetuosity safely tided over.

Chapter III

SCENES AND ADVENTURES IN MEXICO

In the spring of '77, rumors of the wonders of South America having reached them, Dr. Marlow and the boys, together with about thirty others, mostly relatives, sold off their stock, bought mules, wagons and other necessities for a long journey, and began a trip overland to the balmy clime and flowery land of the tropics. It was a lovely morning in March when they started on their long journey, the soft south breeze made the tall grasses growing on the prairie nod a farewell to them, and the meadow larks sang a glad carol that the beauties and benefits of the old Lone Star State might live in their memories, as well as the trials and dangers.

The company generally made it convenient to camp at or near some small town, where such a long train of covered wagons and the fine animals ridden by the boys invariably attracted much attention.

One evening while camped at a small town near Fort Worth, an unusually large crowd of visitors came out to see them and among these was a veritable dude and tenderfoot who was out from the New England States on a visit to the wild and woolly West. He was dressed in a regulation soup-plate hat, toothpick shoes, and eye glass and high pressure collar and cuffs, and his effeminate ways and mode of speech were laughable in the extreme to those free westerners there in camp.

George and Willie[1] had pervious to this acquired to a great degree of perfection that art of ventriloquism, and they concluded to have some

[1] Williamson, Jr. was twenty-four years old in the spring of 1877; George was twenty-one.

sport at the dude's expense. Accordingly, as soon as a sufficient crowd had gathered about, all were startled by the sudden and alarming shrieking of an infant, screaming as if in pain. The sound evidently came from somewhere about the clothes of the dude, and all eyes were turned in his direction. Then came the barking and snarling of an angry dog immediately behind him, at which he sprang into the air with an exclamation of alarm, which turned to amazement on finding nothing at his heels but empty air. Then the imaginary baby commenced to yell again from his coat pocket, and one of the little boys from the wagons ran out and offered the dude a nursing bottle filled with milk, at which everybody roared with laughter, and amid the shouts of the crowd his dudeship beat a hasty retreat in the direction of town.

Again, one pleasant evening when all were encamped on the banks of a little stream near Waco, the boys made much sport and fun for the company at the expense of the Irish cook. It was after supper and they were all lying around the camp fires smoking and telling stories of adventures and frontier life, when a deep and ghostly voice from out among the bushes called in thundering tones for Pat to drop those frying pans and come outside. The bewildered Irishman looked up from his work in amazement, and as the voice still called him in loud and commanding tones to come out, he finally gathered up a heavy neck-yoke and made a bound for the brush. "Pat, you're an Irish villain," said the voice. "You steal whisky and get drunk. You're a Pope-hating Fenian and a potato-eating Mick from Cork." Pat by this time was crazy mad and was beating around out in the bushes like a wild Comanche Indian, using more brogue and profanity than would have stocked up a wake, and flying in all directions to meet his imaginary foe. He was given the grand laugh and let into the secret, finally, but didn't take to the joke very kindly and wouldn't speak to Willie or George for a week.

In three months after starting they reached Corpus Christi, where the second cook, a Mexican, disappeared with a horse, saddle and bridle, and what other loose things he could carry with him. It will not do to trust a Mexican.[2]

[2] This racist slur no doubt accurately reflected the view of many Anglo Texans of the period.

Here they found that the troublesome times in Old Mexico[3] would not permit of their pursuing their journey overland, as they had intended, and so the outfits were all sold out for what they would bring and a brig, the Mary Mable, was chartered to take them southward by water. They were two weeks getting started, but finally set sail one Sunday afternoon and headed out to sea.

The placid waters of the Gulf spread out like a sheet of shimmering silver, rippling in the breeze and bathing the feet of the pebbly shore with gentle waves. As far as the eye could reach it spread out in endless rolling billows of liquid green, and finally mingled on the distant horizon with heaven's own canopy of blue. It was an entrancing panorama spread out to view for endless leagues, but soon changed from bright and sparkling calmness to the dark and angry gathering of that most dreadful thing—a storm at sea. Clouds o'erspread the azure sky and snow-capped waves dashed high upon the rocks. The brig touched at Port Isabel[4] to take on a fresh supply of water, and the captain was urged not to proceed further in the face of the gathering storm. At this juncture, to add to the terror of the situation, young Ellie Marlow,[5] while climbing up the rigging like he had seen the sailors do, lost his balance and fell headlong into the angry waves below. Consternation spread among the little band of passengers, women screamed and strong men grew faint, for in addition to the heavy sea the waters were infested with swarms of man-eating sharks which swam around the vessel, awaiting anything that was thrown overboard. A rush was made to lower a boat, but before this could be done Alfred ran across the deck, threw off his coat and hat, jumped upon the rail and before anyone comprehended what his rash intention was, plunged headlong after his brother who was struggling and battling with the foaming waters. A loud shout of encouragement went up as he grasped his brother by the hair, and a score of willing hands were extended with ropes to assist them on board the ship.

[3] Mexico had been in a state of political turmoil since the sudden death of President Benito Juarez in July 1872. The succession to the presidency by Sebastian Lerdo de Tejada was contested by Porfirio Diaz who, after years of struggle, finally mounted an army and marched on the capital, defeating government forces near Tiaxcala in November 1876 (Fehrenbach, *Fire and Blood*, 450–52). Civil unrest was still pervasive in the country early in 1877 as the Marlows prepared to go south.

[4] Port Isabel (called "Point" Isabel by Rathmell) is in the extreme southern tip of Texas, near Brownsville.

[5] Llewellyn, or "Ellie," was ten in 1877.

Fiercer and fiercer raged the gale, high over the sides of the little ship dashed the maddened waves and tumultuous rove the interminable sea. It was one of the worst storms known to that latitude, and for sixteen days they were tossed ruthlessly about, completely at the mercy of the wind and waves. Food and water also began to get scarce, and had to be issued in small allowances from day to day, in order that the store might be husbanded and actual hunger averted. Toward the close of the sixteenth day the storm abated somewhat, and that evening the approach of the pilot boat was hailed with delight. The pilot succeeded in boarding the brig, while his boat and crew of five men attempted to lead the way across the dangerous bar of the Tuxpan. This proved a hazardous undertaking, for only a few moments had passed until their boat capsized and threw the five struggling sailors among high rolling waves that resembled snow-capped mountains. By the help of parties on shore three were saved, while the others were drowned and dashed on the rocks along the coast. After crossing the dangerous bar the brig's crew went ashore and towed her up stream to Tuxpan,[6] a distance of twelve miles, where a guard was placed over the vessel until the custom house officials could examine the baggage of the passengers for goods which might be smuggled from the United States. This search was very thorough, trunks, boxes and bundles were overhauled and minutely examined, and not an article, book, picture or scrap of writing was overlooked. About the only bit of writing among the baggage was some exceedingly ardent love verses in Charley's trunk which he had written about the undying and everlasting affection he had proposed to cherish for his Indian sweetheart back in the Territory, and this was immediately pounced upon by the lynx-eyed officials, who thought perhaps it might be some state document aiming at the overthrow of their government. None of them could read a word of English, so Dr. Marlow was called upon to explain the purport of the innocent little love ditty. He explained and explained, and in three languages—the English, broken Mexican and finally profane, but the more he tried to explain the denser it all grew to the officials, and finally, after all the English speaking people on board had tried a hand at explaining, it was confiscated and carried off, and Charley's poor little

[6] Tuxpan, in the state of Veracruz, lies some 400 miles south of Port Isabel.

love letter is probably filed away to-day among the secret archives of the Mexican government, and no doubt is regarded as a document of great treasonable anarchistic importance.

Tuxpan is a typical old Mexican town and a curiosity to Americans. The little dingy streets are but seven feet wide and are paved with little round cobblestones about the size of an egg. The buildings are small and of no particular architecture, being built of wood and adobe and strung along the little streets as though they had dropped from above and stayed in whatever position they landed.

Mexicans of every size, age, sex and condition crowded around our little party of explorers as they passed down the thoroughfares, talking and jabbering like a lot of magpies and asking if they had any American calico, American domestic, American cigars or American liquors. Dr. Marlow accepted for the party the very cordial invitation of the U. S. consul to spend a few hours at his home, while the Mexicans carted their goods in wheelbarrows to the place they intended to stop, about two miles out of the city. It was pleasantly located, and the weary and storm tossed travelers greatly enjoyed the quiet and rest afforded by this shady and picturesque retreat.

After spending a very pleasant day at the consul's mansion, they took possession of a place they had rented from a Mexican and prepared to settle down once more. The country seemed to them like a veritable Garden of Eden, so profuse grew the flowers, so rank the vegetation, so luscious the fruits and so immense the vegetables. Here grew the finest fruits and vegetables they had ever dreamed of. Sweet potatoes grew to the length of two and one-half feet; they gathered cucumbers from vines that measured two feet in diameter; there were beans growing on vines which were seven years old, and cotton stocks towered thirty feet high. Irish potatoes grew eighteen inches thick and three feet in circumference; mango trees six feet and upwards in diameter, while fruits and berries were simply phenomenal in size. There were lemon and orange groves where the decayed fruit lay on the ground to the depth of a foot and one-half, and dates, bananas, grapes, figs, plums, and all other fruits could be had for the gathering. Tomatoes grew large and luscious and wild in the woods, without cultivation and many other native fruits and vegetables of which they had never heard. They cooked bananas like

Americans do potatoes, frying them in slices. Butter was very scarce, but the fruit of what is known there as the butter tree answered as very good substitute. It was a queer country, filled with queer people and abounding in queer sights.[7]

The little colony tarried at the place they had rented for a few weeks and then separated into families. Dr. Marlow, wife and six sons and a young fellow who had been with them since leaving the Indian Territory, by name of Wm. McDonald, moved about eight miles further up the Tuxpan river, where the Doctor purchased a piece of land, as all agreed that they had gone far enough south. They made the trip to their new homes in small boats, rowed by the natives, and gathered shells and stones and various curiosities for relics of the country along the route. Their houses were built of cane, like unto that which is used for fishing poles in the United States, only there the cane was in shape of logs and grew upwards of a foot in thickness, being used almost entirely for building purposes. Tubs, buckets and measures were also constructed from this cane, the logs being sawed off first just below a joint and then as far up above the joint as the depths of the vessel required. The houses were thatched with palmetto leaves, as the air was so very moist that a shingle roof would rot out in a very short time. The Marlow house was a fair sample of all others on the farms and plantations of that country, nearly all of them being built square and low, constructed of the cane logs and thatched with the fibrous leaves of the palmetto plant. In cleaning out the room, an infant's grave was found in one corner, and upon inquiry it was learned that one of the curious customs of the country was to bury the infant dead in one corner of the dwelling house.

Their yard was surrounded by beautiful and towering trees, numerous among which were coffee trees, which almost constantly showered down upon them a rain of big, plump coffee berries. All around the foliage was dense and tangled and a veritable jungle of flowering plants and lofty trees gave the entire country the appearance of one immense kingdom of fruit and flowers and rank vegetation. At any spot an animal could be staked out with a thirty-foot lariat and though it remained

[7] It appears that the Marlow brothers, in relating their Mexican experience to William Rathmell, could not refrain from exercising the time-honored Texan penchant for the tall tale.

unchanged for seasons, it could not lower the grass which grew in such profusion. The air is so very moist and warm there that when a weed is pulled out of a garden, unless it is burned, it never stops growing, but takes root wherever it happens to fall. If a cord of wood is cut and piled up, in a few days it will put forth sprouts and leaves and if left corded any length of time will grow branches and proceed to establish a little forest of its own.

Occasionally some of the richer classes of Mexicans would build their homes of stone or adobe, and these structures in a few years became so thickly covered with moss that it would have been necessary to dig into their sides a foot or more in order to learn of what they were constructed. The moss was beautiful, heavy and of a light green, and hung about the doors and windows in a long feathery fringe which was at once odd, handsome and picturesque. As soon as they were settled they gathered a large quantity of pepper, coffee, allspice, tobacco and ginger. All of which had to be scalded to stop its growth.

Wild animals were very plentiful, and where the Marlows lived, a person was not safe outside the house after sundown. It was anything but pleasant, to say the least. To reside in a place where one did not dare to venture out to go to town after supper without running the risk of being torn to pieces and devoured by a ferocious wild cat or tiger. It was about as safe in the woods, though, as in the town, for to venture out in the city after dark would surely invite being held up and robbed, and perhaps worse. The woods were filled with a specie of wild chickens, much resembling grouse or the chickens of the Texas prairies, but it was dangerous to hunt them on account of the vast numbers of wild beasts and enormous snakes to be encountered. The great branches of the banyan trees bend over until they touch the ground, where they take root and grow upward again, and clinging to these branches can always be found monster boas and other terrible snakes, awaiting the coming of any stray animal which might pass beneath. Deer are their easiest prey, though horses and cattle are seized upon and devoured with much relish. The natives always carry forked sticks when in the woods, with which they pin a snake to the ground with an ease and dexterity born of long practice. None of our friends ever cared to try the experiment, not relishing running the risk of playing Jonah to a snake as big as [a] Minnesota saw log.

Naturally enough in a country like this a great deal of sickness is prevalent. Fatal fevers, malaria and diseases peculiar to tropical regions abounded on every hand and carried away victims by the score. About two months after arrival the entire Marlow family, one after another, were stricken with that dreaded Southern plague, yellow fever, and a regular epidemic of it spread over the country. The natives of the little town died at the rate of twenty to thirty a day, and Dr. Marlow was on the go day and night. He had very good luck, as a rule, with his patients, and succeeded in pulling through all the members of the company who had come down with him from the United States.

One day before they themselves were taken down, George and Charley were out around Tuxpan and met four Mexicans carrying a dead native, a victim of the fever, to a hole hastily prepared for his uncoffined body. The natives insisted that the boys help them carry their dead, but knowing that to touch the loathsome thing meant disease and probable death, they promptly refused, whereupon hostilities were declared, the body was unceremoniously dumped on the ground and a shower of rocks flew in the direction of the boys. They happened to be carrying a bag of coconuts, and so returned the fusillade with compound interest. The air was filled with stones, coconuts and Mexican profanity. But soon the boys were victors of the field, for every time one of their ripe coconuts came in contact with a Mexican head it shattered into a hundred fragments, made an ugly bump and nearly drowned the unlucky native in its sticky milk. During the time they remained at this place Dr. Marlow amassed quite a small fortune from the practice of his profession, the locality being one of the most unhealthy on earth. At one village, just across the river from the Doctor's place, only three persons out of a population of over three hundred survived the dreadful scourge of yellow fever.

The ravages of this horrible disease was such that the Marlows decided to leave the country and seek a more healthful spot on earth whereupon to make a home. Accordingly, after being there about three months, they employed natives to take them down a lagoon to Tampico. The craft used was a flatboat, eight feet wide and thirty feet in length, and it was so heavily loaded that the top lacked hardly an inch of being down to the water's edge. In this precarious condition, all the more dangerous because of the large numbers of man-eating alligators which infested the lagoon, the whole company made the journey of a hundred and twenty miles to a bit of land nine miles from where they were expecting to go, where they employed other Mexicans with pack-mules to help them across the country. While unloading the boat, one of the natives took a great fancy to a couple of earthen crocks which Mrs. Marlow had brought from the United States, and offered to give her a horse for them. The horse being worth about sixty dollars, she did not hesitate long in making the trade.

Their intention was to reach Tampico,[8] purchase teams and wagons, and then make their way back to Texas overland, none of them relishing the job of returning by the water as they had come, owing to the rough weather experienced, the tempestuous sea and dangers of the angry deep. They had never seen a wagon at Tuxpan, or, indeed, any kind of a vehicle except wheelbarrows, as the means of conveyance was entirely by pack-mules, but they had no doubt wagons could be obtained at the larger town, although nothing resembling a wagon road appeared in sight at any time [other] than a small pack trail.

The company reached Tampico the eighth day after starting, the Doctor and others who had bought property near Tuxpan leaving it to whoever wanted to take possession, taking with them very little else than wearing apparel. They visited the American consul here and endeavored to procure a guide and guard across the country, but found the Minister had not enough soldiers to guard himself much less furnish any to them, and as they could not make the trip without a strong guard they abandoned the idea, left the two horses they possessed standing in the street and took passage on a Liverpool steamer bound for New Orleans. They enjoyed a pleasant and safe journey, which was continued from New Orleans to Shreveport, and from thence to Willow Springs, Texas.[9]

Two years later, after a pleasant and prosperous residence in various parts of the Lone Star State, they again took up the line of march for

[8] Tampico is one hundred miles north of Tuxpan.

[9] Four Texas counties have had small communities called Willow Springs: Van Zandt and Rains in the northeast and San Jacinto and Fayette in the southeast (Tyler, *New Handbook of Texas*, 6:1001). It is unclear which of these towns is referred to here.

Colorado, in search for the shining gold and silver of the mines, the pure mountain air, and the pleasures of travel and the chase. Arriving at Sheridan's Roost,[10] they paused among the soldiers to rest a bit and to give Willie, who was sick, a chance to recuperate. But Willie was a frail little fellow and grew worse instead of better in the high altitude of the mountain country, and shortly afterwards was laid to rest where the bright columbines blossomed and the pine trees on the foothills sung a requiem.

This was in '79 and during the Leadville boom. That great silver camp was attracting the attention of all America, and indeed the whole world, and thousands were flocking thither in quest of fortunes.[11] The Marlows, however, stopped for half a year at the picturesque village of Pueblo,[12] and then proceeded south to Las Vegas, New Mexico, where they took a large tie and grading contract on the Atchison, Topeka and Santa Fe railway.[13] Next they moved to Albuquerque, pausing there only because the Apache Indians were on the war path and prevented them making a journey to El Paso.[14] The government finally succeeded in quieting the Indians, and in the spring of 1880 they again found themselves in their old Texas home. On this journey they traveled eighty miles one day while being unable to obtain water, and then paid fifty cents a head for the stock to drink. A good bit of the country traversed was known in those days as the Great American Desert, which, although in late years has been made to "blossom like a rose" through irrigation and the onward march of civilization, at that time stretched away as far as the eye could reach in one unbroken sea of stunted grass, sand, sage brush and alkali—a most unsightly and forbidding sight. The Indian, the buffalo and the coyote were fit inhabitants, for such a desolate waste of country, and none but the hardy pioneer would have ever possessed the nerve and fortitude to attempt its reclamation from its natural denizens.

[10] No settlement of this name is known to have existed in Colorado. A small village in the San Juan Mountains of Colorado where Charley and George Marlow would eventually settle was originally called Chattanooga, but later became known as Sheridan Junction after Jim Sheridan opened a hotel, saloon, and livery stable there. Pack trains over Red Mountain to Ouray and wagons to Silverton were outfitted here (Wolle, *Stampede to Timberline*, 434). "Sheridan's Roost" may have been a corruption of Sheridan Junction.

[11] In 1875 it was discovered that a black mud which had hampered the sluicing operations at an almost deserted gold mining camp called Oro City, high in the Colorado Rockies, was actually carbonate of lead containing a high concentration of silver, and a great rush was on (Blair, *Leadville*, 20–21). At 10,000 feet above sea level, a new city called Leadville blossomed almost overnight.

By 1879 there were twenty thousand people living in Leadville or the surrounding area (Ibid., 58).

[12] In the spring of 1879, two rival railroads were contesting for the right-of-way to booming Leadville through the spectacular mountain defile called the Royal Gorge. While their lawyers fought the battle in the courts, officials of the Atchison, Topeka & Santa Fe and the Denver & Rio Grande Railroads were hiring gunmen at three dollars a day to fight it out on the ground. On June 11, 1879, a pitched battle was fought at Pueblo where a force of Santa Fe men under W. B. "Bat" Masterson held a Rio Grande roundhouse under siege of Rio Grande warriors (DeArment, *Bat Masterson*, 148–54). The two oldest Marlow boys, George twenty-three, and Charles, twenty-one, lovers of action and adventure, fearless, and adept with weapons, would have made perfect candidates for the railroad recruiters and it is quite possible that employment as mercenaries in the Royal Gorge War was the reason for their stay in Pueblo. It is also probable that they hired their guns to the Santa Fe, as they were awarded a grading contract with that line immediately afterward.

[13] The Santa Fe Railroad, building south from Colorado, reached Las Vegas on July 4, 1879 (Bryan, *Wildest of the Wild West*, 98).

[14] In September 1879 the Southern Apaches, led by their chief, Victorio, broke out of the Mescalero Reservation, south of Albuquerque, triggering a war that lasted until June 1880 when the remnants of the tribe fled into Mexico. An estimated two hundred settlers and soldiers were killed in New Mexico during this period and a similar number in Old Mexico. At least one hundred of Victorio's band also died (Lockwood, *Apache Indians*, 229–31).

Chapter IV

AN INDIAN CHASE—MARRIAGE AND DEATH

The next four years was spent near old Fort Sill, in the Indian Territory,[1] where the five brothers worked for the heavy cattle barons of that section on their immense ranches, some of which included whole townships. Little change had taken place in the Territory since they had resided there, years before, and the same wild life prevailed.[2]

[1] The military post called Fort Sill was established in 1869 on the west bank of Cache Creek in southwestern Indian Territory (Nye, *Carbine and Lance*, 84).

[2] The Marlows found that Texas longhorns were still coming up the trail and they resumed their former occupation of rounding up strays and running off bunches of cattle whenever possible. In September 1881 Harry H. Halsell came through with 1300 head and had a run-in with the family that he related in some detail in 1937:

> We camped at noon in some wooded country on Hell Roaring Creek, and the wild appearance of the country makes the name appropriate. Passing on through the timber, the herd stopped for the night on a running stream called Rush Springs. The boss of this herd was Mat Laughlin, and he had as a side partner, a great big rough fellow, whose name was Charlie Hardwick. These two had left the herd about three or four o'clock in the evening, and it developed afterward they had gone a few miles southeast of Hell Roaring Creek to the Marlow Camp. There they found Martha Jane Marlow and a "boy of sixteen," probably Boone or Epp. Two boys, about twenty and twenty-two [Alf and Charley] were away from the camp when Laughlin and Hardwick rode up. Now this Marlow family had a herd of cattle, about one hundred and twenty-five head, near their camp. This bunch of cattle was probably all strays, picked up by these people as they were lost out of trail herds. Laughlin told the woman they wanted to examine the herd. She said, "There are none of your cattle in our bunch, and you let them alone." They told her they would examine the herd anyway. The boy, a very brave lad, grabbed Laughlin's bridle rein, and the woman drew a pistol on him. Hardwick drew his gun and told the boy to turn loose and the woman to put away her gun, and both did so. The two men loped out to the herd and started to cutting out some cattle. The woman fired at them with a needle gun, which is a long-range gun, and the men left in a hurry. By this time the other two Marlow boys came up and began firing long-range guns and chasing the two men. Just before this fight and on arrival of her herd at Rush Spring for the night, I had found out one of my cows and a young calf were missing. Late in the evening, about sundown, I had returned to the

One day while George was in Fort Sill, drawing some money due him for work, he met with an adventure which came near costing him his life and scalp. He had drawn his money and was about to start on the return trip to the ranch where the family lived, when he was accosted by an Indian, who said: "You steal Indian's pony." "Indian lies," responded George. "I bought my pony and it is mine." The redskin loudly and vehemently insisted that the pony was his, however, and angrily grasped the bridle with the evident intention of taking the horse away from George. George did not come of a family that feared any mortal man, much less an Indian, and so, shoving a revolver under the startled aborigine's nose, informed him in unmistakably plain language that unless he disappeared in less than half a minute he would be sent on an eternal mission to the happy hunting grounds. At this juncture four other Indians came up, accompanied by their interpreter, and the latter spoke up and said: "You seem to be having some trouble, young man, what's up?"

"Yes," replied George, his eyes flashing fire and his finger resting lightly on the trigger of his six-shooter, "this miserable redskin claims my pony, but he is not going to get it by a large majority, and if you don't want his hide filled full of holes you better take care of him." The interpreter jabbered awhile with the Indians in the guttural lingo, and then, turning to George, said:

"They claim that this pony belongs to them and that it was stolen from them. They want you to go with them to the commanding officer[3] about the matter, and you better go, as that is the best way to settle it without a row."

---

noon camp on Hell Roaring to hunt for my cows. As I rode through the woods on the way, I saw two men coming at full speed toward me, and as they passed. Laughlin said, "The Marlowes [*sic*] are after us; you had better come on." I went to the creek, found my cow, and returned to camp by 10 P. M. We stayed on Rush Creek until noon next day. While we were eating dinner two fine-looking cowboys rode up, got down off their horses, went to the chuck wagon and loaded their plates with bacon, beans and bread, and filled two cups of coffee. They sat down conveniently near their horses to eat their dinner and chatted with all the boys just like they were old acquaintances. Ordinarily, there would have been nothing unusual about this circumstance if it had not been that these very two young men were the ones who had been shooting at our boss and his friend the evening before. It appeared to me to be one of the coolest and bravest acts I ever saw" (Halsell, *Cowboys and Cattleland*, 129–31).

[3] The post commander at Fort Sill in 1882, the year of this incident, was Colonel Guy V. Henry (Nye, *Carbine and Lance*, 245).

"All right," said George, "I will go with them before the commanding officer, but I warn you that the first copper-colored whelp that lays hands on this horse will be turned into a good Indian the next minute."

So they all went up to the officer's quarters, where the interpreter stated the case. He said that a few days previous someone had stolen a horse from the Indians, and that they had recognized it in the one George was riding, and asked that it be delivered over to them.

The officer listened to their side of the case and then, turning to George, asked:

"Where are you from, young man?'

"About thirty-five miles from here."

"What have you been doing?"

"Working for Ed. Walsh on the big ranch up the country."

"How long have you had that pony?"

"About six months."

"Well, if you let these Indians take your horse it's your own fault. You may go now."

"Thank you, sir," replied George. "If they get my horse, you may rest assured that I'll keep the flies off them while they are doing it."

He sprang into the saddle, put spurs into the pony's flanks and, swinging his hat with a whoop, was out of the Fort and over the prairies like a flash. In a moment he was half a mile away, and, turning in the saddle, saw the five Indians coming in hot pursuit. Then the race began. It was five to one if it came to a fight and so much depended on the horse's speed. There were but four cartridges in his revolver, and as it would be impossible to kill five Indians with that, the race meant life or death to him. On and on they went, now lengthening, now shortening, the distance between them. The Indians urged their ponies up to their utmost speed, yelling like demons all the while, occasionally sending a bullet ahead at the flying George, and seemingly sure that it was only a question of time until both horse and rider would be theirs.

On and on over the prairies rushed pursuers and pursued, bounding through the tall grass, leaping over any obstruction and galloping with the speed of the wind toward the big ranch thirty-five miles away.

At one time the distance between them was easy rifle range, and George drew his lone revolver with its four loads, determined to make as desperate a fight for it as possible, but just at this juncture and as the foremost Indian was endeavoring to get sight along the barrel of a gleaming Winchester, his pony plunged a foreleg down a hidden coyote hole and turned a complete summersault, throwing the yelling redskin heels over head about ten feet in the air. He lit with a soul-stirring crash that must have loosened every bone in his body, and the delay occasioned in catching the pony and getting started again gave George another half mile in the lead.

When about ten miles out from the Fort, he saw ahead of him a wood wagon with two men on it, and as he got within hailing distance he shouted to them to give him some cartridges for his revolver. One of them held out a cartridge belt at arm's length, which was about half full of loaded shells, and George leaned over and grasped it as he flew by with a rush and shout. In the next instant both he and the Indians were far ahead of the wagon, and going at the top of their speed on over the country. Fifteen miles of the mad race had been made—twenty—and now like a speck on the horizon George saw a solitary horseman, going in the same direction he was. He spoke encouragingly to his jaded horse, who stretched his neck and responded with increased efforts to lessen the distance between them and the objective point. Soon they drew near the horseman ahead, and George shouted to him and motioned for him to wait. The startled traveler gave one glance over his shoulder, saw George coming at a breakneck pace and closely pursued by the five yelling Indians, and, putting spurs to his own horse, he dashed ahead as fast as his steed would carry him. George saw he could hope for no help from that quarter and as the stranger dashed on and out of sight on his fresh horse, George's tired pony began to show signs of giving out, and he again prepared to do battle alone and single handed with the five redskins so close in his wake. They noticed his slackening of speed, and with yells and whoops like demented demons they urged up their own fagged ponies, and, brandishing their murderous weapons, came on like the whirlwind.

Fifteen miles yet stretched out between them and the ranch. Would the little horse hold out that far? George knew that once he reached the ranch, with the assistance of his brothers, the Indians would soon be repulsed, and again he urged on his pony with voice and spur.

Whiz! a bullet cut its way through the brim of his hat and dashed it from his head, and then as he turned in the saddle to return the compliment he came suddenly upon the man he had seen some time before, down in a little valley, and with gun drawn upon him, ready to shoot down the first object that came within range.

With shouts and gesticulations of peace, George succeeded in inducing him to lower his gun, and then dashed in beside him. After a hurried consultation of hardly half a minute they concluded to keep on riding as long as George's horse would hold out and then give them battle. Accordingly they sped on over the prairies, and George's pony, now that he had company, seemed to take new life and strength. In a few minutes they gained in the race, and continued from then on to widen the distance between them and their dusky foes.

The ranch was finally reached, the Marlow brothers heard the shouts and rode out to meet them, and the Indians, seeing this, gave up the chase and turned back. George and the stranger went up to the house to rest from their mad race, while the rest of the boys gave chase to the Indians, who, finding the tables turned upon them, did their best to get out of the way.

George made the flight from the Fort to the ranch, a distance of thirty-five miles, in one hour and three quarters, and still owns and keeps with him the noble little animal which carried him away from the Indians and safely home.

The rest of the boys returned late that evening from their chase after the reds, tired and dusty. They were very reticent in regard to what had transpired, and had but little comment to make about the matter at all, though it was noticed that they brought back quite a supply of Winchesters and revolvers which they didn't have when they started out. The five Indians must have ridden a long distance, for they were never seen again. Perhaps they are still going.

Everything went on quietly at the ranch after this for a year, George in the meantime courting a pretty girl who had stolen his heart away. She was Miss Lillian Berry, who was born in the north part of Kansas, near the Nebraska line, and raised like the Marlow boys, in several different States. She was a young lady of fair accomplishments and prepossessing appearance, and on the 17th day of June, 1883, George and she were made man and wife, in the Indian Territory, on the Washita.[4]

The following spring the entire family made their way to Trinidad, Colorado, where they sold their large herd of cattle and for the first time being out of the stock business.[5]

Dr. and Mrs. Marlow and Charles took the overland trip to California, to visit the Doctor's eldest son, whom they had not seen for years, to benefit Mrs. Marlow's health, and to see the country.

It had now been thirty-five years since the Doctor had mined a fortune in gold from the California placer diggings, and many were the changes which he noted. Now, it was a land of plenty and the onward march of civilization could be plainly marked on every hand. Then himself and party had killed and eaten their mules to keep from starving; now, fine hotels at reasonable rates were plentiful in San Francisco. Then, he had paid five hundred dollars for the privilege of making a bed for one night on a dining room table for his sick brother. The old mining and pioneer days of the Golden Gate country had faded away forever, and in their place the church, the college and the mart of commercial traffic had stepped. This was not to the taste and long habits of the Marlows, and so, after a pleasant visit of a few weeks, they returned to Colorado, joined the rest of the family at Trinidad and all journeyed back to their old Texas home, via the Indian Territory. Here the grim angel of death came and marked for its own the loved husband and father, and on the 12th day of April, 1885, the good Dr. Marlow passed over the dark river to the other side. It was a sad and darkened household then, for the sunshine of a good man had gone out forever, and with bowed heads and bended knees they laid him to rest beneath the grass-covered prairies of the Lone Star State he had loved so long and well. The soft south wind to-day moans through the long grass a requiem, and the wild flowers nod their jeweled heads above the spot which marks his eternal resting place on earth.

[4] Lillian May Berry, the daughter of an army sergeant, was born and raised in northeast Kansas (Ledbetter, *Ordeal*, 6). The U.S. census records indicate she was born in May 1863, and that she and George Marlow were married in 1885, not 1883 (1900 U. S. Census).

[5] Significantly, the Marlows trailed their stock all the way to Colorado rather than driving them to the closer cattle markets in southern Kansas. Questions regarding altered or defaced Texas brands were much more likely to be raised at Caldwell or Dodge City than in far-off Trinidad. The brothers were subsequently indicted for stealing a large number of Indian horses in March 1885, and these may have been part of the stock driven to Colorado.

Chapter V

BOONE KILLS A MAN—TERRIBLE BATTLE WITH WOLVES

After the death of the Doctor, Mrs. Marlow, her four sons[1] and George's wife moved to a place on the Fort Worth & Denver railroad, where the boys took a grading contract.[2] At this place Alfred made the acquaintance of the woman whom he afterward married—a Miss Venie Davis, who was a handsome Western lass, brave and true-hearted, and who proved entirely worthy as a wife and life companion.

After completing their contract with the railway the boys took a very desirable claim near by, close to the Navajo mountains,[3] and while Mrs. Marlow, George's wife and Boone remained to care for their stock, and Alfred and his bride were off on a little wedding tour and visiting some of her relatives, George, Charley, Ella [*sic*: Ellie] and a hired man proceeded to the new claim to erect dwelling houses thereon.

It was at this time that a tragedy occurred which cast a gloom over the lives and happiness of all our little band of Westerners, broke up their plans and home and made one of them a fugitive.

[1] It is not explained here why only four sons were present, but this probably was the period mentioned later in the book in which George went alone to scout out the San Juan country of Colorado.

[2] The Fort Worth and Denver City Railway Company had been chartered as early as 1873 to build a line from Fort Worth to Denver, but a series of legal and financial difficulties resulted in delays and work was stopped near Wichita Falls in 1882. Construction resumed in 1886 and the line was built diagonally across the Texas panhandle to join the Denver and Rio Grande at Pueblo. The connection was completed in March 1888 (Tyler, *New Handbook of Texas*, 2:1124).

[3] In Wilbarger County, Texas, close to the Indian Territory line.

One evening when Boone was returning with the cows,[4] he stopped to see his sister Elizabeth, who, with her husband,[5] lived a short distance from his mother's, and as his horse neared the house and came to a standstill, a man named James Holstein[6] came out of the house and at sight of Boone drew a revolver and commenced shooting at him without a word. Boone did not know the man or understand the attack, but as the bullets from the six-shooter began to whistle uncomfortably near to his ears, he hastily dismounted, drew his Winchester from his saddle, and, resting it over the horse's back, took hurried aim and fired. True to his aim the bullet sped straight to its mark and the man without a cry or a groan threw up his hands and dropped dead in his tracks, shot through the heart.[7] Elizabeth and her husband rushed out of the house at the sound of firing only to see Boone standing on the defense with a smoking rifle in his hands, and the man Holstein lying dead on the ground, weltering in his blood.[8]

"Oh, Boone, what have you done?" exclaimed Elizabeth, as she ran to her brother's side, while her husband knelt by the side of the stricken man to examine his wound.

"In God's name, sister," replied Boone, "who is that man, and why did he seek my life?"

"I do not know. He is a stranger, who stopped to enquire the way, and he was half drunk, too. He must have mistaken you for someone else."

"Well," responded Boone, "It was a sad mistake for him, and one which has cost him his life. God knows I am sorry for it, but it was done

[4] According to Barbara Ledbetter, Boone at this time was one of a group of horse wranglers who had come to Vernon in Wilbarger County from ranches north of the Red River to have a good time. With him were Robert Martin, Dick Sheppard, Henry Levitte, L. A. Meade, T. H. Addison and George Lowery (*Ordeal*, 7, 167).

[5] Elizabeth "Eliza" Marlow had married a man named Gilmore (Ibid.).

[6] This name has been variously reported as "Holstein," "Holdson," and "Holton." Ledbetter, without identifying her source, says that the man was named James Holston, that he was a native of Mississippi, and that together with his father and brothers he had made several cattle drives up the trail to the Kansas railheads from central Texas (Ibid., 167–68). It is quite possible that the name was given correctly by Rathmell, and the man was the son of Sim Holstein, a well-known trail driver (Hunter, *Trail Drivers of Texas*, 405, 442).

[7] According to the account related by Ledbetter, when the man brandished a revolver, Boone, "a quick-drawing daredevil," beat him to the draw with his pistol and shot him dead. Mounting up, the wranglers rode out of Vernon, leaving "Holston" dead in the street with a bullet in his head (Ledbetter, *Ordeal*, 7, 167).

[8] The Gilmores did not reside in Vernon at this time, but across the Red River in the Indian Territory, according to the Ledbetter account (Ibid.).

in self defense, and it was only a question of his life or mine. What is to be done?"

"You had better seek safety," said Boone's brother-in-law, "for, though you were perfectly justified in the act, there is no telling in this country what trouble and difficulty may result from it."

This, under the conditions and circumstances, was good advice, and Boone hastily prepared to follow it. "You poor devil," he remarked, turning the dead man over on his back, "I'd give a thousand dollars if this hadn't happened, but it is your fault, not mine." Then mounting a fresh horse, and examining well his arms, he sped over the prairies to his mother's home. Hastily informing them of what had transpired, thrusting some money they handed him into his pockets, and buckling on an extra brace of revolvers, he kissed his mother and, putting spurs to his horse, was gone.

Some blamed him, poor boy, for haste and lack of judgment, but no trouble grew out of the affair. Perhaps he was hasty, but when one is being shot at point blank at ten paces, time is short in which to stop and reason and form plans, and rather than be shot to pieces by a drunken wretch it is not unlikely that the average man would have acted as Boone did under the circumstances.

This trouble of Boone's so upset the others of the family that in a short time after they drew up their claims and started for Colorado. None of them had ever committed a violent act before, and although they fully exonerated Boone they were grieved and cast down over the unhappy and deplorable event.

Trinidad was again their objective point, and they sold all the stock except about thirty head of horses, and prepared to make the journey overland. Among the horses kept was the pony which had carried George safely away from the five Indians, and another which was equally a pet. This latter, Shoat, was a prime favorite with them all, and a most remarkable little animal. A noble horse or dog is man's truest friend, we all love them, and to the pioneer in new countries these trusty allies are almost as brothers. Shoat was so called because he was a stocky little fellow and never weighed over 650 pounds at best. He was as knowing and intelligent as many men, and acted more like a human being than an animal. He was an inseparable companion for the boys, and followed them around everywhere, whether in the country or in town. At a word from them he would enter any store or building, climb up stairs, lie flat on his side to be dragged under a wire fence, and in fact do anything he was told to do. When informed that he was sick he would lie down and roll and groan, and roll his eyes as though in great agony, and positively refuse to get well again until copious doses of medicine in the shape of cake or sugar was applied internally. He always followed them on their hunts and expeditions over the country, and if a deer was roped onto his back he would carry it home as fast as he could go, and after being unloaded would strike out to find the boys again. In case they had broken camp and moved farther on in the hunt, Shoat never experienced any difficulty in nosing around in the grass and striking the trail, which he followed with the unerring surety of a hound until he found them. Big prices had often been offered for him and as often were refused.

At Trinidad the entire family were again united, as Boone turned up at that place, and together they set out, after purchasing oxen, new wagons and other overland necessaries, for No-Man's-Land, a neutral strip of the public domain lying between Colorado and the Pan Handle of Texas.[9] Here the five brothers took up some claims, which they worked to great advantage in connection with hunting and trapping. The wild game abounded here in great confusion and consisted of elk, deer, antelope and wolves, the latter being very large and ferocious.

The boys were generally accompanied on their hunting excursions by a dare-devil sort of fellow, by name of Thomas Bull, and it was [on] one of these occasions that an adventure happened [to] them which came very near terminating not only the life of Thomas, but of themselves, and thus abruptly ending this story. The party had struck camp near a rocky

[9] "No Man's Land," also called "The Neutral Strip," or officially "The Public Lands," was a region bordered on the south by the Texas panhandle, on the east by the Cherokee Strip, on the north by Kansas, and on the west by the Territory of New Mexico. Measuring 168 miles east to west and 34 1/2 miles north to south, it would eventually become the panhandle of Oklahoma. But in the 1880s it was a land without laws or courts, lying outside the jurisdiction of any of the surrounding states and territories. It became a favorite haunt of outlaws and fugitives and therefore attracted the Marlows (Chrisman, *Fifty Years*, 15, 310).

Deputy U.S. Marshal Ed Johnson, who would later play an important role in the Marlow saga, led a posse of Texas manhunters into No Man's Land in 1886 after some "criminals who had been run out of the Arbuckle Mountains." He later said that one of those specially deputized for the trip was Sheriff G. T. Douglas of Wilbarger County who was looking for Boone Marlow for murder, but "Boone was not to be found, as he was continually on the dodge" (Johnson, "Deputy Marshal Johnson," 7).

gulch, whose massive and frowning walls towered far above them, and along whose base flowed a clear brook of sparkling water. It was a lonely but picturesque spot, and one well calculated to delight the lover of the chase. While the rest of the men attended to the horses and built a big fire of sage brush and branches of dead trees, young Bull announced his intention of looking around to see if he could not shoot a deer for supper.

"You had better wait until someone is at liberty to go with you," said Charley, "for I have heard that there is a den of the fiercest wolves imaginable around this neighborhood—regular man-eaters."

"Oh, I'm not afraid of wolves," said Tom, as he cocked his trusty rifle and took aim at an imaginary foe, "and besides. I won't go far so if you hear me blaze away, you may come out and help me to skin the deer, or wolf, or whatever it happens to be. Maybe I'll slaughter an elephant or two for supper."

He had not been gone many minutes before the boys heard the familiar ring of his Winchester on the still evening air.

"I guess Tom has got his elephant," remarked Alfred, continuing to fold up some blankets and arrange his couch for the night. Then the first report was followed by another and another in quick succession, and a shout was also heard, mingled with the angry howl of wolves.

"I'll bet Tom is treed by a pack of wolves," said Alfred, dropping his blankets and reaching for a gun, "come on, boys, let's see about him," and they all followed him and dashed down the gulch on a run toward the sound of the firing and the yells.

As they turned a bend at the foot of the gulch a most horrible sight confronted them. A pack of over half a hundred maddened wolves were snapping and snarling, leaping and howling all around Tom, who stood in the center of them with gun clubbed, dealing blows right ant left and making as desperate a fight as he could.

"Give it to 'em, boys," sang out Charley, "don't miss a shot!"

Bang! Bang! Crack! Crack! Rang out the rifles, and five of the ferocious beasts rolled over in death agony, only to be set upon by the rest and torn into shreds and devoured. Another and another volley was poured into them, and then with revolvers and clubbed guns a charge into their midst was made. They were great, hungry, gaunt, wild-eyed beasts, crazed by the smell of blood and the taste of flesh, and with fierce yelps and howls they sprang at their antagonists with foaming and wide open jaws. It was a fierce and hard-fought battle while it lasted, and the crack of the revolvers, the yells of the wolves, and the shouts of the men turned that spot of earth into a hell. Tom, weak and bleeding, relinquished his broken and useless gun and, in a last desperate effort, grasped a giant wolf by the throat as it sprang upon him, and together they rolled over and over among the snapping horde around them.

Hatless, with broken rifles and clothes torn to shreds, it was a sorry little group that stood there when at last the wolves were beaten off. With scratched and bleeding limbs they stood among the torn and mangled carcasses of thirty or more of the blood-thirsty pack, and looked around for Tom. He was found bleeding and unconscious, with the grip of death upon the throat of a monster wolf, whose red tongue hung out upon his breast and eyes staring from their sockets, showed that Tom certainly meant to have company if he was killed. They carried him back to camp, and, after dressing his ugly wounds and forcing brandy down him, he came to and was soon able to sit up on the couch of blankets and furs and tell his story.

"Well, you see," he said, looking mighty pale and weak from loss of blood and the hard fight he had made. "I walked along in hopes of seeing a deer, and never thought any more about what you had said about there being a den of wolves around here somewhere, when all of a sudden a great gaunt-looking fellow boldly rose up from the ground almost at my feet and emphatically refused to let me pass. It was then I remembered what had been said about the den of them, but I reasoned that my Winchester was well loaded and that probably there wasn't more than a half dozen any how, and I ought to be eaten up if I couldn't kill that many. I stood and pondered whether to shoot and run the risk of bringing out several more of the brutes, [when] the one in front of me snapped and snarled so ugly that it made me mad and I up and let him have it. All the time he never took his glaring, yellow eyes off of me, and I took good aim and fired. The smoke hadn't cleared away yet 'til it looked to me like mor'n a hundred of the snarling devils were around me. They fell upon the wolf I had shot and tore him into fragments. I knew this couldn't last long, and that I would have their undivided attention next, so I went to shooting as fast as I could, and when my loads gave out I clubbed the gun and prepared to kill as many of them as possible before they got me down. Then you fellows came up. And you know the rest."

Chapter VI

A DARK AND DIABOLICAL PLOT

While still out on the hunt mentioned in the preceding chapter, and three or four days after the terrible experience with the wolves, the memorable blizzard that swept that section of the country with its wintry blasts in '87 came upon them and caught them far from home and entirely shelterless. Many settlers and hundreds of head of stock froze to death in that terrible storm, and every living creature suffered from the chilling blasts of its icy breath.[1] Our little hunting party tied all the blankets they had in camp over the shivering forms of their horses and then turned them loose, while for themselves they dug a deep pit and stretched a wagon cover over it. During the night they worked incessantly to keep a roaring fire in one end of their hole in the ground, and this they were enabled to do because of having over two hundred pounds of buffalo tallow to feed its flames. It was a dark and terrible night, and one which will remain in the history [memory?] of its survivors as long as they live. When those mighty blizzards of snow are blown over the great tracts of level and unprotected prairie lands in howling hurricanes that

[1] The most memorable blizzard to strike the south plains during the decade of the '80s was a killer storm that swept down out of the north in January 1886, with sub-zero temperatures, high winds and heavy snowfall. Range cattle died by the tens of thousands, and a number of humans, caught away from shelter, froze to death or lost limbs. The winter of 1887 was also severe but the "memorable blizzard" in that country was the "Great White Ruin" of the previous January (Sandoz, *The Cattlemen*, 258–67).

freeze and blight everything in its path, it is an occasion of horror, suffering and death.

Shortly after this Charley also took unto himself a wife,[2] a most estimable young lady whom all were glad to welcome into the family circle, and in the following summer the Marlow brothers sold off their claims in No-Man's-Land and started back to the Indian Territory. Charles and Alfred obtained permission of Agent White,[3] of the Kiowa reservation, to move onto a place held by Sunday Boy, a Kiowa chief,[4] and prepared to settle down to farming and cattle raising. They had been acquainted with the old chief for about ten years and were on the best of terms with him, and he was very much pleased when he found they intended locating on a part of his domain.

It was a custom among this tribe of Indians to hold a big pow-wow before allowing a white man to settle upon the lands of their reservation, and if he was not agreeable to them in every particular, they made life miserable for him until he left the country. So when Charles and Alfred and their wives arrived they found about two hundred Indians congregated and making preparation for a big medicine dance. The ceremony was a most nonsensical affair and lasted two days and nights. The medicine men of the tribe rigged themselves up in fantastic garb, danced around the fires and yelled and shrieked like demented demons, while the others painted their ugly faces and followed suit by dancing, whooping and making fools of themselves on general principles. Sunday Boy's interpreter, a young Indian who had been to school and learned a few things pertaining to civilization, reported every few hours to the boys what progress was being made towards coming to a decision, and finally announced that the tribe gave its gracious permission for them to settle upon the reservation lands. The boys were then invited to a grand

[2] According to the 1900 U.S. Census, this marriage took place in 1888. Emma, Charley's wife, told the enumerator that she was born in July 1863 in California. Her oldest child, Maggie, was born in Missouri in July 1885, three years prior to the marriage. The family, however, gave Barbara Ledbetter an 1884 date for the marriage of Emma Coppenbarger and Charley Marlow (Ledbetter, *Ordeal*, 8, 168).

[3] Eugene E. White was a special agent of the Indian Department (Raymond, *Captain Lee Hall of Texas*, 252).

[4] This Kiowa's name was Sun Boy (Pai-taly), an important chief. In 1872 he was one of a delegation of Comanche and Kiowa chieftains who visited Washington on a junket arranged by the Indian Commissioners (Nye, *Carbine and Lance*, 159–60). In 1877 he was one of ten chiefs for whom the commissioners built a $600 home, and was even important enough to be recorded on the Kiowa hide calendars (Ledbetter, *Fort Belknap Frontier Saga*, 271).

feast, but as Indian fare was not relished very highly by them, they declined with thanks. The houses on the reservation were built for the Indians by the government, and were furnished with cooking stoves, but none were used, the red-skins preferring to live in their tepees and cook out of doors by their camp fires.

The Marlows had many friends among the various tribes of the Nation, especially among the Comanches, and were looked up to and respected as white men who would not harm the Indian, but who would do good to him and teach the ways and wonders of the Great Father's people.

The Comanche tribe loved the boys because of a kindness they had at one time shown their chief, and an Indian never forgets a kindness any more than he does an injury. One morning while after their horses Charley and one of the other boys ran across an old Indian who was wandering around in the timber and evidently lost. He had been wandering around for two days and nights, trying to find the camp of his people, but being very old had got completely turned around. The old chap would not own up to being lost, however, but struck his breast proudly and stoutly affirmed that it was the wigwams of his tribe that were lost, not he. The boys had noticed a party of Indians camped a few hours' ride up the country, and rightly guessed they were the old chief's band, so they made known to him that they would conduct him to where his lost wigwams were, and after taking him to the house, where the women prepared for him a hearty meal, they saddled him a horse and set out in the direction of where they had seen the Indians camped a few days previous. After a ride of a couple hours they came in sight of the camp, and although the chief uttered no further demonstrations of joy than a guttural grunt, his face lit up with pleasure at the sight of his tribe, and the boys felt amply repaid for their time and trouble. When the Indians saw their chief coming in charge of white men, they mistook the situation and supposed he was a captive, and rushed out with wild whoops and drawn weapons to rescue him. This was soon changed to shouts of joy and grunts of approval when they learned from the old chief the true state of affairs and ever after there was nothing too good for the Marlows that lay in their power to give or do.

* * * * *

Leaving the Marlow family attending to their stock and at work on the ranches in the Indian Territory, we will now change the scene, and ask the reader to follow us while we go back a few weeks and enter a certain United States Marshal's office, in the little town of Graham, Young county, Texas,[5] where a deputy stands reading a letter. Let us look over his shoulder and read also:

Sheriff's Office
Trinidad, Colo.

Deputy Ed. Johnson,
Graham, Texas:

Look out for the five Marlow Brothers, who are endeavoring to get away with forty head of horses, stolen from this place.

Doc Burns, Sheriff[6]

The man who reads has but one hand, otherwise is a large, powerful man, with a keen but wicked eye, a square, dog-like jaw, and the general appearance of an unscrupulous and designing scoundrel. He lost his hand by being shot while engaged in a drunken debauch in a house of ill repute in Wichita Falls, a year prior to his introduction at this time, and the reader will learn later on how he lost the other, for at the time of writing this history he has neither hand, and cannot even feed or dress himself.[7]

[5] Young County, in north-central Texas, lies largely in the area of the Western Cross Timbers, but the northwest section is in the West Texas plains. Originally created in 1856 with the town adjacent to Fort Belknap as the seat, it was named for Colonel William C. Young, an early Texas military and political figure. The county was reorganized in 1874, and the seat moved to a town founded by Gustavus and Edwin S. Graham two years before. Graham, in southeastern Young County, with a population of about 600 in 1888, was notable for being the site of the United States Federal Court for the Northwestern Counties of Texas, August 1879 to March 1896 (Tyler, *New Handbook of Texas,* 3:273–74; 6:1130–32).

[6] William T. Burns was elected sheriff of Las Animas County, Colorado, in November 1887 and served one two-year term (Maiden, "Sheriffs of Colorado Counties 1858-1958"). Ledbetter writes that W. T. "Watermelon" Burns was sheriff at Trinidad as early as 1870 and was a lawman off and on for twenty years (Ledbetter, *Ordeal*, 171).

[7] The subject of this excoriating introduction is Edward W. Johnson, a career peace officer who was thirty-four years old in 1888. A native of Clark County, Arkansas, and the son of a Confederate soldier, he married nineteen-year-old Caddo E. Wilson on Valentine's Day, 1877. He first pinned on a lawman's badge at Arkadelphia that same year. In 1880 he located in Texas, where he took a deputy's job under longtime Clay County Sheriff G. Cooper Wright. When William Lewis Cabell took office as U.S. marshal at Dallas in 1885, among the new federal deputies he appointed were his son, Ben F. Cabell, Lon Burrison, John Goodman, John Miller, and Ed Johnson. Burrison and Johnson were assigned to work out of the federal court at Graham. On February 27, 1888, Johnson was involved in a gunfight with a man variously identified as Bob or Frank James in which James was killed and Johnson lost his right arm. Johnson was charged with murder, but was acquitted in a trail the following November. Despite his handicap, he was kept on as a federal officer, a position he held for four years. His son characterized him as

As he reads the letter a plot as dark and damnable as ever disgraced the annals of crime forms itself in this man's brain—a plot which will make him the revolting spectacle which he is to-day, and one which is to create untold trouble, misfortune and misery to innocent men and women, besides causing the ruin and downfall of all connected with it. This plot was against the lives of the Marlow brothers.

---

a serious man who "seldom ever joked but was high-tempered and quick to resent an insult" (Johnson, "Deputy Marshal Johnson," 6–9, 52; Ledbetter, *Ordeal*, 196; *Fort Worth Daily Gazette*, February 29, November 17, 1888). The loss of Johnson's other hand will be discussed in the notes to Chapter XV.

Chapter VII

THE PLOT DEEPENS— THE MARLOWS IN CHAINS

Had E. W. Johnson known how terrible and disastrous would be the result of the dark scheme he planned that bright August day in 1888, he would have paused ere making so fatal a move, but alas! He could see nothing but popularity and gain as an outcome, "for," he soliloquized, "if I go up to the Indian country and arrest these five brothers I will make myself popular with the cattle men, and the $50 apiece for their arrest and ten cents milage on each bringing them down will net quite a neat little sum besides. But the warrants! What am I to do about the necessary papers? Bah! What does it matter? If I have to show a warrant I will manufacture one for the occasion.[1] Yes, I will do it, and my friend Sam Criswell is just the man to assist me in the undertaking. It will be hard on the Marlows, but will be the making of me."

He puts the letter in his pocket, not thinking that he has been thinking aloud, and that the very walls have ears sometimes, and saunters out into the city in search of his trusted ally, Sam Criswell.[2]

[1] Warrants for the arrest of Alf, Charley, Llewellyn and Boone Marlow were issued at Graham by F. W. Girand, U.S. Commissioner for the Northern District of Texas, on August 18, 1888, and turned over to Deputy Marshal E. W. Johnson. The brothers were charged with the theft, in the Indian Territory, of nineteen horses from Bar-Sin-da-Bar, a Caddo Indian. The complaint was filed August 8 (Case No. 238, *The United States v. Alf Marlow, et al*).

[2] This name was spelled "Creswell" in the *Graham Leader* and was copied by Sonnichsen (*I'll Die Before I'll Run*, 201). Raine (*Famous Sheriffs*, 37) spelled it "Cresswell." Although Carrie J. Crouch referred to "Sam Cresswell" in her account of the Marlow troubles (*History of Young County*, 119), she included in her biographies of Young County pioneers a family named "Criswell," to which Sam certainly belonged (Ibid., 187). The name was spelled "Criswell" by

What Johnson meant by making himself popular with the cattle men may here be explained by stating that in Northern Texas the rich cattle barons practically ruled the country, and the officers who "stood in" with them soon became wealthy and influential. They had formed an association for mutual aid in preventing thieves from raiding the ranches and running off the cattle, and Johnson had been employed by this association in this capacity.[3] The country was infested with bands of thieves and marauders whose desperate and lawless acts were practically unchecked as yet, as Johnson had made but little headway against these "Rustlers," as they were termed. So he determined to arrest somebody on charge of horse-stealing, fearing the stock men would lose confidence in his ability unless he arrested someone once in awhile, and knowing full well that in that frontier region it was easier to convict an innocent man of horse-stealing than a guilty man of murder. He learned that the Marlow boys owned a large number of horses, and thought that because of their nomadic life it would be an easy matter to swear them into the penitentiary.

The Marlow brothers were but boys then, some of them not yet grown,[4] and with the exception of Boone's trouble, already mentioned, had never by word or deed been guilty of the slightest violation of the laws. And why should they? In the Texas Pan-handle all the good horses that one could wish ran wild, and could be had by lassoing them. Deer were as plentiful as the trees; there were turkeys without number and

---

Ted Johnson, who knew the family well. "Sam Criswell," he said, "was a brave fellow and had been with my father almost continually on his trips to the Territory" (Johnson, "Deputy Marshal Johnson," 53). Johnson's deputy is identified as Samuel H. Creswell by Barbara Ledbetter in her account (Ledbetter, *Ordeal*, 13).

[3] In February 1877, primarily in response to depredations by cow thieves, the Northwest Texas Stock Raisers' Association was organized at Graham by three pioneer cowmen, C. C. Slaughter, James C. Loving and C. L. "Kit" Carter (Sandoz, *The Cattlemen*, 216–21). Three hundred cattlemen attended the first meeting held February 15 and 16 (Crouch, *History of Young County*, 137–38). Among the measures agreed upon was the employment of stock detectives or "protection men" to be paid by the association. These "association men" were expected to look out for the interests of all members and to hunt down and harass cattle and horse thieves wherever they could be found. Since this private security work coincided to some extent with public police responsibility, municipal, county, state, and federal officers sometimes were secretly on the payroll of the cattlemen's association. This is the charge made against Deputy Marshal Johnson by the Marlows. It is repeated by Ledbetter, who says that he was paid $150 a month by the cattlemen (Ledbetter, *Ordeal*, 196). No evidence is cited in either book to substantiate the charge.

[4] This is a transparent attempt to gain the reader's sympathy for the "boys." In August 1888 the five Marlow brothers ranged in age from thirty-three (George) to twenty-one (Llewellyn). They were definitely all grown, and were tough, frontier-hardened men.

game of every description swarmed the country in flocks and droves. The hides and furs from the different wild animals brought them a goodly store of money, which[,] having no particular use for it, they laid by for future days. If they saw a horse that pleased their fancy they had ample means to buy it at any time. They had no incentive to be dishonest, in the first place, and in the second place, it was against their teachings and their frank Western nature.

In a few days after the receipt of the letter read in the preceding chapter Johnson, Criswell and a posse of deputies started out on their unrighteous mission. Johnson received a second letter, written in the Sheriff's bold scrawl, bearing the Trinidad post mark, which was forwarded to him from Graham, Texas, and read as follows:

Deputy E. W. Johnson,
Graham, Texas.

I find that I was mistaken in regard to the forty head of horses. The parties owning them have since found them. They had only estrayed. I remain,

Yours truly,
Doc. Burns, Sheriff.[5]

After perusing the contents of this letter carefully, he roughly thrust it into his pocket, thinking little or nothing more about it, where it remained for months, only to be brought up against him as a witness of truth.

How much better it would have been for all had this unscrupulous deputy explained the situation clearly to his posse, and with them returned to Graham. But no! he had his plans laid, had men to assist him to put them into execution, his desire to "put a new feather in his cap" by arresting somebody grew stronger and stronger, and the idea of returning without accomplishing his purpose did not enter his mind.

Johnson had never seen the Marlow brothers, knew nothing about them, and in fact did not pretend to know anything himself, and after becoming acquainted with them had the grace to admit that "he liked the boys very well." Still, for a bit of popularity and a few dollars he

[5] Raine accepted the story of the original communication from Sheriff Burns, but was dubious with regard to this second message and the allegation by the Marlows that Johnson "pigeonholed" it (Raine, *Famous Sheriffs*, 27). Ted Johnson, in his version, made no mention of either message.

would swear them into prison, and was the means of the two younger of the five brothers losing their lives. Besides five other known deaths, making seven in all from the same cause.

Johnson and posse reached the place where Boone, Ellie and Mrs. Marlow were living one Saturday in August.[6] At the time of their arrival Boone and a young fellow by name of Metz[7] were gathering corn in a field near by, while Ellie had gone over to a neighbor's.

There was, consequently, no one at the house except the old lady. The day was very warm and she cordially invited them into the house out of the sun. They asked for water, which she drew from the well near[by] with her own hands, never dreaming that she was supplying the wants of men that would in a short time take her sons away to their death.

Her love for her boys was as their love for her, and each other—fierce and consuming. Not one of them would have hesitated to fight a regiment in defense of the other. Of a Spartan nature, she rejoiced in the stern and lofty denunciation of the Jewish prophets. Her religion taught her to demand an eye for an eye, and a tooth for a tooth. All she asked of the world was for it to let her and hers alone, but if wrong were done them, forgiveness was strange to her nature.

Johnson pretended that he wanted to hire the boys to drive some cattle for him, and asked where he could find them, and if they would be in soon. The reader will see by this, that in spite of their roaming, Gypsy-like life, they did a great deal of work at times. They worked for the sake

[6] According to Ted Johnson's account, Deputy Marshal Johnson made two trips into the territory during the summer of 1888 after the Marlows. On the first trip, made in the company of two deputies, he had been advised at Fort Sill by Indian Agent Lee Hall "that the Marlow Brothers were a bad bunch, heavily armed, and would not surrender easily." Hall "insisted on sending one Indian Police and two soldiers with them" said Johnson. But the boys were not at the Marlow place when the officers arrived. The women said they were away trading in the Pottawatomie country. Johnson led his posse after them, but they were not to be found, and he returned to Graham (Johnson, "Deputy Marshal Johnson," 7). This trip, however, could not have taken place as stated. Indian Agent Lee Hall, under a cloud of allegations of financial improprieties, had been relieved of his duties in October 1887 (Raymond, *Captain Lee Hall*, 252). The trip could have been made prior to this, however. Later, in the summer of 1888, Johnson "got a tip" that the Marlows were home, working their crops. Accompanied by Deputy Marshal Lon Burrison and possemen Sam Criswell, Marion A. Wallace and David "Dink" Allen, he returned to Indian Territory. At Fort Sill the posse was reinforced by two Indian policemen and an unspecified number of soldiers (Johnson, "Deputy Marshal Johnson," 7). One of the Indian policemen reportedly was a son of the famous Kiowa chieftain, Santana (Ledbetter, *Ordeal*, 13).

[7] This man is identified as William Montcrief by Ledbetter (*Ordeal*, 9).

of working only, and not for the cash they received, for money they as little regarded as a man would water in a country where it was plentiful. The unsuspecting woman told where each and every one of the boys were and when she expected Boone and Elsie [Ellie] to return, never once thinking that they would be arrested, and why should she, for none of the boys, with the exception of the killing of Holstein by Boone, in self defense, had ever broken the laws of the country in the smallest degree.

After about an hour Johnson and posse took their departure, saying that perhaps they would meet Ellie on the way, return with him and talk over whatever bargain he and they might make with Boone, who they hoped would be back when they returned. On finding Ellie they ordered him to throw up his hands. This order was repeated the third time before he made a move to obey, so astonished was he.

After taking Ellie prisoner, they proceeded to the cornfield, where Boone was at work. As they passed the house on their way to the field, the ever watchful mother perceived by Ellie's indignant look that something was wrong, and as the cavalcade neared the house she ran out and demanded an explanation. They paid no attention whatever to the poor old lady, but kept on in the direction of the field, the mother following on foot as fast as her aged steps would carry her.

After arresting Boone, and the young man with him, Johnson left the party with directions to unload the corn as he wanted the wagon to convey the prisoners back to Anadarko,[8] while he rode back to meet the mother, who was slowly plodding along toward them, and when in speaking distance he informed her very decidedly that she wouldn't be allowed to go any nearer the wagon.

"Sir," she said, "I have started to my sons, and I shall go in spite of anything you or anybody else can say or do."

"I tell you, Mrs. Marlow, that you shall not go to your thieving sons. Of course, though. You know what they have done without my enumerating their crimes. I am having your wagon unloaded to carry them to the agency, and you won't see them before they go, either. Do you understand?"

[8] Anadarko, thirty-seven miles north of Fort Sill, was the site of the Government Agency for some 4,000 Comanche, Kiowa, Wichita, Apache, and Caddo Indians (Raymond, *Captain Lee Hall*, 229).

"Stand out of my path, sir; I am going at any risk."

"I tell you that you are not, and I don't care to be seen standing talking to you. You had better be moving along toward your shanty."

"I tell you, sir, that I started to see my boys, and see them I will, or die in the attempt." With that she darted past with more agility than one would think she possessed and gained the wagon before he could prevent her.

A few seconds later Johnson came up and ordered the prisoners (they had been handcuffed before) into the wagon. The mother in spite of all their orders and curses followed. The prisoners were chained down to the wagon, making it impossible for any of them to drive. The roads being very sloppy and muddy, they endeavored to ride as close to her as possible, by which means they were able to splatter mud and water over her. The party seemed in a great hurry, but their hurry effected [*sic*] the old mother very little, and in spite of all their curses, blows and threats, she took her own time.

When within a quarter of a mile of Anadarko the prisoners were removed from the wagon, Johnson for some cause or other preferring to walk them into town. Here the boys persuaded their mother to go to a friend's house, a short distance from where the halt was made, take the team and place them in safe keeping till they were needed again, stay at the place over night herself and come to see them the next morning. Johnson had found by this time that he made but little headway in managing her by harsh treatment, so decided to change his tactics and accordingly told her that she could see the boys as early the next morning as she desired; so, bidding them an affectionate farewell until the next morning, Johnson moved away with them, leaving the aged woman standing alone in the fast gathering darkness. When she could no longer see them she climbed into the wagon and drove to the friends'. After a sleepless and miserable night, she, just as the sun was rising, made her way to the place where Johnson had told her the prisoners were to be incarcerated for the night. After a long and tiresome hour or more, she was let in by Johnson himself, who very politely asked her to return to her home, get the boys a change of clothes, and return in the afternoon as early as she liked, and that then she could see the boys and have a long talk with them besides. The disappointed old lady turned away with a throbbing heart to retrace her steps, having taken no nourishment since the noon before.

By 1 o'clock she was once more at the jail, only to be informed by the person in charge that Johnson, with posse and prisoners, had been on their way to Fort Sill for about four hours.

In speaking of it afterwards Mrs. Marlow says: "Disappointment or grief very rarely kills. When I was told that this man Johnson, who had showed so plainly to me of what kind of material his being was constructed, had taken my dear children away, I felt as though I was choking to death. My heart stood perfectly still for a few moments, then beat so rapidly and fast I thought it would burst out of my bosom. But I did not die then or afterwards, either, when Charley and George came home to me in the early morning of a cold, gray Sunday, with such ghastly, blood stained faces and hands that I could hardly believe that they really lived, and I was told that two more of my darling boys lay dead on the hard ground in a dark and lonely place where their poor bodies had been riddled with bullets without mercy, and yet at another time while I watched by the side of a third dear son that had been robbed of his life by a man whom he had befriended as a dear brother in many instances, and still I never died of grief, yet I would have gladly laid down this troublesome life if my other two could have gone, too. No, trouble rarely kills. It is a means of torture that makes one long to die, but that is all."

Johnson and posse with prisoners reached Fort Sill in the afternoon. Here they remained until the following morning when they went twelve miles [to] town to Sunday Boy's place where Charley and Alfred were arrested. This was on the 29th of August, 1888.[9] Both places were searched for fire-arms. In all was found one shotgun belonging to Boone, that had laid wrapped in a bed sheet so long that it was rusty, proving that it

[9] This account differs substantially from that given by Ed Johnson as related by his son. In the Johnson version, the posse, upon arrival at the Marlow place, caught Charley, George, Alfred and Llewellyn unarmed and away from the house and effected their arrest. Boone was not there. The altercation with Mrs. Marlow was mentioned: "The womenfolk . . . started with guns to the field. . . . It took considerable argument and persuasion to convince the mother that the other two were under arrest, and before she would give up the guns." Johnson said the party and their prisoners stopped at Fort Sill the first night of their return trip. The next day, when they started back to Texas, was August 29, according to Johnson ("Deputy Marshal Johnson," 7).

was used but seldom. From Ellie they took a six shooter and a Winchester, the same from Alfred and Charley, making seven pieces in all.[10]

At Sunday Boy's place young Metz was turned loose.[11] They had only kept him from informing the other two boys of the arrest of Boone and Ellie. Charley's and Alfred's wives were placed under guard and sent to Anadarko, where they joined the poor old mother, while Johnson and posse with the four brothers started to Graham, a distance of seventy-five miles, in a lumber wagon.[12]

The Marlow brothers were accused of stealing 130 head of horses from an Indian by name of Bar-Sin-da-Bar.[13] When examined, this old Indian testified that he did not own that many horses and had lost none at all, and that "Marlow men no steal Indian man's horses anyway, because he have better horse he get somewhere else, but Indian man think white mans steal (meaning Johnson and posse) if Indian man don't sleep with one eye open." During this trouble the boys' Indian friends came to the front like true friends indeed. Old Sunday Boy wanted to

[10] "I remember my father telling me about the enormous amount of firearms the Marlow brothers had in the house when arrested—buffalo guns, .45 six-shooters, shotguns and carbine rifles—all of the best makes and plenty of ammunition. Most of this was taken and left at Fort Sill" (Ibid., 8). In reporting the arrest, the *Graham Leader* said that the Marlows "had in their possession a goodly number of the best Sharp's rifles, and if Mr. Johnson had failed to get the 'drop,' they would, no doubt, have made it lively for the posse" (September 6, 1888).

[11] There was no mention of Metz (or Montcrief) in the Johnson account. Barbara Ledbetter says that the man was brought to Graham and jailed with the Marlow brothers. A day later he was released (Ledbetter, *Ordeal*, 14, 166).

[12] Johnson said he rode in a hack with the ironed prisoners while the other officers rode horseback. The next night was spent in camp just across the Red River in Texas. Here, according to Ted Johnson's account as related by his father, the brothers tried to escape:

> The Marlows were shackled in pairs and handcuffed. Everyone except my father and Wallace were sleeping on pallets on the ground. The guards took two hours relay on watch. The guard that went on duty at two o'clock in the morning went to sleep sitting against a tree, with a Winchester across his lap. During the night one of the prisoners had slipped the handcuffs and seeing the guard asleep, he quietly awakened the others and they, in whispers, planned their escape. They were to take the breast yoke from the tongue of the hack, as they were sleeping close to it, knock the sleeping guard in the head, take his arms, kill Wallace and Johnson, and force the others to release their chains. Then disarm and take the hack and horses and make their escape. Whether this plan would have worked or not we do not know, but we do know it would have been a desperate fight. But Wallace happened to awake and hearing the whispers of the prisoners awoke Johnson and they made a search of them, to find the handcuffs slipped. They relocked the handcuffs and sat up the rest of the night themselves. (Johnson, "Deputy Marshal Johnson," 7)

[13] On September 5, 1888, additional warrants were issued for the Marlows, charging them with theft in March 1886 of "about 20 head of horses, the property of Black Crow, a Comanche Indian," and "13 head of horses, the property of Washington, a Caddo Indian." When indictments were filed on October 17, the brothers were charged with two thieving forays on the herds of Bar-Sin-da-Bar. On March 10, 1885, they were said to have stolen five mares, ten geldings, three fillies, and one foal with a combined value of $640; six days later they reportedly stole nine

pledge all of his stock, lands, and squaws for Charley's and Alfred's freedom, and many others offered as much according to their positions. These offers were all refused on the plea of its being unlawful to take an Indian on a white man's bond.

While the women were being held at Anadarko, from what cause they never knew, George, who was ignorant of the trouble his brothers had been so suddenly thrown into, came into Anadarko on some business connected with the ranch where he was putting up hay. As soon as Agent White, before mentioned, knew of his arrival he placed him under arrest, saying that he had been ordered to do so by Johnson.

Again his Indian friends proved how sincere their regard was for him; every nicknack or sweet that they thought he would eat was brought to him. On the seventh day of his imprisonment the women of the Marlow family were placed under a guard and conducted across the country to Red River. About four days later George was released. The women had left Shoat for him to overtake them on, and here George practiced a

---

mares, six geldings, two fillies, and two foals with a total value of $512 (Case #235, *The United States v. Alf Marlow et al*).

Johnson's account contains no mention of the Colorado horse theft charge so emphasized by Rathmell. That there was such a charge is substantiated by news items announcing the arrests. The *Graham Leader* (September 6, 1888) reported that the brothers were "charged with horse stealing in the Territory and Trinidad, Colorado." Said a special dispatch to a Fort Worth paper from Trinidad on September 22:

> Word has been received by Sheriff Barns [*sic*] that a gang of seven horse thieves among whom were the five Marlow brothers, well known characters of this region, had been captured in the Indian Territory by Deputy United States Marshal Johnson, and were now held in Texas. With the gang were recovered twenty head of horses, the majority being recognized by the brands as belonging in this section. The depredation of the brothers have been going on for some time, but it seems impossible to get hold of them. They will probably soon be brought to Trinidad and tried for their crimes. (*Fort Worth Daily Gazette*, September 23, 1888)

Later writers have added to the confusion surrounding the arrest of the Marlows. Carrie J. Crouch wrote that "there were no charges against any of the Marlows except George," but that "in addition to George, Johnson decided to bring the other four brothers . . . back from Indian Territory to Graham for trial in Federal Court" (Crouch, *History of Young County*, 116). This assertion was repeated by Sonnichsen (*I'll Die Before I'll* Run, 195). Interesting also is the apparent disagreement in the various accounts as to which brothers were jailed at Graham and when that jailing occurred. According to Johnson, "As Boone was not at home at this time (August 1888) the four arrested were Charlie, George, Alf, and Lep." Boone was not taken until December when he "was arrested by soldiers at Fort Sill, Indian Territory, and was brought to Graham by Johnson and placed in jail about December 12, 1888" (Johnson, "Deputy Marshal Johnson," 7, 9). Crouch (*History of Young County*, 116), followed by Sonnichsen (*I'll Die Before I'll Run*, 195), reported all five brothers jailed at once by Johnson. The Rathmell version—that Charley, Boone, Ellie and Alfred were brought together from Indian Territory by Johnson and that George was arrested weeks later—is in agreement with the stories in the *Graham Leader* and court records and has been repeated by Raine, Ledbetter and Shirley (*The Fighting Marlows*).

little deception on his Indian friends, quite a crowd of whom gathered around to see him off.

"Friends," he said, as he slyly whispered in the wise little horse's ear, "if this horse lays down I will see my squaw before 10 o'clock tonight." Shoat understood the whispered communication, instantly stretched himself out, to the amazement and delight of the superstitious Indians. After a few more little mysterious passes, to make them more firmly believe in his ability as a great prophet, he struck out in the direction the women folks had gone four days before. The Indians had given him a lunch of cheese and crackers, and at noon he halted long enough for Shoat to eat this, eating nothing himself. About 6 o'clock Shoat began to sniff the air, and seemed to take on new life. George gave him the reins, and at 9 o'clock sharp he ferreted them out, camped off the road a little distance. Between 8:30 in the morning and 9 o'clock that night this little fellow had carried George ninety-five miles. The friendly Indians had not left them, and seemed as happy as the poor lonely women when George and Shoat came in. They thought they could out-ride a white man when it came to riding fast or long distances, but this trip fairly astonished them, and when a few days later they returned and told how he had overtaken them on the same day that he had left Anadarko, they were more ready than ever to believe that he was a great prophet.

George's next work was to reach Graham, where the United States Judge of the northern district of Texas held court for the convenience of the Panhandle and other counties on the northwestern frontier of Texas.[14] George wanted to take all their stock, if possible, for as soon as he reached Graham he intended to have the other boys cleared of this trouble and thought the stock might be useful to turn into ready money. The brothers had been able to prove where each had been bought and at what time, so had no fears of being detained for any great length of time.

[14] This judge was Andrew Phelps McCormick (1832–1916). Admitted to the bar in 1855, McCormick served in the Confederate Army, was a judge in Brazoria County, participated in the Constitutional Conventions of 1866 and 1868–69, and was elected to the Texas Legislature. In 1879 he was appointed United States judge for the Northern District of Texas at Graham (Tyler, *New Handbook of Texas*, 4:379). Ted Johnson called him "a tyrannical judge" (Johnson, "Deputy Marshal Johnson," 49).

Chapter VIII

WAR CLOUDS— BOONE GATHERS ANOTHER VICTIM

Upon arriving at Graham, George's first efforts were endeavors to provide bail for his imprisoned brothers, but in this he was temporarily balked, and instead was himself thrown into jail with them,[1] by Johnson and Criswell who, having started in, were as relentless as death in their prosecution. In the few days prior to his arrest George had secured the services of an attorney, one Robert Arnold,[2] who subsequently turned

[1] According to the *Graham Leader* of October 11, 1888, Deputy Marshal Johnson arrived in town on October 7 with four prisoners he had brought back from the Indian Territory. Besides Pete Berry, "an old violator of the law . . . for whom Mr. Johnson has been on the look out for a long time," T. A. Atterson, wanted for cattle stealing in Wilbarger County, and Bill Murphy, charged with horse stealing in the territory, Johnson had under arrest "George Marlow, brother of the four Marlows already in custody, who is also charged with horse stealing." The paper noted that Murphy was a nephew of the Marlow brothers and had agreed to testify as a government witness against them. A warrant for George was issued on October 7 by Commissioner Girand and signed by Deputy Marshal Johnson as having been executed that day (Case #234, *The United States v. George Marlow*).

The story as handed down in the family is that George wagoned into Graham about October 1 with a number of family members. Besides the boys' mother, there were the wives of George, Charley and Alf, each with a young daughter. Included in the entourage were Bill Murphy, son of the boys' sister, Nancy, and Pete Berry, brother of George's wife. A hired man, Zane Ousley, also was with the group. It was when George, Murphy and Berry went to the jail with Mrs. Martha Jane Marlow to see the brothers that they were arrested by Johnson and locked up with them (Ledbetter, *Ordeal*, 16–17). The grand jury failed to bring indictments against Murphy and Berry and they were released. Neither would cooperate in the cases against the Marlows as a prosecuting witness. They were told to get out of town and they lost no time in complying. When Zane Ousley came into Graham for supplies, Deputy Marshal Johnson also ordered him to leave and he, too, quickly departed (Ibid., 18–19).

[2] Robert Frederick Arnold, a Mississippian, attended Jacinto College, was admitted to the bar at Fort Worth, and moved to Graham in 1879. He served as judge of the Court of Criminal Appeals, district judge, and county judge (Crouch, *History of Young County*, 174). At the time of the Marlows' troubles he had law offices with attorney C. W. Johnson, the father of Carrie J. Crouch (Ledbetter, *Ordeal*, 17, 218).

out to be a bosom friend of Johnson's. He took the case for $500, which George paid without a word, and would have paid three times the amount had it been asked, as he was ignorant in those days of courts, law and lawyers as an unborn babe. That the Marlows were inexperienced in such things is plainly shown by the fact that they allowed Johnson to arrest and imprison them without a warrant or any other show or proof of legal authority; and again in submitting to the outrage perpetrated by Indian Agent White, when he held George under arrest and forced the innocent and helpless women to leave the country, all without the shadow of authority, right or justice.

About six weeks after George was arrested the Spartan mother succeeded in securing the release of Ellie under heavy bond,[3] who in turn obtained freedom likewise for Charley,[4] and together they raised bail for Boone, giving stock as security to those who became their bondsmen.[5]

After the brothers were all released, George and his wife, with Boone and Ellie, rented a farm near by and went on with their usual work, while Charles and Alfred, with their wives and mother, secured another place fifteen miles out of Graham and some seven miles from the rest of the family.

[3] Epp (Ellie) Marlow was released on bond on October 29, three weeks after George had been jailed. He, J. D. Short and Charles Short jointly signed an appearance bond in the amount of one hundred dollars to insure Marlow's appearance before the next regular term of the district court. Epp made his mark with an X (Case #236, *The United States v. Alf Marlow, et al*). The fact that Charley at this time could not sign his name makes ridiculous Rathmell's assertion (in Chapter III), that he had written "ardent love verses" years before. Charles Short was apparently J. C. Short, whose hardware, tin, and gun shop was the first business established on the south side of the square in Graham (Crouch, *History of Young County*, 269).

[4] Charley gained his freedom on November 30 when he, D. C. Brooks, and John Gilmore signed an appearance bond identical to that of Epp. Like his brother, Charley made his mark (Case #146, *The United States v. Charles Marlow*). Brooks and Gilmore were members of families which would figure prominently in the dramatic events that followed the Marlow brothers' jailing.

[5] On December 6 Alf and George were released on one hundred dollars appearance bonds. Alf made his mark, but George signed his name as G. W. Marlow. Signing with them were D. C. Brooks, O. G. Denson and Frank Herron (Case #238, *The United States v. Alf Marlow, et al*; Case #239, *The United States v. Alf Marlow*). Boone was not freed until December 15. He could write and laboriously scrawled "D. B. Marlow," above the signature of Denson and the X of E. P. (Llewellyn) Marlow, who made his appearance bond with him. Of the five brothers, only George and Boone apparently were sufficiently literate to sign their own names (Case #238, *The United States v. Alf Marlow, et al*). Denson and Herron were prominent Young County citizens. Denson had large land holdings in Young County, much of it planted in cotton; the Marlows were living on Denson property. Frank Herron was a resident of Young County as early as 1876 (Crouch, *History of Young County*, 172; Johnson, "Deputy Marshal Johnson," 9).

Meantime Johnson and Criswell were not idle. If ever the mind of man was employed with the damnable work of the devil, here was an instance. The good will of the cattle barons must be held at any cost, and for this they would sacrifice the safety, reputation and even the lives of a dozen families if necessary. Their next step in the tragedy was to secure the indictment, through perjury, of the Marlow brothers, for the theft of one hundred and thirty head of horses, alleged to have been stolen from the old Indian Bar-sin-da-bar. The evidence, however, being entirely made up of whole cloth, was so weak and unreliable that the State asked for and was granted a continuance of the case.

Johnson and Criswell then began systematically to create unfavorable public opinion against the boys, by appearing before the court and making oath that they were fugitives from justice. They then industriously disseminated the opinion that the Marlows were cut throats, horse thieves and "rustlers," and so diligently did they work on this infamous scheme that they succeeded in a measure in creating the impression that the boys were, to use the parlance of the day, "bad men." A frontier term which stamps its bearer as a wanton murderer, and makes everyone hate and fear him and wish for his death.

This unfavorable impression which two despicable villains lodged in the minds of many people of Young and adjoining counties was largely the cause of the state of terrorism which afterwards prevailed, and which subsequently brought about the terrible battle of Dry Creek, of which we will speak in detail further on.

Not yet satisfied with their work, Johnson and Criswell next went up to Wilbarger, where they heard of Boone's killing Holstein in self defense some years before, and had a warrant issued on this charge for his arrest,[6] and the same was sent to Sheriff Marion Wallace,[7] at Graham, to serve.[8]

[6] Johnson had been aware of a possible Wilbarger County murder charge against Boone for months. In reporting the original arrest of the brothers in September, the *Graham Leader* had noted that "Boone Marlow is also wanted in Wilbarger county for the murder of Holdson in 1886" (September 6, 1888). Deputy Marshal Johnson, Criswell, and F. W. Girand, clerk of the federal court at Graham, reportedly went to Vernon in Wilbarger County, testified at the grand jury hearings there in October 1888, and were instrumental in securing an indictment against Boone for the 1886 murder, which was handed down on December 1, 1888 (Ledbetter, *Ordeal*, 20, 23). A search of the Wilbarger County criminal files disclosed no record of this case (Wilbarger County Deputy Jan Kennon to Robert K. DeArment, March 27, 1991).

[7] Marion DeKalb Wallace was born in Alabama, June 18, 1846, one of twelve children of a prosperous Chambers County farmer and slave-owner. After seeing action in the Civil War under

On the 17th of December, 1888, Boone and Ellie visited their mother, and as the family were at dinner, Sheriff Wallace and a deputy, Thomas Collier,[9] rode up to the ranch for the purpose of arresting Boone. Both men had been drinking freely before they left town, and were considerable the worse for liquor when they arrived at the Marlow farm. They rode up to the chimney end of the cabin, where there was neither door nor window, and Wallace alighted, tied his horse and walked around the house. Collier rode directly up to a window and peered in, and Boone being first to see him, called out:

"Hello, Tom! Light and come in and have some dinner!"

"I'm not hungry," replied the deputy.

"Come in anyway," urged Boone.

Without replying, Collier alighted and walked to the door as though he meant to accept a seat at the table. He stepped in, and as Boone arose to welcome him he exclaimed:

"Boone Marlow, I'm after you!" As he spoke he aimed his revolver at Boone, and fired right in among the women and children.

Boone dodged the shot and grabbed a Winchester that lay on a bed. Collier, seeing Boone possess himself of the gun, and at the same time seeing that his own shot had missed its mark, jumped back and out of

---

Confederate General "Fighting Joe" Wheeler, he went to South Carolina where he married his cousin. He and his wife, Martha, had nine children. About 1876, the family located near Belknap in Young County (Ledbetter, *Ordeal*, 187–88). Wallace was elected sheriff of Young County November 4, 1884, and re-elected November 2, 1886 (Tise, *Texas County Sheriffs*, 557). "Now Wallace was a popular man and liked by many, a great hand to joke but inclined to be a little overbearing" (Johnson, "Deputy Marshal Johnson," 9).

[8] Johnson said that on the way back from Fort Sill with Boone as his prisoner he "notified the sheriff of Wilbarger County by letter, as he passed through Wichita Falls, that he had Boone and would place him in jail at Graham." After jailing young Marlow, he received orders to return to the Indian Territory. Before leaving, he "cautioned Wallace in particular as to Boone and his character. He told Wallace to be very careful with him, as he had killed one man, shot at another, and further advised Wallace to hold Boone in jail until he received the state warrant from Wilbarger County, which he was sure would only be a few days." Wallace ignored the deputy marshal's warning and, when bond was arranged on Saturday, December 15, released Boone. The following Monday the Wilbarger warrant arrived and Wallace, in attempting to re-arrest Boone, fell victim to his gun (Johnson, "Deputy Marshal Johnson," 9). It is one of the bitter ironies of the Marlow affair that had the warrant arrived two days earlier, or Boone held two days longer, the chain of events resulting in the violent deaths of eight men might have been averted.

[9] Thomas B. Collier came from the same Alabama county as Wallace; their fathers had both been justices of the peace there. Wallace and Collier wagoned to Young County, Texas, together and settled in the same area. When Wallace was elected sheriff, he appointed his close friend as deputy. Although the families were inter-related by marriage, apparently Collier was not a nephew of Sheriff Wallace as has been reported (Ledbetter, *Ordeal*, 187–88; Johnson, "Deputy Marshal Johnson," 53; *Graham Leader*, December 20, 1888).

the door. Boone hastily fired a random shot, the ball penetrating the wall beside the door, grazing Collier's left temple and eye, and carried away about four inches of his hat brim.[10] Boone threw another cartridge into his gun, sprang to the door, gun in hand, and, seeing a man near the corner of the porch, with a cocked and drawn revolver in his hand, fired again, hitting Wallace, who was hastening toward the door. This was the first intimation the boys had that Collier was not alone. Boone, seeing a man on the porch, naturally supposed it to be Collier. Wallace fell headlong upon the porch, his pistol remaining cocked by his side.[11]

On looking for Collier, with the determination of putting an end to his cowardly career at once, Boone saw him running away at full speed. Covering him with his rifle, he shouted to the fleeing deputy to come back, a command Collier meekly obeyed.[12]

When he returned Boone said, pointing to the prostrate form of the wounded sheriff, whose head Charley was supporting in his lap:

"Tom Collier, you are responsible for this. You fired on me like I was a dog, and I thought it was you when I fired."

"I know it," whimpered Collier, "but don't let us say anything more about it."

"You cowardly scoundrel, I shan't let you live a minute," replied Boone. "Charley, let me shoot him between the eyes," [he said,] at the same time drawing bead on the spot indicated. Collier crouched down behind Charley and begged piteously not to permit Boone to kill him. Charley, who was in many respects the leader of the brothers, told Boone not to shoot, and the latter reluctantly took the Winchester from his shoulder. Collier continued to cling to Charley till Boone mounted Shoat

[10] Boone's bullet "passed through Collier's hat, just grazing the temple and almost striking the eye" (*Graham Leader*, December 20, 1888).

[11] The story in the *Graham Leader*, received "from the best authority," came, of course, from Tom Collier. According to this version, Boone "grasped a Winchester and fired" the first shot, nicking Collier, just as "the officers both stepped in the door." He fired again and his bullet "entered the side of Mr. Wallace just above the hip, passing entirely through his body." Not until then did Collier draw his pistol and fire, but, "dazed by the powder-burn of the shot aimed at him . . ., he missed his aim" (Ibid.).

[12] Collier said that Wallace "besought [him] to retreat and save himself, telling him . . . it was a fight of three against one and he stood no chance with such odds." Collier said he then "retired a few rods . . . and stood waiting for some one of the Marlows to show his head at the door. But instead of coming out and facing his revolver," they drew on his affection for the stricken sheriff, saying that "if he would lay down his pistol he might come and administer to the wants of his wounded friend and relative" (Ibid.).

and rode off. Before starting he insisted that each of his brothers present as well as those absent, should regard his wish, swearing to him that in case he should be killed while resisting arrest, (for he would never submit to another arrest—he had been treated too badly in the Graham jail, consequently did not propose to try any more jail life,) "not one of you are to raise an arm in revenge for me. Try to let your troubles die out, if possible. I am the one who shot Wallace, and am willing to pay the penalty, though it was an accident."

Turning to the wounded and gasping sheriff, Boone said:

"You believe me, Mr. Wallace—you believe I never intended to shoot you, don't you? I would not have shot any man only for good reasons and in self defense."

"Why did you shoot me, Boone?" asked the wounded man feebly.

"Don't you understand yet that I thought you were Collier?"

"Did you think I was Tom?"

"I certainly did, for had I recognized you God knows I never would [have] fired, for I have nothing in the world, Wallace, against you."

"I forgive you, Boone, and here is my hand," gasped Wallace, extending a trembling hand, which Boone grasped warmly in both his own.

Wallace was carried into the house, where Mrs. Marlow and the other women administered to his wants as best they could. At Charley's suggestion Ellie caught a horse and went to Graham for a doctor, and once in the saddle, he struck into a furious gallop and never drew a line until in front of the physician's office.[13]

Alfred mounted another horse and rode off to summon the neighbors, and Boone, having by this time disappeared miles away toward the distant horizon, Collier sneaked around the house and made tracks in the direction of town, unnoticed by anyone.[14]

[13] Dr. R. N. Price and his son, William, hurried to the scene of the shooting, taking with them the wife of the sheriff (Johnson, "Deputy Marshal Johnson," 9). Dr. Price arrived in Graham in 1876 and was the town's first physician. Born in Virginia in 1827, Price received his medical training in Philadelphia and practiced in Tennessee until the outbreak of the Civil War in which he served as a Confederate surgeon (Crouch, *History of Young County*, 255).

[14] Needless to say, Collier's account of the moments following the shooting included none of the dialogue and drama detailed by Rathmell. Collier said simply that while he tried to ease the sheriff's suffering, Boone "very deliberately" mounted a horse and rode away (*Graham Leader*, December 20, 1888).

The wounded sheriff suffered a great deal, and though he bore up with the strength and fortitude of a brave man, he could not suppress an occasional moan which the pain forced from his blanched lips. The women staunched the flow of blood, bathed his face and hands, gave him cooling drink and watched over him so carefully that they did not mark the flight of time until they were surprised by the sudden return of Deputy Collier with a crowd of men at his back. Among the men were several of the boys' bondsmen, and they immediately turned the lads over to the tender mercies of Collier, who gave them to understand that they were again prisoners. George, who was seven miles away on his farm when the shooting occurred, had been summoned by Alfred, and the two arrived just in time to be arrested with Charley. Ellie, having started the doctor off in haste to attend to Wallace, remained in town to tell others of what had happened, and was thereupon arrested and thrown into jail without comment or investigation.[15] So in a few hours after that terrible drama of that December day the Marlow brothers again found themselves in custody and confronted by a more serious charge than before.[16] Not all of them, either, as Boone was well out of the country, and was never again seen alive by any of them except his mother and three sisters-in-law.

Upon the arrival of the doctor the wounded sheriff was placed in a hack and removed to Graham, where he lingered between life and death

[15] Ed Johnson recalled that it was Alfred who rode into town for the doctor, was arrested and jailed there, and the other three brothers were jailed the next day. Johnson, however, was not in town at the time of the shooting and his memory may have been faulty since he got the details secondhand after his return (Johnson, "Deputy Marshal Johnson," 9). The *Graham Leader* reported only that "one of the Marlow brothers came to town and brought the news and was promptly locked up" (December 20, 1888).

[16] On December 31, 1888, Charley, Alf, and Epp Marlow, "charged in two counts with complicity in the murder of Sheriff Wallace" were brought before Justice J. S. Starrett, examining magistrate, given until January 4, 1889, to procure testimony, and remanded to jail without bail (*Graham* Leader, January 3, 1889). At the preliminary hearing on January 4 before the same magistrate, evidence was heard and arguments made: "It is the theory of the State that [the three brothers] were present, aiding and abetting in the offense, if not actual participants, [while] the defense contends that Boone Marlow did the shooting without the advice or assistance of his brothers" (Ibid., January 10, 1889). At the conclusion of the hearing Charley, Alf, and Epp were again remanded to jail "in default of bail in the sum of one thousand dollars each to await the action of the grand jury" (Ibid.). George, who was not present at the Denson house at the time of the Wallace shooting, had been arrested with his brothers. As he was not charged in that case and had been freed on bond in the horse theft cases, it is unclear on what grounds he continued to be held.

for just a week before he died. He was shot on the 17th and buried on the 25th. [17]

Sheriff Wallace was a popular man and leading citizen and had treated the Marlows kindly while they were in his care before they were released on bail, and after they were released he was a frequent visitor to their home, and not one of them would have intentionally harmed him.[18]

After the boys were again arrested, Young Ousley, the same young man that assisted George in bringing the stock down, returned to help the women in any way he could. Johnson, fearing that this young man would be of some use to them, gave him a given length of time to quit the country, which threat had its desired effect. This left the four women alone.

The Marlow brothers had ceased to fear Johnson because of the reputation of the man in general. Some of the best citizens had expressed their opinion of him to the effect that he amounted to very little as a man of honor.[19] Among these was the late sheriff, who expressed himself thus:

"All Johnson wants is your stock; he will let you alone when he gets all your money. He isn't apt to molest a poor man. Yes," he continued, as he seemed to recollect some past villainy of Johnson's, "the infernal rascal has forged many a warrant to make a few dimes."

[17] Boone's bullet had pierced both of Wallace's kidneys and he evidently died of uremic poisoning. During the week prior to Christmas he drifted in and out of consciousness. "When the dread delirium came on he seemed to take up his work again," said the *Leader*. "He trailed thieves and murderers and often from his ravings his nurse discovered that his detective instinct led him in his delirium upon the imaginative trail of his own murderer" (December 27, 1888). Wallace died at 10:00 on the morning of December 24 and was buried on Christmas Day (Ibid.).

[18] In emphasizing the point that Wallace was shot accidentally, Rathmell and the Marlows are evidently unaware of an inconsistency in their story. Supposedly, Boone fled after the shooting because "he had been treated too badly in the Graham jail," but now it is asserted that Wallace "had treated the Marlows kindly while they were in his care." Bill Ribble, a neighbor of Denson, told C. L. Sonnichsen in 1944 that Collier had mistreated Boone at the jail and for that reason Boone tried to kill him. Wallace stepped in front of Collier just as Marlow fired (C. L. Sonnichsen Papers).

[19] Bill Ribble was one of these, describing Johnson in 1944 as "about the sorriest man that ever was" (Sonnichsen Papers). Johnson's son, of course, presented an entirely different view of the relationship between the officer and the citizenry. "I want to say here that God never created a nobler or better class of people than the old-timers of Young County," he wrote. When the Johnson family was in dire financial straits in later years, "many are the ways [these people] helped us until we finally got to where we could make our way" (Johnson, "Deputy Marshal Johnson," 53).

Chapter IX
REWARD FOR BOONE, DEAD OR ALIVE— HIS ESCAPE

A large reward was offered for the capture of Boone Marlow, dead or alive, and in consequence the country swarmed with men eager to obtain this reward, either by fair means or foul.[1] Boone soon learned of this, and fearing detection, he retraced his steps back to the home place and hid for the time being in a large stack of wheat straw, half a mile from the house. He tunneled into this big hill of straw for quite a ways, and excavated a room in its interior large enough for all practical purposes. No one ever dreamed he was in the neighborhood, though a crowd of men and officers seeking his life because of the high reward were continually about the premises, thinking no doubt that perhaps he might seek to communicate by some means with his family, and thereby leave some clue by which he might be traced and hunted down.

Food was conveyed to Boone by Charley's wife, who displayed more courage and nerve than is usually shown by womankind, and showed herself to be a true heroine. This brave and true-hearted little woman made the trip from the house to the stack under cover of the darkness

[1] Young County posted a reward of fifteen hundred dollars for Boone's capture; the state of Texas offered an additional $200 if the fugitive were delivered "inside the jail door of said county" within six months (Crouch, *History of Young County*, 117; *Graham Leader*, December 27, 1888). The murder of a fellow officer and the lure of the reward money quickly drew lawmen from neighboring counties. The day after the shooting, Sheriff John J. Douglass of Stephens County arrived in Graham with a posse. From Jack County came Sheriff George W. Moore at the head of another large posse. The *Graham Leader* called for "all good citizens [to] turn out and assist in [the] capture" (December 20, 1888).

every night shortly after midnight, going around by different routes each night and stealing through the trees and past guards and spies with the stealth of an Indian and the silence and swiftness of the air. How she ever managed to escape detection was a mystery, as at no time were there less than fifty to seventy-five men prowling around day and night, and watching with sleepless eyes for any sign or clue of Boone or his whereabouts.[2]

George's wife, Lillian, had moved over, after his arrest, in order to be with the rest of the women, and to assist in any possible way in bearing the terrible burden of sorrow and distress which had fallen upon them all.

None save themselves can realize how these four helpless and defenseless women suffered and were tortured by the official and the hordes of reckless men who continually hung around the neighborhood of the ranch and made life miserable for them in a thousand ways. They overhauled everything on the place and in the house, and nothing was too sacred to escape their prying eyes and ruthless hands. They would come into the house and tear down pillows and poke around the beds with their guns, and tear up the floor, under pretense of hunting for Boone, but really more to irritate and madden the poor half-crazed women than anything else. There was not a box, trunk, closet or drawer that escaped their pilfering hands. There were many volumes of valuable medical works and a few hundred dollars worth of medicines which the family kept in tender remembrance of the good old Dr. Marlow, and these were tumbled about and as roughly used as everything else in the house, until Mrs. Marlow became desperate at the insults and ill usage heaped upon them, and with the help of the girls dug a deep grave one dark night in the bed of a ravine and buried them, preferring them to go to decay to being polluted by the vulgar touch of drunken and insolent moneyed blood-hunters.

Many a night did these helpless and terrified women carry their beds into the woods and pass the night huddled together in tears and trembling fear, rather than remain in the house and run the risk of having it burned over their heads.

[2] The extent of the surveillance of the Marlow house obviously is greatly exaggerated. Given the number of men said to be watching the house, it is unbelievable that Emma Marlow could take food to Boone's hiding place night after night without detection.

With all their braggadocio and daring talk of how anxious they were to meet Boone, not any twelve of them would have dared to stand before him, or make any demonstration against his life or safety, unless it were from ambush or in some cowardly manner behind his back. Boone was but a little fellow, scarce five feet in height, and slender build,[3] but his nerve and bravery in the face of danger was so well known and respected in that country that none cared to provoke his wrath or get within reach of his unerring Winchester. They were all very brave, however, when it came to insulting and browbeating defenseless women, and so for weeks this gang of disreputable hounds howled around the Marlow residence, kept themselves two-thirds drunk all the time and made day and night hideous with their noise and boasting threats.

After remaining in hiding in the straw stack for three weeks, a listener and witness to about all that was transpiring around, Boone concluded to change his hiding place to one nearer the house, mentally vowing vengeance upon the first man he saw offering insult to his mother or any of the women who were like [his] own sisters to him. So he looked well to his trusty Winchester and the next night communicated his desires for a change of location to Emma when she same with his daily allowance of food. It was a hazardous and extremely difficult undertaking for him to make his way among nearly a hundred guards and spies who surrounded the house for a radius of a mile or more, ready to shoot him like a dog at sight, but Boone knew no such word as fear, and so at about the hour of midnight he crept silently and cautiously out from the stack and like an Indian stalking a foe crawled through the brush and into the grove of trees. With the silence of death he made his way toward the ranch yard, and finally crept within the shadow of the house. Hastily making his way to the door, he whispered his mother's name, and the ever watchful woman was at the door in a moment. All crowded around

[3] The *Graham Leader* of December 20, 1888, provided a description of Boone:

> A man of about twenty-three years of age, weight about 145 pounds, height about 5 feet 7 inches, hair light, eyes blue, light complexion paled by three months confinement in jail, wears a very small mustache and no whiskers. The fore finger of his right hand is cut off between the first and second joint. When last seen he had on a light drab overcoat with gray wolf fur on collar and sleeves—wore high-heeled cow-boy boots and is slightly bow-legged. . . . He is well armed and will no doubt resist to the last.

The Marlow brothers were all small, "short, wiry, roughly dressed men with blond hair and blue eyes" (Sonnichsen, *I'll Die Before I'll Run*, 192).

him and silently and joyously welcomed him as they drew him quickly into the room and made doubly fast the door.

Silently and in whispered conversation were the succeeding hours passed, and in darkness, for they dared not light a lamp. The poor old mother clung to her boy as though in constant fear that he would be torn from her and put to death, and all together they huddled in the darkened and barred room and discussed plans to meet and cope with the worse than perilous situation.

At about an hour before daybreak Boone crept cautiously out from the house and silently made his way under cover of darkness to an old corn crib near by, where he secreted himself under a pile of corn fodder which had already been carefully examined by the men hunting for him. From here he could command a view of all that went on, and was comparatively safe from discovery for a few days at least.

When the morning was more advanced, Lillian started out for the farm of A. G. Denson,[4] where all their horses were pastured, intending to get a horse by some means if possible, and aid Boone to escape from the neighborhood. Their movements were so closely watched that this was no small undertaking, as suspicion would be aroused by a breath of air. Upon arriving at the ranch Lillian informed Mr. Denson that she would like to get one of the saddle horses to make a trip to town, and that worthy gentleman, suspecting nothing, readily gave his consent and allowed her to pick out one to suit herself. She chose a small jet-black horse belonging to Ellie, as being the best for the purpose. Shoat was among them, but he was so well known all over the country that it would have been a very easy matter to trail him wherever he went.

After securing the horse, the next thing was to manage in some way to communicate with Boone without raising the suspicion of the guard, which seemed to have doubled that day.

By very unconcernedly taking an empty bed tick out of the crib and industriously cramming the dry fodder into it, under cover of the noise they made among the rattling blades, they were able without detection to communicate their plans to Boone and that night about 10 o'clock

[4] Oscar G. Denson. The initials are given correctly in subsequent references. The Marlows were living on property owned by Denson, a forty-nine-year-old Georgia native who would prove to be the family's staunchest ally in their Young County troubles.

Boone emerged from the corn blades and once more ran the gauntlet. He reached the house in safety, where the anxious women awaited him with bated breath, realizing what great risk he ran of being discovered; and they knew that detection meant death to many, for he would sell his life as dearly as possible.

This horse of Ellie's was as black as night, with the exception of a tiny white spot in his forehead, which Boone covered with tar from a wagon wheel that stood in the yard. The horse was equipped with Ellie's saddle also. When ready to start, Boone once more bid them never to think of him if killed and above all things, he said as he held his weeping mother in his arms, "If I am killed, never, never let one of the boys try to avenge my death." Then gently forcing the aged arms from around him, he hastily kissed the three noble sisters who had been all an own sister could have been to a dearly beloved brother, mounted and passed out of their sight. Many minutes the four women stood and listened to the muffled sound of the horse's feet as long as the faintest echo could be heard. Then the sisters gently led the lone and heart broken mother into the dark and gloomy house. Besides the clothes he wore, Boone carried with him an overcoat, muffler, testament and one gun—a Winchester.[5]

The next morning Lillian reported to Denson that she had tied the horse to the wheel of a wagon which stood in the yard, intending to start very early the next morning on her errand, and upon going out at daylight found the horse missing. Thinking that he had worked himself loose and was feeding somewhere in the near neighborhood, she had searched the country thoroughly in every possible place she thought likely for him to be, and she was afraid he was stolen, and guessed she wouldn't go to town at all now, but look for the missing horse.

If Denson suspected that she was deceiving him, he never made it known by word or action, so the report gradually went the rounds that the horse had been stolen by some unknown party or parties.

[5] A man named J. H. Griffiths later reported seeing Boone near Henrietta, Texas, about January 18 and purchasing this Winchester (*Fort Worth Daily Gazette*, January 29, 1889).

Chapter X

ESCAPE FROM PRISON—RECAPTURED

When the four brothers were taken to jail in Graham they were stripped naked and their clothes searched for arms or weapons of any description. Then they were shoved roughly into a small steel cage and locked and barred in with extra precaution. The turnkey and other jail officials and peace officers seemed determined to make their existence as miserable as possible, and every possible indignity and insult that could be devised was heaped relentlessly upon them. Their friends and even their mother and wives were denied admittance to them, and not a message or article of any kind was allowed to be transmitted either to or from them. The food they were given was of the coarsest kind, and not enough of it to have satisfied the hunger of one man, much less that of four strong and stalwart men like the Marlows at this time.

As day after day passed under this treatment, the realization that they were to be starved to death like rats in a cage forced its way upon their minds with all its horrors, and smarting under a hundred other insults, taunts and indignities, it is no wonder their free Western spirits rebelled, and that they resolved to make a bold break for liberty.

Among the prisoners was a man named Speers,[1] who had managed in some way to conceal a large pocket knife upon his person when he

[1]This name was usually spelled "Speer" in later accounts (Crouch, *History of Young County*, 117; Raine, *Famous Sheriffs*, 31; Sonnichsen, *I'll Die Before I'll Run*, 199). It was spelled "Spear" in some of the court records which gave his first name as John. Ledbetter identifies him as John Frank Spears (*Ordeal*, 45, 166). In January 1883 Spears had been convicted on two counts of

was incarcerated, and this he stuck into the end of a broom handle and poked it through the bars of his cell and across the corridor to the cell of the Marlows, and with it they commenced the work of digging out.

There was another man in the cell with the Marlows, named Cummings, who had been jailed for some small misdemeanor,[2] and they all took turns working with the knife each night to cut away the wall which lay between them and liberty, concealing the opening being made by means of a blanket in the daytime. They had a sheet of iron to cut through, as well as the wall, which was necessarily very slow and tedious work, having nothing but the pocket knife in the way of tools,[3] but they were strong and determined, and worked away steadily through the long hours of each night, thinking as each chip of iron or piece of stone dropped out that it was just that much nearer to liberty and freedom for them. It took them just a week to cut a hole through large enough to crawl out of, and then everything was cleaned up nicely so that the turnkey would not be suspicious, and plans were laid to escape that night. The guard was watched that day with anxious eyes, but he showed no sign of suspicion, and so after all were asleep the boys tore their blankets and tied them into long strips to form a rope on which to descend through the opening they had made to the jail yard below. One end of the blanket rope was made fast to the timbers of the room near the hole, and the other lowered to the ground, after which Alfred clambered out and slid down in safety. The others followed quickly and silently, Cummings bringing up the rear. Once on terra firma again, Cummings separated from the Marlows, he taking a northerly direction and making good his escape,[4] and they striking out in the direction of their home, fifteen miles distant.

The night was bitter cold, and, having no overcoats or wraps, they suffered keenly from the icy blasts that swept unbroken over the prairie

---

larceny in Tarrant County, Texas, and was sentenced to a pair of two-year prison terms (*Logan v. United States*, 271).

[2] Marion Cummings was charged with taking stolen property into the Indian Territory (*Fort Worth Daily Gazette*, January 16, 1889; Ledbetter, *Ordeal*, 46).

[3] "Some person on the outside certainly furnished the prisoners with tools to work with. The cage is the best of chilled iron and it takes the very finest tools to have any effect on it" (*Graham Leader*, January 17, 1889).

[4] Three days later Cummings was still at large but Sheriff Collier was "confident of capturing him" (Ibid.). Evidently he was never recaptured (Ledbetter, *Ordeal*, 47).

and through the timber. They took a circuitous route to avoid detection and were thus forced to be out in the cold all night.

At daybreak they came in sight of home, and the smoke curling upward from the chimney in the old familiar house was a sight that gladdened their hearts and put new life into them.[5] They quickened their steps and had almost reached the ranch yard, when with the suddenness and unexpectedness of a flash of lightning a posse of men rounded the trees on horseback and rapidly bore down upon them. It was Collier and his posse, and a dozen others, who had been on guard around the house that night and had espied the boys the moment they came out of the timber.

The Marlows were totally unarmed, and resistance against twenty or more heavily-armed men was useless, so when sternly commanded to halt on penalty of instant death, they had no other course left but to submit. It was bitter medicine to be thus captured again when in sight of home, but there was no alternative, and at the point of a dozen revolvers and Winchesters they were turned around and marched back to town and to prison. All unconscious of their escape, their mother and wives were preparing the morning meal, less than half a mile distant.[6]

Upon again arriving at the jail they were first searched and then taken in a body to a blacksmith shop, where they were shackled and chained together, two and two—Charley and Alfred, George and Ellie. When the job was done and they were again locked in the jail, this time another cell, Sheriff Collier said:

[5] The "old familiar house" had been the abode of the Marlows for less than five months and most of that time the brothers had been in jail.

[6] A dispatch from Graham to Texas papers reported that the Marlows escaped at about 8:00 on the night of January 14 and were recaptured on the "evening" of the 15th (*San Antonio Daily Express*, January 16, 1889; *Fort Worth Daily Gazette*, January 16, 1889). If the brothers did indeed head back to their house after escaping jail, they should not have been surprised to find Collier's men waiting for them; the Marlow cabin would have been the first place the officers would investigate when the break-out was discovered. Said the *Graham Leader*: "As soon as the discovery was made, Sheriff Collier sent a posse to Mr. Denson's farm where the Marlows live, and with another posse struck the trail and followed it to within a short distance of the house where the Marlows were captured and brought back" (January 17, 1889).

Ted Johnson said there were three different search parties out after the Marlows: "They were keen woodsmen and would use rocks to travel on when they could, but they were trailed down about daylight at the mouth of Connor Creek, about twelve miles southeast of Graham, where they were hidden under a large projecting rock. When commanded to do so, they came out and gave up, as all they had was an old cheap pistol. Charlie Marlow laughed and said the reason they broke jail was to try and get bond, but the suspicion was that they intended to stay in hiding all day and ride out at night" (Johnson, "Deputy Marshal Johnson," 9).

"Now, damn you, I guess you'll not get away again."

The feeling throughout Young county on account of the shooting of Wallace was intense. At his death the demand for vengeance was general, and the enemies of the Marlow boys were quick to take advantage of it to secure their ends. Collier, in whom as chief deputy was lodged the authority of the sheriff, and who on the death of Wallace succeeded to that office,[7] joined hands with Johnson and Criswell to bring ruin on the Marlows. Collier led a party in search of Boone,[8] and talked constantly of his fear that a mob would take the Marlows from the jail and lynch them. This was the first mob talk that was heard; but when a week later Wallace died, the conspiracy for the mobbing of the jail and lynching the Marlows was in full progress. The leading spirits in inciting the mob, besides Collier, Johnson and Criswell, were John Leavels, the deputy sheriff to collect taxes under Wallace and Collier;[9] Ben Williams, son of the county judge;[10] Sam Waggoner, a constable;[11] Morrison Wallace, a nephew of Sheriff Wallace, and appointed by Collier to be jailer;[12] Clint Rutherford,[13] Robert Holmes,[14] Bruce Wheeler,[15] Dink Allenk [*sic*],[16] Will Hallice,[17] Frank Harrison,[18] Pink Brooks,[19] Verner Wilkerson[20] and several other citizens.[21]

[7] Reported the *Graham Leader* of January 3, 1889: "Mr. T. B. Collier made his bonds as Sheriff and Tax Collector and was qualified Friday, December 28. Tom is a faithful officer, and all predict that he will make a good sheriff. There was no opposition of any note to his appointment and he seems to be the choice of the people."

[8] Several posses were in the field searching for Boone. The one headed by Jack County Sheriff Moore found Boone's jaded horse only a few miles from the scene of the shooting. The officers believed Boone had exchanged it for a better mount (*Graham Leader*, December 20, 1888).

[9] This name has been given many spellings. Later, quoting court records, Rathmell spells it "Lewell." This may have been a misprint, as it was given as "Levell" in the Supreme Court records (*Logan v. United States*, 269), a spelling also used by Crouch (*History of Young County*, 118). The name is given as J. Y. Leavel in the *Graham Leader* (January 31, 1889). Sonnichsen spelled it both "Leavel" and "Leavell" (*I'll Die Before I'll Run*, 200, 204). "Level," as Ted Johnson spelled the name, came from Alabama and was an expert bookkeeper (Johnson, "Deputy Marshal Johnson," 9).

The name was properly John Y. Leavell. In 1883 Leavell had been arrested with two others, Monroe Chambers and one Nickleson, on a rustling charge and held in the Graham jail for a month. When Nickleson died mysteriously in jail, Leavell and Chambers beat the charge, successfully blaming the dead man for the crimes. By 1885 Leavell was employed as turnkey at the jail and during that year found himself guarding his former henchman, Chambers, who had been arrested once more for theft. Leavell later married the widow of Bee Williams (the former Alice Woods) and moved to Pecos County, Texas. He served as a deputy under Sheriff R. B. Neighbors during the bloody Frazer-Miller feud which plagued Pecos County in the mid-1890s, and later was six-term sheriff of neighboring Reeves County, 1896–1908. Still later he served two terms as judge of Reeves County (*El Paso Times*, May 2, 1896; Tise, *Texas County Sheriffs*, 436; Ledbetter, *Fort Belknap*, 269; *Ordeal*, 189-90).

[10] This was William "Bee" Williams as correctly given by Rathmell later. "Ben" was evidently a misprint which was repeated by Raine in *Famous Sheriffs*, 34. Bee was the son of Harry D.

Williams, a Texas pioneer who served in the Confederate Army and fought Indians both before and after the Civil War. An early resident of Young County, Harry D. Williams established his home at Belknap and served as county clerk and judge. Bee's older brother, Henry C. Williams, served six terms as sheriff of Young County, from 1892 to 1904 (Ledbetter, *Fort Belknap*, 269; Johnson, "Deputy Marshal Johnson," 53; Tise, *Texas County Sheriffs*, 557).

[11] Samuel V. Waggoner was constable at Graham (Crouch, *History of Young County*, 117). Ted Johnson described him as "a whole-souled fellow, a cowpuncher, and a native of Texas" (Johnson, "Deputy Marshal Johnson," 53).

[12] Marion A. Wallace was called by some "Little Marion" to distinguish him from his uncle, Sheriff Marion D. Wallace (Johnson, "Deputy Marshal Johnson," 10). Raine copied Rathmell's "Morrison" error (*Famous Sheriffs*, 24), but later correctly referred to him as "Marion" (Ibid., 37). Sheriff Tom Collier appointed Wallace a deputy the day after assuming his new duties. "Marion is a quiet unassuming young man of steady habits and we confidently predict will prove worthy of the trust confided in him," said the *Leader* of January 3. In later years Marion A. Wallace worked as an inspector for the Cattlemen's Association of West Texas, stationed at Midland, and ran a cattle spread of his own in northern Young County (Johnson, "Deputy Marshal Johnson," 53). In 1904 he was elected sheriff of Young County and served three terms, from 1904 to 1910. Elected again in 1914, he served six more years as sheriff (Tise, *Texas County Sheriffs*, 557; Ledbetter, *Ordeal*, 188).

[13] Clinton Thoeodore "Clint" Rutherford (1866–1907) was the son of former Tennesseean Clinton Rutherford (1819–1904), a veteran of both the Mexican and the Civil War, and an active member of the Southwestern Stockraisers' Association. On January 17, 1907, long after the Marlow troubles, Clint Rutherford was shot and killed by a man named A. P. "Pick" Stewart. Rutherford had allegedly made improper advances toward Stewart's wife (Wilene Smith, *Descendants of Clinton Rutherford*; Crouch, *History of Young County*, 171; Ledbetter, *Ordeal*, 159, 195).

[14] Robert Holman was called "one of our leading attorneys" by the *Graham Leader* and his subsequent arrest as a member of the mob came as "a great surprise to most of our people" (November 5, 1890). Ted Johnson considered him "a fine fellow and a good lawyer" (Johnson, "Deputy Marshal Johnson," 53). Holman was one of the few Young County residents who could trace his lineage to Texas colonists; his grandfather, Jesse Burman, after serving as a militia captain with Stephen F. Austin, had been awarded one of the first land grants by the Mexican government in 1823. In Graham, Holman had law offices with Robert Arnold and C. W. Johnson. After the legal battles resulting from the Marlow affair, and the tragic deaths of three infant children, Holman, his wife, the former Gabriella Delaney, and their two surviving children moved to Pecos in west Texas. They went from there to Las Vegas, New Mexico, where Holman practiced law. He died at El Paso in 1897 at the age of forty-three (Ledbetter, *Ordeal*, 177–78).

[15] Wheeler was single, a partner in the cattle business with W. O. Clark. "Bruce was a fine fellow and liked by everybody for his business ability and generosity. I believe he came from Tennessee" (Johnson, "Deputy Marshal Johnson," 53).

[16] This is obviously a misprint. David "Dink" Allen was born at Belknap in 1859, married Jennie B. Simpson and fathered nine children. He died in Young County in 1952 (Ledbetter, *Fort Belknap*, 251).

[17] Will Hollis. This is given correctly later by Rathmell. Raine compounded Rathmell's original error by calling the man "Mill Hallice" (*Famous Sheriffs*, 34), but later named him correctly (Ibid., 37).

[18] This was another name of many spellings. Raine (*Famous Sheriffs*, 34–40) and Sonnichsen (*I'll Die Before I'll Run*, 201–2) accepted Rathmell's spelling. Johnson called him "Harminson" and said he was "a frontier Texan [who] ranched up close to the line of Archer County" (Johnson, "Deputy Marshal Johnson," 53). He was actually Columbus Frank Harmonson, born in 1857, the eldest of the eleven children of William Perry and Ann (Harper) Harmonson (Ledbetter, *Fort Belknap*, 263).

[19] Lewis Pinkney "Pink" Brooks (1841–1931) at the age of twelve rode a mule from his native Georgia to Texas. He was a Confederate veteran and a hard-core Democrat (Ledbetter, *Fort Belknap*, 285; *Ordeal*, 203). Ted Johnson knew and admired the venerable pioneer: "Old Uncle Pink Brooks, who lived on the Brazos River just below Fort Belknap . . ., fought Indians before and after the Civil War. He was a man above reproach and a law-abiding citizen. His old sandstone residence is one of the oldest in Young County. Not many years ago the *Dallas News* portrayed his picture on the front page with pick and shovel in hand, under the shade of a tree, referring to him as the man who dug the Brazos River, with the excuse of the river being so crooked being

that Uncle Pink in his daily labor followed the shade of the trees" (Johnson, "Deputy Marshal Johnson," 49).

[20] In contemporary newspaper and court records this man's first name has been given variously and erroneously as Verna and Vernon and his last name asWilkerson. The errors have been repeated by later writers. His true name was Verner Wilkinson (1856–1897) and he was the son-in-law of war veteran and cattle association activist Clinton Rutherford (Wilene Smith, "Descendants of Verner Wilkinson." Ms. Smith is the great-great-granddaughter of Clinton Rutherford and the great-granddaughter of Verner Wilkinson.). Wilkinson, a native of Iowa, had a farm and cattle ranch in the northern reaches of the county (Ibid.; Johnson, "Deputy Marshal Johnson,"53). Following the Marlow affair, he sold his 319-acre farm and moved to Wilbarger County, Texas, where he became an officer of the law (Ledbetter, *Ordeal*, 159), then on to Briscoe County, Texas, and finally Woodward County, Oklahoma. On October 24, 1897, he was shot to death in a gunfight with Abner J. Chapman in a dispute over pasture fencing (Smith, "Descendants of Verner Wilkinson").

[121] This list includes all those who subsequently were formally accused of mob participation with the exception of Eugene Logan, W. R. Benedict, Dick Cook, and Jack Wilkins.

Chapter XI

LYNCH LAW— AT THE MERCY OF THE MOB

Stronger and stronger grew the sentiment against the Marlows. The officers who had in the beginning started out to ruin them left no stone unturned to accomplish their purpose, but actuated by the hope of gain and personal aggrandizement they spread abroad every lie and innuendo which could suggest itself to their fertile and scheming minds.

Here were four innocent men in prison—men who had never in their lives committed wrong by word or deed—yet they were manacled and ironed like desperados of the worst type, held in prison under the charges of theft and being accessory to the heinous crime of murder, and outside the people were worked up and so incensed against them that they already thirsted for their blood, and muttered threats of lynching them could be heard on every side. The death of Wallace and their subsequent escape from the jail of course intensified this feeling, and things began to assume for them anything but a roseate hue.

On the night of January 17th the trouble which had been brewing came to a climax, and the jail was turned over to an organized mob by the peace officers already named. The details of the lawless project were carefully planned, and it was decided to work quickly, quietly and systematically. No shots were to be fired, as that would arouse the town and perhaps cause the recognition of those forming the mob.

The mob was to do its work in darkness, and the identity of its members was to be kept secret. Alibis were arranged by which one could prove by another that he was not at the jail, and Sheriff Tom Collier and Constable Waggoner swiftly rode away after the attack with the pretense of serving a warrant, these things being prepared beforehand. After the town was quiet the mob went to the jail.

The prisoners had been ordered to bed earlier than common on this night, and most of them had been asleep when the mob arrived. Presently they heard the men coming up the stairs from below. There were two cells in the jail at this time, known as the north and south cell. The south cell was so damaged by the Marlows when they made their escape a few nights before, that all the prisoners were in the same cell on this night. The mob came to this cell and made every effort to get the Marlows from among the other prisoners and get them outside at the same time. They were afraid to shoot, as they would alarm the town. They tried to force the other prisoners to shove the Marlows out, but they would not try it, although the mob held guns and pistols to their heads and threatened to blow their brains out. The prisoners were apprehensive of a mob and took the crowd for what it really was. In the afternoon of the 17th Collier had been in and ironed Speers and Burkhart,[1] two other prisoners, and told them that they should not be hurt, "But I swear to you those Marlows shall catch hell," he added. The mob was disguised, but their disguises did not prevent the prisoners from recognizing in them the jail guard and several other peace officers of the town. John Leavels was in the lead (Leavels was turnkey) and unlocked the door.[2]

Leavels told Charley to come out, that there was a man out there who wanted to see him. Charley and Alfred walked up to the door, one on each side, but Speers spoke up and said:

"Don't you see it is a mob? They are disguised. Don't go out."

Charley said: "What do they want with me, Leavels?"

"I don't know what they want," replied Leavels, "Come out and see."

[1] William D. Burkhart, like the Marlows, was charged with larceny in the Indian Territory (*Logan v. United States*, 265).

[2] Of course the story told later by the jail guards was entirely different from that of the Marlows: "The first warning the guards had of [the mob's] presence, was the opening of the door and the pointing of a dozen guns at their heads, with a demand to surrender—a demand with which they readily complied. Then the mob made them go up and open the cages and call all the prisoners out except the Marlows" (*Graham Leader*, January 24, 1889).

Charles declined to go out at all. Eugene Logan[3] had a gun drawn on Speer's back. Speers told him if he meant to kill to shoot him in the face and not in the back. Logan said he would not kill him if he would put Charley Marlow out of there. This Speers, as the others had done, refused to do.

"I have lain here every night and wanted water," said George to Leavels, "and when I begged for some you said that the keys were in the office and that you could not get it for me, and now you let men in here to kill us."

"Mr. Leavels is here under arrest," said Logan.

Martin[4] brought in a lantern to show Logan where to shoot Charles, as he said. Martin jabbed Speers in the side with his gun and said:

"Shoot Speers; he wants to die."

At last one of the mob, tired of delay, made a rush for Charley Marlow. He didn't get him, however, for as he entered Charley struck him a terrific blow on the head with his fist, knocking him headlong through the door and against the stone wall of the prison, where he fell unconscious on the floor. The mob started back in dismay, but presently the man revived and gasped.

"Take me out, Frank," (meaning Frank Harmison) "for I am bleeding to death."

[3] Eugene Logan was one of the guards at the jail. Born in Tennessee in 1843, he moved from Hill County to west Texas with his wife, Anna, two daughters, and one hundred head of cattle in 1879 and established a ranch on Boggy Creek, a mile from the Brazos, where three more children were born. In 1885 the Logans moved to Belknap where in the ensuing years five more children entered the family. After the Marlow affair in which he became a principal figure, Logan was an inspector for the Cattlemen's Association and held several jobs as a lawman. He claimed to have served a stint in the Texas Rangers, but no record of this service has been found. The New Mexico town of Logan, between Tucumcari and Dalhart, Texas, is said to be named for him. When last seen by Ted Johnson, he was running a rooming house at Dalhart. He died May 9, 1935 (Johnson, "Deputy Marshal Johnson," 53; Crouch, *History of Young County*, 232; Ledbetter, *Ordeal*, 193–94).

[4] Phlete A. Martin was born September 7, 1864, in North Carolina. In 1883 he shot and killed a man named William H. Reeves, Jr., and the following year was convicted of felonious homicide and sentenced to six months in the Iredell County jail in that state. Upon completion of his sentence, Martin went to Texas where he studied law, was admitted to the Young County bar in 1886, and quickly elected county attorney. On April 25, 1889, during the Marlow uproar, he married Lois Graves, eldest daughter of *Graham Leader* editor J. W. Graves. After the ordeal of the various trials, he practiced private law and became general manager and chief editor of the newspaper. In 1902 he was elected again as county attorney, and later became district attorney for the 30th Judicial District of Texas, and later still, district judge. He was judge of the 89th District Court at Wichita Falls for fifteen years and in 1935 was appointed to the Texas Court of Civil Appeals (*Logan v. United States*, 271; Ledbetter, Ordeal, 179–81; Crouch, *History of Young County*, 243–44).

The mob returned, picked him up and carried him down stairs. This was young Robert Hill, and he died two days later of inflammation of the brain. Charley's blow did the work.[5]

Speers told Clift[6] to screw off the water pipe in their cell. He got it and gave it to Alfred Marlow.[7] The mob returned shortly and called all the other prisoners out, there being four, leaving the Marlows in the cell alone. The men taken out were put in the south cell. The mob then went down stairs, only to return after ten minutes. In the mean time the Marlows arose and stood side by side, determined to make as good a stand as possible. Clift, in the south cell, crawled out through the hole that the Marlows had cut, it not having been repaired, and started down stairs, saying that he was going down town and let the people know how they were being treated.[8] The mob met him on the stairs and sent him back to the cell. The mob returned with Leavels in the lead, swinging a lantern in one hand and the keys in the other. With the mob at his heels he unlocked the door, while George endeavored to dissuade them from their purpose.

"Men," he said to the guards, whom he recognized in spite of disguise, "we are prisoners and you should protect us from the mob. We have done none of you any harm. Neither of us killed Wallace, as Collier knows, and when our brother shot him he knows it was meant for himself; and Collier knows also that when our brother expressed his sorrow for

[5] "George Marlow related this incident about Bob Hill to me," wrote William MacLeod Raine. "He was very definite as to details. He said that young Hill died two days later from concussion of the brain. I have not been able to verify this" (Raine, *Famous Sheriffs*, 36).

The *Graham Leader* of January 24, 1889, reported that "Robert Hill, oldest son of Mr. J. G. Hill, died of congestion of the brain last Friday." Young Hill, described by the paper as "a promising young man of good morals [who] was generally liked by his acquaintances," died on the day following the lynch party's attempt on the jail, but no mention was made of the death having resulted from that abortive affair.

Ted Johnson said it was rumored that young Hill (whose name he remembered as George) died a few days later from injuries received at the jail. "The cause of death was reported as brain fever. All was kept very quiet as the Hills were . . . pioneers of Young County and respectable people." He said the dead man's father, "Uncle Jack" Hill, was a former Confederate soldier and an ex-sheriff of Young County (Johnson, "Deputy Marshal Johnson," 10). He was mistaken in the last assertion, however. John George Hill, while never sheriff of Young County, did serve as a deputy during the term of Sheriff William T. Bunger (Tise, *Texas County Sheriffs*, 365; Ledbetter, *Ordeal*, 54).

[6] Louis Clift was also charged with larceny in the Indian Territory (*Logan v. United States*, 265). The first name is sometimes spelled "Lewis."

[7] Johnson alleged that Charley used this pipe to strike young Hill (Johnson, "Deputy Marshal Johnson," 10).

[8] It is not clear how Clift could go down the inside stairs after passing through the hole the Marlows had cut. This hole, according to the account of the escape, led to the outside.

the mistake, the sheriff extended his hand in token of forgiveness, of his own free will. Some of you have mothers and wives. Do you think they would be pleased to see you engaged in such unlawful work?"

The longer he talked the louder and more wicked the mob cursed them, so he gave up all hopes of accomplishing anything by reasoning, and the four stood there waiting, resolved to die fighting.

Marion Wallace started into the cage to bring Charley out. The mob thirsted for his blood, as Collier had spread the report that Charley instead of Boone had killed Sheriff Wallace.[9] On reaching the door Marion Wallace noticed that Alfred, the strongest of the lot, had a big joint of lead water pipe in his hand. Seeing Alf standing there ready to brain his assailants as fast as they entered the cage, Wallace stopped and backed away. When challenged to go in, he said:

"I'll be d——ed if I'm going in there to be killed."

Some of the mob then got a rope and tried to lasso the brothers, but the Marlows were up to that trick, and it could not be worked. The mob then poked their guns through the bars and threatened to shoot them if they did not come out quietly, which the boys refused to do. They were punched and struck with the guns, but the men holding them did not dare fire, for fear of rousing the town. Tiring of this sport, the mob abandoned the attempt to dislodge them and left the jail. The Marlows talked the matter over, and though they had recognized their assailants, they decided to disclaim all knowledge of them, hoping by that course to secure their own safety.

About one hundred yards from the jail was a cemetery, in which the mob had hidden four ropes with nooses, which were found afterwards.[10]

A short time after the mob had left the jail, the guards removed their disguises and returned, laughing and telling the prisoners how they scared the mob away. They wanted to know if any of the mob had been recognized, but the prisoners claimed to know nothing of their identity.

[9] "It seemed that the friends and relatives of Wallace wanted to lay the murder of Wallace on Charlie" (Johnson, "Deputy Marshal Johnson," 10). The *Graham Leader* said in its account: "It is now certain that they intended to lynch the whole quartet of Marlows, and were simply prevented from doing so by the bold stand the prisoners made" (January 24, 1889).

[10] The ropes were used to lead the guards to the graveyard, according to the story in the *Leader* (January 24, 1889).

After retiring from the jail the leaders of the gang hit upon a new plan, in accordance with which they aroused the town at 5 o'clock the next morning and gave a well-fabricated account of how a gang of desperadoes from the Indian Territory, led by Boone, had ridden into the town in the night and made an attempt to capture the jail and rescue the four brothers. They told how the attempt had been foiled by the watchfulness and courage of the faithful jailer and his guards.[11]

During the next day these startling "facts" were telegraphed to United States Marshal Cabell, at Dallas, Texas.[12] He wired his deputy, Ed Johnson, to remove the Marlows to Weatherford, sixty miles distant, for

[11] Sheriff Collier and Sam Waggoner were out of town at the time of the mob attempt on the jail according to most accounts (Raine, *Famous Sheriffs*, 35; Sonnichsen, *I'll Die Before I'll Run*, 199). However, Ted Johnson recalled that it was Waggoner who notified his father that night that a masked body of men had attempted to *release* the Marlow brothers from the jail but had been driven away. "I remember very distinctly my father telling mother that the story was all bosh and that he suspicioned violence instead of release, and would go and get some help to guard the jail until daylight. He at once secured four more guards and went to the jail, at which time Charlie Marlow told him the particulars" (Johnson, "Deputy Marshal Johnson," 10).

The attempt on the jail took place on a Thursday night. The weekly *Graham Leader* appeared on Thursday, so a full week passed before proprietor Jonathan Webb Graves could publish an editorial commenting on the episode. In the issue of January 24 he deplored the mob's action as "a disgraceful affair." Although the Marlows were "a desperate set of ruffians," they were, he said, still entitled to their day in court and the protection of the law. Perhaps Graves forgot that the Marlows had already been convicted without trial in the pages of his paper, which had characterized them as "a family of five noted thieves and cut-throats" (*Graham Leader*, December 20, 1888). Perhaps he also forgot that only six months before he had suggested that lynch-style treatment might be appropriate for horse thieves: "Horse stealing seems to be the prevailing disorder with a certain class just now," said the *Leader* of July 26, 1888, "and perhaps nothing short of the hemp will cure the malady."

While not commenting upon these previous remarks, which some might have considered inflammatory and possible contributors to mob violence, Graves did admit to finding the attempt on the Graham jail

> more amusing than serious, and comic rather than tragic. The unsuccessful assault on the cage, the resistance of the four Marlows, the retreat of the lynchers, and their leading the guards away with ropes tied in hangman fashion, all present a mixture of tragedy and comedy, with a strong preponderance of the latter. It is thought by some that they did not intend to hang any one, but . . . simply to frighten them. No matter what the plan was, it was a most dismal failure, and doubtless the would-be executioners went home heartily ashamed of their night's work, fully realizing that they had made a most complete fiasco. . . . It is to be hoped that this thing will not be attempted again.

As he penned his piece, Graves apparently did not know that Robert Hill had died as a result of the jail assault; he certainly could not foresee that it would run in the same issue as another Marlow brothers story which was neither amusing nor comic, a story he would headline: "A Horrible Affair. Five Men Killed and Four Known to Be Wounded."

[12] William Lewis Cabell (1827–1911), born in Virginia, was a West Point graduate in 1850. At the outbreak of the Civil War he resigned his U. S. Army commission to enter the Confederate Army as a major. Rising to the rank of brigadier general, he was twice wounded and later captured by Union forces. After the war he studied law and was admitted to the bar in 1868. He was elected mayor of Dallas in 1874 and held the office at intervals until appointment by newly elected President Grover Cleveland as United States marshal for the Northern District of Texas. He served in that capacity from July 1, 1885, until April 9, 1889 (Tyler, *The New Handbook of Texas*, 1:880).

safe keeping. This answer was received on Saturday, January 19th, a date remembered by many with sorrow.[13]

Immediately the mob leaders got together and again laid plans for the next attempt. A new and larger mob was organized and the guards agreed to offer no resistance when attacked. It was decided to get the prisoners outside before another attack should be made. There were six of these so-called guards, three of whom were chosen by Ed Johnson and three by Collier. Johnson selected Criswell, P. A. Martin and John B. Girand, son of a United States Commissioner at Graham.[14] Collier chose Marion Wallace and Will Waggoner,[15] and Will Hollis,[16] all of whom had been members of the jail mob. It was a party organized in the name of justice, but intent upon revenge.[17]

On the evening of the 19th Collier and Johnson notified the Marlows that they would be taken to Weatherford that night. While they were waiting to start they were all re-ironed. Clift and Burkhart were ironed together and the Marlows were fastened as before. Alfred asked what guards they had, and when they were informed by Johnson their hearts sank within them. They had recognized all of these as a part of the men bent on their death, yet they decided that they would stand a better chance outside if attacked than in, so rather favored the change.

When Clift tried to put on his boot over his irons he found it necessary to remove the top; so, tearing it off, he said:

"Here, Leavels, I will give you this to remember me by."

[13] Upon receipt of his order from Cabell, Deputy Marshal Johnson held a strategy meeting with Major Francis Washington Girand, U. S. Commissioner and clerk of the federal court at Graham. Also present was the postmaster, a man named Taylor. It was agreed to leave with the prisoners under strong guard that same night and "to get part of the guards from among the friends of Wallace, to prevent ambush and also to prevent them from organizing a party of violence" (Johnson, "Deputy Marshal Johnson," 10).

[14] John Barton Girand was the young son of F. W. Girand, whose title of "Major" had been acquired during his service with the Confederate Army. Major Girand arrived in Graham with the establishment of the federal court there in 1879 and the appointment of his first cousin, A. P. McCormick, as district judge. Girand served as U. S. Commissioner and clerk of court until after the transfer of the court to Abilene in 1896. His son, John Barton, saw service as a deputy U. S. marshal before replacing his father upon his resignation as clerk of the court (Crouch, *History of Young County*, 205).

[15] This was Sam Waggoner. Raine repeated the error of Rathmell, referring to "Will" Waggoner (*Famous Sheriffs*, 37), but later correctly called him "Sam" (Ibid., 43).

[16] Mentioned in Chapter Ten as "Will Hallice."

[17] In addition to those named, Johnson enlisted John Leavell and Eugene Logan as guards for the trip. All were given "the strictest orders of secrecy" (Johnson, "Deputy Marshal Johnson," 10).

"All right," said Leavels, "I will take it, for you will be on the pauper's field before daylight anyway,"

"Oh, nothing; they will take you to Fort Smith and I won't see you any more."

Just before starting, Eugene Logan, one of the jail guards and a leader of the mob, called out:

"Oh George!"

"What do you want?" answered the man addressed.

"Sing me a song. I'm going to leave you to-night, and want to hear you sing again."

George sang and Logan complimented him on his voice, and added:

"I'm going home to-night, boys, to recruit, and hope the mob won't get you."[18]

This man was just from a meeting of the leading conspirators, where all the details had been arranged to waylay and assassinate the prisoners.

At 8:30 o'clock Johnson and some of the guards came up after the prisoners. He told them that no one knew of their removal excepting the three or four guards around the jail and those who were going along. Upon reaching the ground floor they found about fifteen men standing around, and on going outside they discovered thirty more.

[18] "Logan said at the time he was summoned, that he would have to go home and change horses, but that he would be at the jail on time. But for some unknown reason, he was not at the jail when the time arrived to leave," said Johnson. While not making a direct accusation that Logan was the culprit who mobilized the mob, Johnson left that implication: "Now, there were good horses in those days and good riders and somebody snitched" (Ibid.).

William Rathmell, who became acquainted with George and Charles Marlow in Colorado, wrote and published the first book-length account of their extraordinary story in 1892.

Wilson Williamson Marlow, doctor, rover, and father of the fighting brothers.

Martha Jane Marlow, long-suffering mother of the boys.

The five Marlow brothers on horseback, circa 1887. Left to right: George, Boone, Alfred, Llewellyn, Charles.

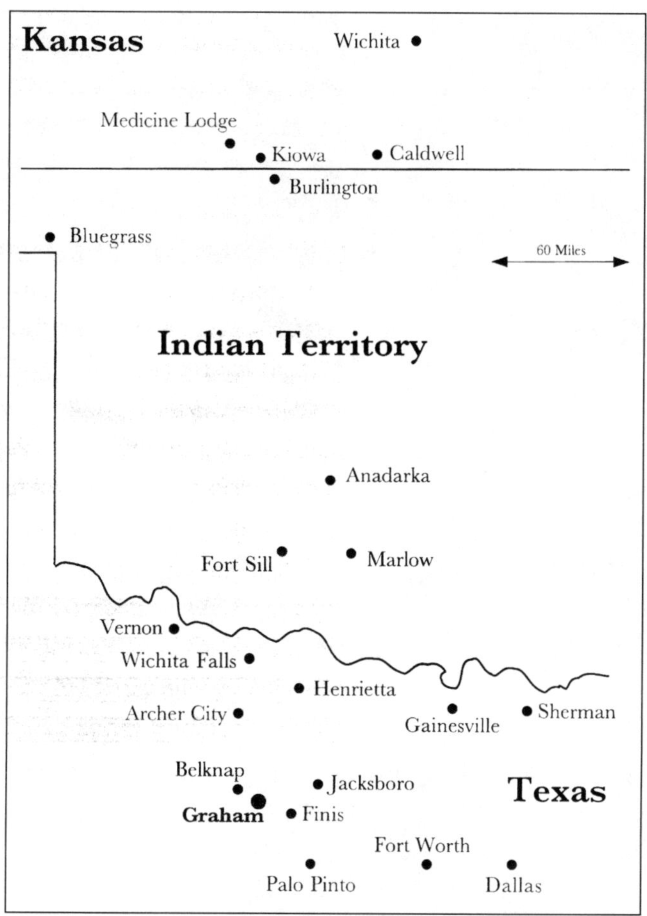

Map of the haunts of the Marlow brothers in Texas, Indian Territory, and Kansas. Map prepared by Rosemary DeArment Walter.

Graham, Texas, in the 1880s.

In a photograph taken before he lost his arm in a gunfight, Deputy United States Marshal Edward W. Johnson is shown (left) with two fellow law officers, Texas Ranger Lorenzo K. Creekman (center) and Parker County Deputy Sheriff E. A. Hutchison (right).

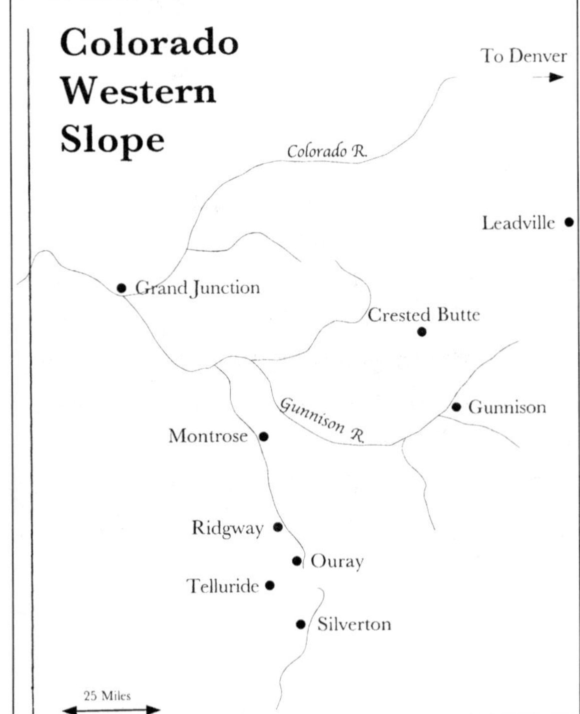

Map of the Colorado country in which George and Charles Marlow were active. Map prepared by Rosemary DeArment Walter.

Ouray, Colorado, as it looked about the time George and Charles Marlow arrived there.

Charles (left) and George Marlow at the time of the great mob conspiracy trial.

Crested Butte, Colorado, scene of the big strike in 1891.

Sheriff Cyrus "Doc" Shores, seated, with Deputies George and Charles Marlow (left to right).

Chapter XII

REMOVAL AND FINAL ATTACK— BATTLE OF DRY CREEK[1]

The prisoners feared a mob worse than ever when they saw the crowd, and asked Johnson if he would arm them if they were attacked.

"Yes, I will," he said.

There were two hacks and a buggy in sight. The six prisoners and driver got into one of the hacks and started, Clift and Burkhart, who were chained together, occupying the front seat by Martin, the driver, who was unarmed, for fear the prisoners might take his weapons from him when the attack was made. The four Marlows occupied the back seats.[2] In the second hack were the two deputy marshals, Edward Johnson, a kinsman of ex-Attorney General Garland,[3] who had command of the party; Sam Criswell and the other guards, who were all heavily armed.[4]

[1]The chapter title under the heading "Chapter XII" was inadvertently omitted in the Rathmell edition.

[2] The lead vehicle was a three-seated hack driven by P. A. Martin (not "George" Martin as stated in Crouch, *History of Young County*, 118, and Raine, *Famous Sheriffs*, 37). Beside Martin sat Louis Clift (called "Pitts" by Johnson) and William Burkhart, chained together at the ankles. George and Ellie were paired and ironed together in the second seat. Charles and Alfred, also connected by leg-chains, occupied the rear seat (Johnson, "Deputy Marshal Johnson," 10).

[3] Augustus Hill Garland of Tennessee (1832–1899) served in the Confederate Senate and was elected governor of Arkansas in 1874. He was appointed attorney general in the cabinet of President Cleveland in 1885 (*National Cyclopaedia of American Biography*). Although this was the same year that Ed Johnson secured his appointment as a deputy U. S. marshal, there has been no confirmation that he was a "kinsman" of Garland.

[4] The second hack, a two-seater, contained Deputy Marshal Ed Johnson, his regular posseman Sam Criswell, Deputy Sheriff John Leavell, and young Johnny Girand, a guard. "This hack," said Johnson, "contained all the extra arms, such as Winchester rifles and a supply of ammunition. Next came the buggy with Special Guards Marion A. Wallace and Sam Waggoner. Two mounted

Criswell, fearing that the prisoners were not secure, was in favor of tying them to the bottom of the hack by a rope being run through their shackles and passed through the bottom of the hack. But this was not done, which proved to be a fortunate thing for the prisoners.[5] The hack in which they rode drove on ahead of the others and out of sight. The prisoners became quite uneasy at finding themselves so far from the guards, chained as they were, with nothing to defend themselves against an attack, and with a driver whom they knew to be one of the leaders of the mob of the seventeenth. They had no faith in the guards, yet hoped against reason that they would be armed, if not protected. George remarked that the other hack was not coming, to which Martin said:

"They will catch up presently."

A few hundred yards farther the other hack came in sight. The vehicles moved slowly along the road until they came to a small stream called Dry Creek, two miles from Graham. On the opposite side of the creek was a long lane, separating two pastures covered with large trees and brush about as high as a man's head. The banks of the creek were steep and high.

The procession halted within a short distance of the creek. The guard hack drove alongside of the other one and Johnson alighted, saying:

"Maybe the boys would like a drink."

Handing a flask to George, he shouted at the top of his voice:

"Boys, have a drink."[6]

The bottle went the rounds, the prisoners taking a little in their mouths and instantly spitting it out, fearing it contained poison.

The prisoners now made the discovery that not one of the guards wore an overcoat or had a lap robe. This scant clothing for a sixty-mile ride on a cold January night looked very suspicious, to say the least. Clift had a blanket over his lap, which he offered to share with Martin,

---

special guards, Will Hollis and Eugene Logan, brought up the rear of the procession. Logan still had not appeared when the procession left the jail, but caught up with Hollis about a mile out of town" (Johnson, "Deputy Marshal Johnson," 10).

[5] Ed Johnson would later say that "one of the guards suggested . . . he handcuff the prisoners, but being of a suspicious nature [he] refused to do so, and told Charlie Marlow that he would leave their hands free, for which Charlie thanked him at the time" (Ibid.). Ted Johnson suggested that decision is prima facie evidence that, although his father may have had forebodings, he did not conspire in the events to come (Ibid., 49).

[6] George Marlow would later claim that this was a signal to the waiting bushwhackers (Raine, *Famous Sheriffs*, 38).

but the driver said that he didn't want anything in his way. Taking in all these suspicious points, Charles said:

"Boys, we will be mobbed in fifteen minutes."

"Ed, you will arm us?" said George.

"Yes," he said, "and die with you."

"You will certainly arm us, Ed, if it comes to so bad as that?" said Charles.

"Yes, I will."

"Boys," said Charley, "that mob is lying in some thicket close to us."

They knew a plot was afloat for their destruction, and nerved themselves with the determination to sell their lives as dearly as possible when it came to the worst. Martin started up and the other hack followed. The assertions of the guards did not deceive Charley Marlow. As their hack emerged from the creek bed and climbed the ascent he saw the trees and bushes on the south side of the lane, the moon shedding a bright light over them.

"Boys," he said again, "we will be killed; the mob is hiding somewhere in that brush."

Hardly were these words out of his mouth when the leader of the mob arose from the brush and shouted:

"Halt! Hold up your hands!"[7]

A sheet of flame leaped out of the bushes, the reports of a score of rifles rang out upon the still night air, and a crowd of armed men sprang out from the bushes and ran yelling to the foremost hack.

"Here they are," shouted Martin as he scrambled from the hack. "Take the whole six of them."[8]

At the first alarm Charley and Alf jumped over the side of the hack away from the mob and hobbled as fast as their chains would permit to the hack where the guards were handing their guns and six-shooters to

[7] Johnson said the command to halt came "just as the front hack with prisoners and the second hack of guards reached the far side and the top of the creek bank (the buggy and horseman still being in the creek bed)" (Johnson, "Deputy Marshal Johnson," 11).

[8] Martin "surrendered at once," according to Johnson. Of course, being unarmed, he had little choice. "Seeing part of his guards jump out and run and his trusted old Deputy (Sam Criswell) badly excited," Ed Johnson "knew at once that he was doublecrossed." He claimed to have fired the first shot, killing one of three masked men who converged on his vehicle. He said he shouted for the Marlow brothers to come to his hack "where there was plenty of arms, and to fight for their lives" (Ibid.).

the mob. Charley wrenched Johnson's revolver from him[9] and Alfred grabbed hold of the barrel of a gun belonging to one of the mob. Charley drew the pistol on the man holding the other end.

"Don't shoot," begged this man. "I am a guard."

"Let it loose, then," demanded Charley, and he gave it up.

George and Ellie were the next to gain the ground. As they landed, a man heavily armed passed them and George jumped upon his back, bore him to the ground and seized a pistol and Winchester. He passed the pistol to Ellie, cocked the gun and shot the man in the back as he started to run. The mob formed a semi-circle around the two hacks and fired a volley upon the Marlows, who were standing back to back. The famous battle of Dry Creek had begun.[10]

Clift was a man who feared nothing, while Burkhart was extremely cowardly. Clift was shot through the thigh at the first onslaught, while trying to take a gun away from one of the mob. This might not have happened if he had not been so hampered by Burkhart, who, after Clift was wounded, crawled under one of the hacks, dragging the half-conscious man with him and yelling "murder" at the top of his voice.

The Marlows then fired a telling volley into the ranks of the mob, and one man was seen to fall and crawl off into the brush, while another, shot through the pistol hand, jumped up and down in the road, cursing like a pirate. The mob, disconcerted by finding the boys armed and ready to fight to the death with undaunted courage, beat a hasty retreat into the timber to get ready for a grand charge which should annihilate the boys at once. They reappeared in a few moments, whooping and yelling like Indians, and firing as they advanced. Alfred fell when this volley was fired, stone dead, shot fifteen times through the head, body and shoulders.

[9] "Someone from behind or at the left side grappled Johnson's pistol, which he held onto until he was pulled from the hack. He being one-armed, the pistol was wrenched from him." Johnson never believed it was Charley Marlow who grabbed his sixshooter. "My father has told me many times," said Ted Johnson, "that while he did not know the man who wrenched his pistol, he *did know* it was *not* Charlie Marlow. He was of the belief it was one of his own guards" (Ibid.).

[10] Johnson did not last long in the fight. Soon after he had been stripped of his pistol, "someone from behind opened fire on [him], the first shot taking effect in his only hand, literally tearing it to pieces." Seeing a man firing at him from close range with a Winchester, Johnson, defenseless, beat a retreat to the creek bed. "He called to the man that he was wounded and unarmed," but the assailant "took deliberate aim and shot at him nine more times, and he could hear every one of them whine." Afterward he found "there were three separate bullet holes through the front lapel of his overcoat and one through his hat and another bullet completely cut a plaited hair watch chain in two" (Johnson, "Deputy Marshal Johnson," 11).

A man passed them closer than the rest, firing point blank several times at Ellie, who, mortally wounded, threw down his empty revolver, snatched a Winchester from George's hands, brought it to his shoulder while he reeled in agony and fired at the man who had shot him, and fell headlong to the ground at the same time, never to rise again.

George was shot through the right hand, the ball striking his gun and knocking it against him with such force that he was nearly paralyzed for a moment. Charley was unhurt.

One brother in each chained pair had been shot down, and lay stark and cold upon the ground, still grasping in death their weapons. The two yet alive were rendered desperate by the slaughter of their brothers, and continued to fire shot after shot at their foes.

George, as soon as he recovered his self-possession, rested his rifle upon his wounded arm and again poured a regular fusillade into the ranks of the scattered mob, working the lever of his magazine with his left hand, as a result of which two more men fell prostrate in the road, and lay where they fell. Others, wounded, ran off shouting and cursing with pain and leaving a trail of their life blood behind them. The mob scattered in all directions and again disappeared among the trees and underbrush,

Glancing back along the road in the direction of Graham, Charley [*sic*: George] saw in the creek bed what he took to be a buggy. It was hardly discernible in the obscuring shadows of the creek banks, but he raised his rifle and was about to fire, when Charley said:

"Don't shoot down there. That's the buggy and those are the guards."

George shifted his aim and fired into the brush. At the same instant from the gloomy depths of the creek bed came a flash and report of a Winchester, and Charley sank to the ground.[11] George then fired quickly at the buggy, which instantly disappeared down the bed of the stream.

George alone was left standing. He called to Ellie, but the poor boy was fast bleeding to death, and gasped with his expiring breath that he could never get up again. He called to Charley, but there was no response. He shouted aloud to Alfred, but only the echo in the lonesome trees answered—Alfred was dead.

[11] Charley's wounds were inflicted by a shotgun, not a Winchester rifle.

George stood there alone in the cold January night, while the moon looked down upon the upturned faces of the dead, and the mournful wind moaned a solemn requiem through the shivering branches of the leafless trees. Himself wounded and bleeding, with one hand shot through and useless, chained to one dead brother and two more lying apparently dead a few feet away, his hope was forlorn, yet his courage undaunted, and in a frenzy of anguish and pain, he shouted aloud to the retreating mob:

"Come back! Come back again, you cowardly hounds! We have plenty of ammunition and no one is hurt. Come on! Come on!"[12]

One man of that panic stricken mob turned back. It was Frank Harmison, considered the gamest man of Young County. Wounded and numbed at the first volley of the Marlows, he had just recovered himself when he heard George's challenge, and rose and drew his six-shooter.

"Where are you going?" asked another of the mob.

"I'm going back to have it out," was Harmison's reply.

"Don't go; you will be killed," continued the other.

Frank Harmison did not heed the warning. He walked quickly through the woods, and stepped out into the road. George saw him coming. Harmison halted when he saw George, and the two men faced each other in silence. Then, raising their guns, fired simultaneously, then again and again. At each shot George advanced a step, dragging after him the dead body of Ellie, to whom he was chained. At the fifth fire Frank Harmison leaped into the air and fell lifeless in the road, shot squarely between the eyes.

So intently was George watching Harmison's advance that he failed to see a tall man step from the shadows of the trees, hardly ten paces away, and raise his pistol to shoot him, but Charley, who had regained consciousness by this time, fired on the tall man, hitting him in the leg. Then began a duel between the two—Charley Marlow and Eugene Logan, the former lying on the ground, the latter standing. They emptied their six-shooters without fatal effect. Charley was not struck at all, but Logan was hit three times and badly hurt. The last time Logan was hit he fell, but had strength enough left to crawl into the shelter of the brush.

[12] Said Johnson: "The mob could be heard leaving through the bushes, the Marlows begging and cursing them as cowards to come back and finish the job" (Ibid.).

The battle of Dry Creek was ended.[13] Three of the mob lay dead in the road, Frank Harmison, Sam Criswell, and Bruce Wheeler. Johnson, Logan, and Clint Rutherford were badly wounded. Alfred and Ellie Marlow had been killed. Charley, who had been shot down, struggled up, half sitting and half reclining on the body of his dead brother, gasping for breath. He was shot through the lungs.[14] George made his way slowly back to his living brother's side, and the two brothers grasped each other by the hand.

"Charley, our brothers are dead and their souls are in Heaven," said George. Then, as he looked upon the faces of the two men whom in life he had loved so well, George was seized with a paroxysm of rage, and once more he defied the mob to come in sight, but none heard him save Eugene Logan, who had crawled off into the bushes to hide, and Martin, the driver, who was skulking in the bushes in fear of his life. When the paroxysm had spent its force, George knelt down by his dead brothers, baring their breasts, and putting his ear to their hearts in the vain hope that he might hear a faint fluttering. He was doomed to disappointment, for Ellie had drawn his last breath a few minutes before, while Alfred had been past human hope a still longer time.

George looked inquiringly at Charley, who directed him to hunt for a knife. Searching the dead body of one of the mob, he found a big clasp

[13] The fight lasted twenty or thirty minutes with "constant firing from the mob and the Marlows." When the shooting stopped, Johnson made his way to the creek bed and got some water to quench his extreme thirst. Said Ted Johnson:

> He could hear the moaning of the wounded and could recognize the voice of Charley Marlow. Knowing the awful thirst of a wounded man, he got his hat full of water and . . . started up the bank and called to the Marlows who he was and that he had some water for them and was their friend. In reply Charlie Marlow told him, friend or foe, that if he valued his life, to stay where he was or leave—and as a reminder, sent a bullet whizzing over his head. (Ibid., 11, 48)

It is not explained how a one-armed man with his only hand "literally torn to pieces" by a bullet could carry a hatful of water.

[14] The *Graham Leader* of January 24 ticked off the casualties: "Alf and Epp. Marlow, prisoners, Sam Cresswell, guard, Bruce Wheeler and Frank Harmison, of the mob, were all instantly killed; Deputy Marshal Johnson shot in the hand—a painful but not dangerous wound; Charley Marlow seriously shot in the breast and jaw; George Marlow shot in the hand; Clift, another prisoner, shot in the thigh, and Eugene Logan, Constable Belknap Precinct, and one of the mob, shot in the breast and arm, which may prove fatal. . . . It is thought that others of the mob were hurt, but none of them have been reported."

Fifteen-year-old Ted Johnson joined a crowd at the battle ground the morning after the fight and the sight made a deep impression on his memory. "Pools and spots of blood were to be seen in many different places. . . . There were many trees marked by bullets and I believe it would be safe to say one could have counted a hundred or more bullet marks on the large oak trees" (Johnson, "Deputy Marshal Johnson," 48).

knife,[15] whetted it on a stone lying by the road, and handed it to Charley, who had the use of both hands. Charley then unjoined the shackled ankles of his dead brothers and freed himself and George.[16] After freeing themselves at such cost, the brothers made their way to the hack, Charley leaning heavily on George. Clift and Burkhart were in before them.

After helping the half-fainting Charles in, George gathered up all the ammunition he could find, climbed in beside Charles, ordering the cowardly Burkhart to drive for his life if he was not wounded. To this he replied that he was not wounded in his hands, by which George supposed that he was shot somewhere else. Handing him a six-shooter, he told him to take that and use it if he had a chance. Burkhart drove the hack until they reached Finis,[17] where they stopped before a house and asked to stay the night. This request was refused by the man that was asked, who went inside and hastily closed the door. George climbed out and got an ax from a near wood pile and on the hack tire broke Clift's and Burkhart's shackles. To their astonishment, as soon as Burkhart was released he ran off into the thick brush, having not received so much as a scratch. The Marlows have never heard from him since.

A short time after leaving Finis, Charles became so ill they halted to let him die, thinking it impossible for him to live longer. Clift and George each raised him up by an arm, thinking to benefit his breathing. This move caused him to cough a quantity of clotted blood, which helped him so much that it was repeated with the same favorable results.

When they first stopped, Charles seemed to quit breathing altogether. George shook him frantically, begging him to speak to him and asking him if he was going to give it up. A very decided shake of the head was his only answer. George understood that he was not going to give up, and believed that if possible, although it looked very unlikely just then, with his iron will, he would recover. After bathing his face and hands in

[15] "They got hold of a knife—it is thought one of the other prisoners took it out of Cresswell's pocket. . . ." (Ibid.).

[16] Charlie Siringo wrote that the "flat stone on which the ankles were unjointed was later taken to the United States Marshal's office in Dallas, where it was kept on display for many years. And may be there yet. On one side it showed the bloodstains" (Siringo, *Riata and Spurs*, 211).

[17] The Marlows' initial intention was to flee the county, but Charley's serious condition forced them to return to the Denson farm to get help. Finis was a small community established on Rock Creek in the southwestern corner of Jack County about 1880. Only a few years after the Marlow affair it lived up to its name and disappeared (Horton, *History of Jack County*, 133).

water that George brought from an icy little stream near, he felt so much better that they thought it best to try to reach the farm, where the mother could care for their wounds. After inquiring their way several different times, they finally reached the ranch of O. G. Denson, roused him from his slumbers and explained to him all that had happened. He started back in consternation when he beheld their muddy clothes and blood-stained faces and hands, and did not recognize them until they spoke. Denson told them to hurry down to their mother's place and he would follow them there immediately, and accordingly they started for home. They had traveled about twenty-five miles during the night, and were well-nigh exhausted from fatigue and loss of blood.

Home was reached in the cold grey dawn of the morning, the old mother and the other women awakened and hastily informed of all the circumstances, and the wounded men made as comfortable as time and circumstances permitted.

Chapter XIII

THE STORY IN A NEW YORK PAPER, IN JUNE 1891

We make a chapter here from a detailed statement of the facts now being narrated, which appeared and was elaborately illustrated in the National Police Gazette during the summer of 1891.[1]

HUNTED IN THE LAW'S NAME.
FOUR MEN IN SHACKLES AGAINST A HUNDRED.
BORDER LIFE IN TEXAS.
THE FAMOUS MARLOW MOB CASE.

There is no more startling story in all the turbulent annals of the southwest than the one that will be told when the "Marlow mob" cases are called up at the next term of the United States Supreme Court. Ex-Attorney-General Garland will appear for the defendants in the case, which comes up before the final legal tribunal on a writ of error.

The official records of the case, which are on file in the Supreme Court, will, it is asserted, disclose an astounding conspiracy, which, started by designing men, finally led a whole community into a series of criminal transactions, and stained the history of [a] Texas county with blood. The story, now told for the first time, would certainly be incredible if it were not supported at all points by official records.

[1] Rathmell chose to enclose this entire article in quotation marks to show it was copied from the *National Police Gazette*. However, he also used double quotation marks instead of single to enclose direct quotes within the article, making for confusion in reading. For clarity I have removed the marks enclosing the article, which continues to the end of the chapter.

In 1885 five sons of Dr. Marlow, a Missouri man, who had moved to Texas, were living with their mother, near where the Indian Territory, southeastern Colorado, northeastern New Mexico, and northeastern Texas come together.

Their names were Boone, George, Alfred, Charles and Lewellyn—the latter better known as "Epp." Of these all but Boone married soon after. The boys led a semi-nomadic life, and were the types of frontier plainsmen—brave, honest, shrewd and loyal. Their love for each other amounted to a passion, and was only second to their devotion to their grey-haired mother, a remarkable woman and a descendent of Daniel Boone.

They roamed over the country at will, sometimes home as the exigencies of their life demanded, sometimes working, sometimes trading horses, and living chiefly on game, fish and maize.

Late in August, 1888, the first step was taken in the series which led to the bloody affray at Dry Creek. Two deputy United States marshals—Edward W. Johnson and Sam Criswell—went to the Indian territory and arrested four of the Marlow boys on the charge of stealing 33 head of horses from Ba-sin-Da-Bar,[2] a Caddo Indian. The theft was said to have been committed in 1885. George Marlow was away on a trading expedition.

The arrests were made without evidence whatever, as was afterward proved, but simply because the officers had failed to connect any of the "rustlers" with the theft, and felt as if they must make some kind of showing in order to hold their official positions.

The four Marlow boys were carried to the jail at Graham, the county seat of Young county, where the United States judge of the northern district of Texas held court for the convenience of that and adjoining counties.

When George Marlow heard that his brothers were arrested, he rounded up the cattle, and taking his mother, wife and child, and the wives of Charles, "Epp" and Alfred, went directly to Graham. When he endeavored to procure bail for his brothers he himself was imprisoned.

It was then that the Spartan nature of Mrs. Marlow, the mother, showed itself. She went out among the Young county farmers, secured bail for her

[2] The spelling is slightly different here than in other references.

boys, securing their release one by one. She obtained a cabin on the farm of O. G. Denson, about twelve miles southeast of Graham, and there she and her daughters-in-law were joined by the sons as soon as they were released. The United States marshals knew they had no evidence against the Marlow boys, and so must rely on prejudice. They circulated the report that the Marlows were all bad men. By methods which on their very face bore the stamp of unfairness, Johnson and Criswell, so the story goes, secured an indictment of Boone Marlow on the charge of murdering J. A. Holton, who had been found dead in a gulch.

The capias for the arrest was sent to Marion Wallace, sheriff of Young county, who, accompanied by his chief riding deputy, Tom Collier, started for the Denson ranch to arrest Boone.

On their arrival Wallace walked around the cabin, while Collier went directly up to the door. Boone Marlow first saw Collier and called out:

"Hello, Tom; 'light and come in and have some dinner."

Collier replied: "I'm not hungry."

"Come in anyway," urged Boone.

Without replying, Collier alighted and walked to the door. He stepped in, and as Boone arose to welcome him, he called out:

"Boone Marlow, I'm after you."

As he spoke these words he aimed his pistol at Boone and fired. Boone dodged and seized a Winchester from the bed. Collier, seeing that he had missed his man, jumped back and closed the door, and Boone fired through the door, the bullet passing through Collier's hat brim. Running to the door, Boone opened it, and seeing a man coming around the corner of the cabin, fired and struck down Sheriff Wallace, who had heard the shots and was hastening to learn their cause.

Wallace had been friendly to the Marlows when they were in jail, and they were overwhelmed with sorrow at the catastrophe. Boone compelled Collier to come back at the muzzle of his Winchester, and pointing to the prostrate form of Sheriff Wallace, whose head Charley Marlow was supporting, exclaimed:

"Tom Collier, you are responsible for this. You fired on me like I was a dog."

"I know it," whimpered Collier, "but let's not say anything more about it."

"You —— scoundrel, I ought to shoot you between the eyes!" thundered Boone, drawing a bead on the spot indicated.

Collier crouched behind Charley Marlow and begged him piteously not to let Boone shoot him. Charley, in many respects the leader of the brothers, told Boone not to shoot, and the latter reluctantly took his Winchester from his shoulder.

Physicians were sent for, and every care was given the wounded officer; but he died a week later. In the meantime all the Marlow boys, except Boone, gave themselves up and were jailed. Tom Collier succeeded Wallace as sheriff of the county, and this circumstance, combined with the indignation and sorrow over the death of his predecessor, boded no good to the Marlow boys. Boone had mounted a horse and was never seen alive again in Texas. A reward of $1,500 was offered for him, dead or alive, but all efforts to find him proved unsuccessful.

The demand for vengeance was general, and when Wallace died, a conspiracy, reported to have been led by Johnson, Criswell and Collier, had been formed for lynching the four Marlow boys. Chafing under the indignities thrust upon them, the Marlows resolved to escape. They procured a large pocket knife, converted the large blade into a saw, and cut their way out of the jail.

They went directly to their families on the farm and went to work. They were arrested the following day, stripped and searched, and when they were dressed, were taken to a blacksmith shop and shackled and chained together, two and two—Charley and Alfred, George and "Epp."

"Now, —— you," said Sheriff Tom Collier, "I reckon you won't get away again."

Two days later, January 17th, 1889, the jail was turned over to a mob, organized and led by the peace officers before mentioned. The Marlows were to be lynched, but no shots were to be fired, as the town would be alarmed and the mob discovered. The conspirators had arranged to swear to alibis for each other if any arrests were made.

The prisoners, who were confined in iron cages, were awakened by rough footsteps. "Boys," said a prisoner to the Marlows, "it's a mob, and they're after you."

The four Marlow boys rose without a word and stood two and two, as they were chained. John Leavels came first, swinging a lantern in one hand and carrying the jail keys in the other. He unlocked the door of the cage, the mob at his heels. He called to Charley Marlow to come out, saying that a man wanted to see him. Charley refused to go. Believing that the mob meant to put them to death, the Marlows had resolved to stand together and die fighting.

At last one of the mob, tired of delay, made a rush for Charley Marlow. He didn't get him. As he entered the cage, Charley struck him a terrible blow on the head with his fist, knocking him headlong through the door and against the wall of the prison, where he fell unconscious to the floor. The mob started back in dismay. Presently the man revived and gasped:

"Take me out of here; I'm bleeding to death."

The mob returned, picked him up and carried him down stairs. The identity of this man has never been positively ascertained, but it was a singular coincidence that a prominent citizen who had been in good health on the morning of the day when the attack on the jail was made, died a day or two afterwards from alleged brain fever.

Marion Wallace, nephew of the dead sheriff, led the mob on their next attack. The mob tried to lasso the prisoners, then poked their heads with the barrels of their rifles, threatening them with instant death if they failed to come out. The attempt failed and the mob went home. Next morning the leaders gave out the story that Boone Marlow, at the head of a gang of desperadoes from the Indian Territory, had attempted to rescue his brothers, but had been foiled by the vigilance of the faithful jailers.

They managed to get an order from United States Marshal Cabell, of Dallas, to have the four desperate prisoners removed to Weatherford, sixty miles distant, for greater security. Another and a larger mob was organized. It was given out that the six guards commanded by United States Deputy Marshal Johnson and Sheriff Collier would not offer any resistance.

The journey was commenced January 19th. Shortly after 8 o'clock the two hacks and a buggy were driven up in front of the jail. The prisoners were brought down still shackled and chained and placed in one of the hacks, driven by County Attorney Martin. In the second vehicle were Ed Johnson, a kinsman of Ex-Attorney General Garland, who had command of the party; Sam Criswell, the other deputy, and two other men. In the buggy were two men, named Sam Waggoner and Will Hollis. The three carriages had not gone two miles before they reached Dry Creek, where the tragedy of the night occurred. The hack containing the prisoners stopped suddenly.

"We'll all be killed in fifteen minutes," exclaimed Charley Marlow.

Johnson and Martin tried to reassure him, but he knew danger was coming. As the hack emerged from the creek bed and climbed up the ascent, he saw the trees and bushes on the south side of the lane; and the moon, now well up, shed a bright light over the scene.

"Boys," he said, "the mob is hiding somewhere in that brush."

Hardly were the words out of his mouth before the leader of the mob rose up out of the brush and shouted:

"Halt! Hold up your hands!"

A sheet of flame burst from the cover, the reports of a score of rifles rang out and armed men ran yelling toward the foremost hack. Martin, the driver, scrambled down from his seat and ran to his horses' heads, crying:

"The —— scoundrels are in there. Kill 'em all."

At the first alarm Charley and Alf jumped out of the hack away from the mob, and ran as fast as their shackled condition would allow to the other hack, where they each snatched a Winchester from one of their guards. George and "Epp" seized a man who was passing and took from him a Winchester and a pistol. The mob, passing to the front and rear of the two hacks, fired a volley point blank at the Marlows, who were standing back to back. The battle of Dry Creek had begun, with one hundred armed men[3] on one side and the four shackled prisoners on the other.

At the first volley by the Marlows one man fell and crawled away, and another, shot through the pistol hand, jumped up and down, cursing. Soon the mob made another rush, firing as they came. Alf Marlow fell dead, with a bullet in his brain, and "Epp" was also stricken down. George

[3] This is undoubtedly greatly exaggerated. There were probably no more than twenty-five involved, including the guards.

was shot through the right hand, but Charley was unhurt. The boys' next volley killed two of the mob. A moment later Charley Marlow sank to the ground, shot through the lungs. Still the intrepid George did not lose his courage. He dared the mob to return to the attack.

"Come on, you cowards; we've got plenty of arms and ammunition, and nobody hurt. Come on, you —— cowards."

One man of the panic-stricken mob turned back. It was Frank Harmison, considered the gamest man in Young county. George Marlow saw him coming. He dropped his empty rifle and picked up the pistol he had given "Epp" at the beginning of the fight. The two men blazed away at each other until Harmison fell in the road, shot fairly between the eyes. He never spoke nor moved afterward.

George had not noticed that a tall man had advanced behind him and had drawn his pistol to shoot him, only ten paces away. Charley regained consciousness just in time to see this new danger, and fired at the new comer, one Eugene Logan. After several shots, Logan crawled into the brush, badly wounded. The battle of Dry Creek had ended.

The surviving brothers, George and Charley, cut themselves from their brothers and made their way to the Denson farm, where they told their story to the agonized women. But they had little time to mourn. The house was fortified for the attack their enemies were sure to make, and due attention was given the wounded brother.

The story, as told by the mob, was that the Marlows had been rescued by Boone Marlow and his followers, and that the men who fell died trying to resist the deliverance of the prisoners.

The cry now was: "Extermination of the Marlows—men, women and children." This sentiment overreached the mark and opened the eyes of some thinking men. Marion Lasater, a Scotchman, was a fast friend of the Marlows.[4] When an attempt was made to arrest them in their home he went to the house, and being admitted, manned a rifle in their behalf.

Sheriff Monroe, [*sic*: Moore] of Jack county,[5] had now come to assist in the siege. He saw the animus and went home disgusted. A reaction

[4] Marion L. Lasater (1847–1892) was a neighbor of the Marlows (Crouch, *History of Young County*, 119).

[5] George W. Moore was the sheriff of adjoining Jack County, having been elected the previous November (Tise, *Texas County Sheriffs*, 277).

set in. The mob camped at a safe distance and waited until Capt. Norton [*sic*: Morton] arrived from Dallas,[6] and then the boys gave themselves up and were taken to court, 1890, on the charge of horse stealing, and were acquitted on that and on all other counts against them. At the next election "mob" and "anti-mob" tickets appeared in the field, the latter being victorious and placing Marion Lasater in the office of sheriff.[7]

Many arrests followed. Indictments were found by wholesale against the participants in the transactions of the mob. Shortly after the Dry Creek battle three desperadoes brought in the body of Boone Marlow and secured the $1,500 previously offered for his capture.[8] Later developments proved that Boone had been poisoned by the brothers of a sweetheart he had found in one of the white families of the Indian territory, who was supplying him with food.

The three men who brought in the body have since been indicted for murder.[9] Sam Criswell, Bruce Wheeler and Frank Harmison were

[6] Deputy U. S. Marshal W. H. Morton.

[7] Marion L. Lasater was elected sheriff of Young County November 4, 1890, and filed for his second term in 1892 when he was stricken with typhoid fever and was forced to withdraw. He died soon afterward (Tise, *Texas County Sheriffs*, 557; Ledbetter, *Ordeal*, 206).

[8] After leaving Young County, Boone headed for the family's old stamping grounds on Hell Roaring Creek in the Indian Territory. At Henrietta, in Clay County, Texas, at the home of a man named J. H. Griffiths, he swapped horses and sold his Winchester rifle. Griffiths, aware that Boone was a fugitive, "had a notion to capture Marlow but did not want to kill him for the reward." Following Boone into Indian Territory, he "put John Derrickson and Jim Beavers on his trail" (*Fort Worth Daily Gazette*, January 29 and 30, 1889).

At Hell Roaring Creek Boone was hiding out with an old girlfriend, Susan Harbolt. The Marlows were well acquainted with the Harbolts; one of the clan, William Harbolt, had also been charged with larceny in Indian Territory and jailed with them at Graham (Ledbetter, *Ordeal*, 90). The two bounty hunters, Derrickson and Beavers, enlisted the aid of Susan's brother, George E. Harbolt, in the taking of Boone. On Monday, January 28, authorities at Weatherford received a telegram from Henrietta stating that Boone had been killed resisting arrest and that his slayers had passed through town with the body the previous day on their way to Graham to collect the reward (*Fort Worth Daily Gazette*, January 29 and 30, 1889). On that same Monday three men arrived in Graham with Boone's body. "I remember this very well," wrote Ted Johnson, "as they drove into Graham and stopped their hack under a large post oak tree at the corner of the Court House Square. A great many people went out and saw Boone. I could see several bullet holes in his chest and forehead, but no blood to speak of" (Johnson, "Deputy Marshal Johnson," 49). At an inquest before the coroner, J. Squire Starrett, a determination was made that Boone had been killed in the Indian Territory while "resisting arrest" on the 24th, and the reward paid (*Graham Leader*, January 31, 1889). The names of the three men are variously reported at "Beavers" and "Weaver;" "Harbolt," "Harbold" and "Harboldt;" and "Dirickson," "Direkson," "Dirreckson," "Deerickson," "Dickerson," and "Kirkson."

[9] During the transport of Boone's body from the Indian Territory to Graham, Dr. W. R. Dunham, who had known the boys, was called to Archer City in Archer County to view the remains, apparently to confirm identification. He later said that he had an opportunity for a "thorough examination" of the body and concluded that Boone "had been poisoned and then shot" ("Memoirs of W. R. Dunham, Jr., as Given to Aulton Durham. August 18, 1936").

Why this information was not forwarded to the authorities at Graham is not clear, but several weeks later federal officers went after the bounty hunters. Deputy U. S. Marshals W. H. Morton shot at Dry Creek; Tom Collier and "Bee" Williams died in prison;[10] Marion Wallace lost both arms,[11] and Eugene Logan and Sam Waggoner are doing long terms in the penitentiary.[12]

The trial of the conspirators and mob leaders was held at Graham before Judge A. P. McCormick. The indictments, drawn by United States Attorney Eugene Marshall, filled 175 type-written pages and required a whole day to read to the jury. The accused were well defended, and were found guilty. Their counsel have carried their case to the supreme court of the United States, and whatever the result may be, the case affords a signal illustration of unscrupulous persecution by public officials and of the tables turned on the persecutors.

---

and H. H. Dickey arrested the three in the Indian Territory and took them to Dallas. Beavers was charged with the killing of Boone and the others as accessories (*San Antonio Daily Express*, February 17, 1889). "It is a curious fact," commented the *Graham Leader* in reporting the arrests, "that everybody who has had anything to do with the Marlows has more or less trouble over them" (February 28, 1889).

Boone's accused murderers were released on $5,000 bail at the March term of court in Graham (*Graham Leader*, March 28, 1889). Later Harbolt was reportedly shot to death and there was no further prosecution in the case (Crouch, *History of Young County*, 119–20; Sonnichsen, *I'll Die Before I'll Run*, 203).

[10] While awaiting trial William "Bee" Williams declined rapidly from the ravages of a form of tuberculosis known as "galloping consumption." In late September 1890 authorities permitted his removal to the family home in Belknap where he was treated by his brother-in-law, Doctor William Benoit Pope (*Graham Leader*, October 1, 1890). At the trial the following month he appeared to be "greatly emaciated, and but a shadow of his former self. He [had] to be carried to and from the courts in a vehicle, as he [was] too weak to walk even the short distance between Judge Williams's residence and the court room" (Ibid., October 29, 1890). Bee Williams, aged thirty-two, died in Belknap January 12, 1891, and was buried at Graham the next day (Ibid., January 14, 1891).

Exactly one month later, on February 12, 1891, Tom Collier, aged thirty-one, died in the hospital ward of the Tarrant County jail at Fort Worth. His fatal disease was reported as typhoid fever, "aggravated if not induced by his confinement in the unwholesome atmosphere of federal prisons." His body was removed to Alabama for burial. In reporting the passing of the controversial former sheriff, the *Graham Leader* noted:

> In justice to him it may be truthfully said that few if any peace officers in this state ever came into office confronted by more difficulties than did Sheriff Collier. The jail was filled with prisoners who made every effort to escape while outside the air was filled with breathings of vengeance toward those who were incarcerated for the murder of Wallace. . . . The escape of the prisoners, the attack upon the jail, and the bloody fight at Dry Creek, followed in quick succession, marking perhaps the bloodiest page in the history of Young county. In the wholesale arrests that followed, Sheriff Collier was taken and held until his death by the federal authorities. His guilt or innocence is a question which has now passed beyond the jurisdiction of the courts of earth. (Ibid., February 18, 1891)

[11] There is confusion here with Ed Johnson. Marion A. Wallace was able-bodied enough to serve in later years six terms as sheriff of Young County (Tise, *Texas County Sheriffs*, 557).

[12] On April 17, 1891, Eugene Logan, Sam Waggoner, and Marion A. Wallace were convicted of conspiracy in federal court and each sentenced to ten years imprisonment and a fine of $5,000. Appeals were filed, but at the time of this publication they were convicted felons (Case #263, *The United States v. Eugene Logan, et al; Logan v. United States*, 276).

Chapter XIV

THE HOME BESIEGED—ONE HUNDRED TO ONE

Brief time was there for the wounded brothers and grief stricken women to lament over the death of their loved ones, for their frail cabin had to be turned into a fortress, and hasty preparations made to defend their home and lives from the blood-thirsty horde which would be sure to arrive before long.

The brave mother was first to recover her self-possession, and commenced without delay for the siege. Charley was faint and helpless, the night's ride having exhausted the little strength his wounds had left him. The only way in which he could breathe was when propped up in a sitting posture, and in this position, with a Winchester across his lap, he sat the following two days and nights. If anyone spoke loud or passed before him, he would instantly grasp his gun deliriously, try to draw it, then finding his mistake, sink back more exhausted than ever. The mother took command, Charley's Alfred's and George's wives doing as she directed. When they had done all they could to put their little cabin in a state of defense, they busied themselves preparing cooling drink for the boys, and quietly awaited the coming of their enemies. Clift was in agony from a ragged wound in the thigh, and leaning on two guns, he continually hobbled up and down the floor, in too much pain to be quiet.

After the rout at Dry Creek all the living members of the mob, except Logan and Martin, fled to Graham as fast as their horses could carry them, and circulated the report that a gang from the Indian Territory, headed by Boone Marlow, had rescued the Marlows after a desperate fight in which some of the guards had been killed and others wounded. This story, shrewdly contrived for the purpose, spread throughout the town and county like wildfire, and roused the people to a demand for vengeance.

Had all the Marlows been killed, and Clift and Burkhart with them, as the mob expected them to be, who was there to dispute this fabrication? This story would have evidently been accepted as the true state of affairs. Of course violent counsels prevailed at such a report and there was no lack of volunteers. "Extermination of the Marlows," was the cry. A deputy sheriff was dispatched to Jack county to procure aid from Sheriff Moore and his posse, and when the sun was about an hour high on the morning after the night at Dry Creek, the avenging cavalcade, with Sheriff Tom Collier at its head, began its march to the Denson farm. They were soon found by the sheriff of Jack county, whose posse numbered thirty men. Collier's force numbered over a hundred before the arrival of the reinforcements.

Collier had demanded surrender of the Marlows, but this they refused. George replied:

"We will give ourselves up to George [*sic*: William Lewis] Cabell or his chief deputy, Captain Morton, and to no one else. And if we are attacked we will defend ourselves to the end."

His words gained additional force when the mob saw the muzzles of half a dozen Winchester rifles projecting through the rudely-cut loop holes. Collier and others of the principal conspirators urged the storming of the cabin. In this crowd was one man who would attract attention anywhere—tall above the average, yet graceful in every movement, clear blue eyes that could blaze and sparkle at an injustice, twinkle with merriment when occasion offered and never faltering under the most searching gaze. He had been one of the posse that had sought Boone at the time of the killing of Sheriff Wallace, always treating the helpless women of the Marlow family with greatest respect, assisting them in every way possible. He had assisted in the recapture of the other four Marlows at the time of their escape from jail, but had heard only one side of the affair then. He had no part in the conspiracy and had not participated in either mob at the jail or at Dry Creek. Collier's denunciation of the Marlows and his declaration that they should be wiped from the face of the earth, men, women and children, so that their names should become extinct in years to come, opened his honest eyes to a clear understanding of the motives actuating Collier and his fellow conspirators. He very modestly called attention to himself and made a few remarks to the crowd. It was the first attempt of his life at a public speech.

"Men," he said, with a slight Scotch accent, "There has been enough blood shed in Young county growing out of this affair. These men," pointing to Collier and the other leaders, "have not brought us here in the interests of peace and justice, but as a mob bent on wreaking vengeance on these men in there, who haven't done anything but defend their lives when attacked. Men, I am tired of this, and I am going down there to that cabin and if these men won't surrender to me, I am going inside if they will let me, and see how they are, and if the cabin is attacked while I am in there you will have to kill me before you get the Marlows."

"Good for you, Marion Lasater!" shouted Bill Gilmore,[1] another brawny and honest frontiersman, "I'll go with you."

The two men walked toward the cabin with their hands extended in token of their peace mission. Lasater asked George Marlow if he would surrender to him. George repeated his answer to Collier.

"Can I come in?" asked Lasater.

"Let him come in," said the mother, "He is an honest man."

Lasater and Gilmore entered the cabin and remained there. After they had cast their lot with the Marlows, the sheriff of Jack county arrived with a posse. He consulted briefly with Collier. Everybody was excited and making suggestions. The favorite plans were to open fire on the frail structure, the walls of which were of thin weatherboarding, and keep it up until everybody inside was dad, or to load a wagon with hay, run it up against the cabin, set fire to it, smoke the inmates out and shoot them down as they emerged from the shelter.

Sheriff Moore disapproved of both of these barbarous suggestions, and a Young county man named James Denty, who had become disgusted

[1] The Gilmores were another family neighboring the Denson property and the Marlows (Crouch, *History of Young County*, 119). John Gilmore had been one of Charley Marlow's bondsmen the previous November.

with the Collier crowd of conspirators, joined him. When the two had passed beyond earshot of the mob, Denty said to the Jack county sheriff:

"You don't seem to understand the affair. Let me tell you how it stands."

Denty then explained this trouble from the beginning to the end, showing up the conspiracy to destroy the Marlows. Without a word Sheriff Moore walked back to where the crowd was.

"Jack county men, mount your horses. If these wronged men would surrender to us we would protect them. Since they refuse to do so, we have no business here."

Collier appealed to him to stay and help him take the desperate Marlows, intimating to the sheriff of Jack county that his motives for leaving might be misconstrued.

"Tom Collier," said Moore as he laid his hand on his six-shooter, "No man will say I am a coward." No man did, for the sheriff of Jack county had proved his courage on the battle fields of the Civil War and in single combat with desperadoes afterward. Collier and the gang were afraid to attack the cabin alone, so contented themselves with camping around it at a safe distance until Captain Morton arrived on Tuesday and removed the prisoners to Dallas.

The Marlows had sent the hack back to Graham in two or three hours after getting home, and asked for the bodies of their dead brothers. This was granted, and about 1 o'clock in the afternoon of the same day Johnny Gilmore brought the bodies of Alfred and Lewellyn home to the sad-hearted ones, prepared for burial.[2] Their graves had been dug in the Graham cemetery. Three more desperate men than Clift, George and Charles were, when the bodies were brought in, would be hard to find, and it wouldn't have been well for one of the mob to have come within their reach.

Alfred was shot fifteen times. Ellie was so shot to pieces that it was necessary to bind strips of cloth about him till he could be dressed for the grave. It was certainly a heartrending sight to look upon—the sorrowing wife and two little children of Alfred, and the old mother

[2] Ed Johnson remembered that although "John Gilmore brought the hack and team from the Marlows and returned them to the livery stable. . ., Uncle Bush Lawrence was hired to take the two dead Marlow brothers to their home on the Denson farm" (Johnson, "Deputy Marshal Johnson," 48–49).

frantically kissing and talking to the still forms of her children, looking so peaceful in death, no trace being left on the regular features of the desperate struggle the night before, for life and liberty, that the other two had gained at such a cost. Later in the afternoon Alfred and Ellie, by George's and the mother's request, were buried at Finis, Jack county, Texas. Quite a number of Jack and Young county men who were at last getting their eyes open to the wrongs of the Marlows, volunteered their assistance, all seeming eager to do as much as possible for them.

Shortly after Lasater went into the cabin, Dr. Price, who had been sent for by the mother, came in. He made a hasty pretense of dressing George's hand, then after examining Charley's wounds, told him he could do nothing without putting him under the influence of an anaesthetic.

"What's that?" feebly inquired Charles.

"Why, put you to sleep," protested the doctor.

"But I don't want to go to sleep," protested Charley, not knowing what moment the cabin would be stormed. "Charley," said George, cocking his six-shooter. "Let him put you to sleep, and if he don't wake you up when I think he ought to, I'll kill him like a dog." The good doctor snatched up his pill bags and very unceremoniously took his departure.

Chapter XV

PRISONERS AGAIN—BOONE MURDERED

On Tuesday morning, in answer to a telegram sent the Sunday before to U. S. Marshal Cabell, stating that they would never surrender to anyone but he or Morton, Morton with his guard arrived.[1] A mattress was placed in the hack they had brought for them, and the brave and self-sacrificing Clift, at his own request, was placed in first in such a position as to hold up Charley, it being impossible for him to breathe only in a sitting position, so the wounded and suffering Clift held him in his arms till they reached the railroad the next day at about 11 o'clock.

After leaving the house a few yards they were met by Collier and his crowd, by appointment, in order to return the guns they had carried away from the battle field. It was prophesied by all that witnessed their departure that Charles would die of his wounds before reaching Dallas.[2]

When about one mile from the Denson farm a man overtook them and asked where they meant to reach the railroad. "Weatherford," said Morton, and, on getting an answer, the man returned as he had come, in a lope.

[1]On Sunday, January 20, Marshal Cabell received a telegram from Deputy Ed Johnson: "Come to Young at once; two Marlows and Burkhart [*sic*] have been found at Denson's. They are all wounded, but heavily armed. They refuse to surrender alive to anybody except you or Capt. Morton. (Signed) E. W. Johnson." The marshal dispatched his son, Deputy Ben Cabell, W. H. Morton, and two other officers to Young County with orders "to protect the prisoners and to prevent their escape." The lawmen took the train to Weatherford and there rented a buggy which they drove all night, arriving at the Denson farm about six o'clock on the morning of Tuesday, January 22 (*Fort Worth Daily Gazette*, January 21 and 22, 1889; *Galveston News*, January 23 and 25, 1889).

[2] "It is thought Charley Marlow will not live to get to Dallas" (*Graham Leader*, January 24, 1889).

Suspecting Collier of laying a plot for another attack,[3] Morton left the Weatherford road a few miles farther on, taking a road leading to Tala Pinto,[4] and reached this place Tuesday night, Morton, guards and prisoners all sleeping in the county jail. None but Morton and the guards were allowed near them. On Wednesday, a little before noon, they reached Gordon,[5] where they were to take a train for Dallas, and on this day they traveled fifteen miles in a cold January rain. Their clothing was saturated in blood, and after being rained on for so long they were a more unsightly-looking trio than ever.

On reaching Gordon, they went directly to the station, and as they were expected, quite a crowd had congregated to get a glimpse of them if possible. The sympathies of this town were with the Marlows. One old soldier, the proprietor of a hotel, insisted upon serving them with dinner at his own expense. One man brought a basin of warm water and bathed George's hand, which was bleeding profusely. Another did the same kind of office for Clift, while others did all they possibly could for Charley. The crowd was so large that the guard lost sight of them for a time, but they knew they were with friends, so contented themselves with standing off and looking on at a distance.

An hour later when the train came, the enthusiastic crowd raised the three men and carried them in their arms into the coach, where they took particular pains to place each in a comfortable position.

They reached Dallas Wednesday night, and the next morning Doctor Carter[6] dressed up their wounds. How Clift and Charles ever survived such treatment is a miracle. They were wounded on Saturday night, and received no medical attention until the following Thursday.[7] On the trip

[3] Morton, "against some remonstrance on the part of Collier, took the Marlows into his custody and removed them to Dallas" (*Logan v. United States*, 274). Deputy Marshal Morton, in an interview after his arrival back in Dallas, said that he had found the Marlows in "a little box house surrounded by Sheriff Collier and his posse." Collier told Morton he had not stormed the house "first because he thought enough blood had been shed, and second, because an attack upon the house would necessarily have resulted in the killing of some of the women and children" (*Galveston News*, January 25, 1889).

[4] This should be Palo Pinto, county seat of Palo Pinto County, lying southeast of Young County.

[5] Gordon, in southern Palo Pinto County, was on the Texas & Pacific Railroad.

[6] This was probably Dr. J. L. Carter, a Dallas physician practicing in the 1880s (Miller, *Bounty Hunter*, 150).

[7] Ted Johnson disputes this assertion, saying that Dr. Price, after ministering to his father's wound the night of the fight, returned the following day and said "he had been down and waited on the Marlows. [He told] my father how many times they were shot but [felt] that under proper treatment he did not consider any of their wounds fatal" (Johnson, "Deputy Marshal Johnson,"

Charles coughed up a bullet, and a short time after coughed up a second, besides having a shot in the neck, shoulder and right cheek near the nose, which made breathing through that organ difficult, and another shot near the eye.[8] Clift was shot through the thigh and hand, but with good treatment and their strong constitutions, they were soon on the road to recovery.

On the Thursday that Dr. Carter dressed Charles' and George's wounds, Boone came to his death by poison administered by the hands of a man whom the Marlow family had greatly befriended a few years before. Five days later the wives of Charley and George, not having heard of Boone's death, went into Graham after clothing and other things belonging to Ellie and Alfred. On hearing of their arrival, the noble Marion Lasater sought them out and told them that Boone's slayers would be in before long with his body. The brave women determined to wait and take him home with them if allowed. The murderer drove in town and up to the court house in a sweeping trot, stopped at the court house and took out a large bundle wrapped in blankets. When the wrappings were removed the body of a man was discovered.

"There's Boone Marlow's dead body. We killed him in the Indian Territory, and we've brought him here to get the reward," said the spokesman.

It required a coroner's inquest to decide whether it was Boone's body or not. Finally it was decided that it was and the reward of $1,500, offered by the conspirators at the time of the killing of Sheriff Wallace, was turned over to the three sneaks—Harbolt, Beavers and Derrickson.[9] Their money did them very little good, as they were indicted immediately in the United States court for the murder of Boone Marlow, and sentenced to long terms of imprisonment.[10]

At about 3 o'clock, the body was turned over to the two lone women, who had to go a distance of about fifteen miles, on a short winter's day,

48). The *Graham Leader* also reported that Dr. Price had gone to the Denson farm and dressed the wounds (January 24, 1889).

[8] Charley Marlow, said Deputy Marshal Morton, "has buckshot in all parts of his body. A shot is imbedded in his head above the left eye and several are in the left jaw. His lungs also contain several shot. The fact that he coughed up a buckshot yesterday will convey an idea." Although he thought Charley and Clift were "in a pitiable condition," Morton had to admire their toughness: "The prisoners have plenty of grit. They bore their wounds in silence throughout the whole journey" (*Galveston Daily News*, January 25, 1889).

[9] See Chapter XIII, n. 8.

[10] See Chapter XIII, n. 9.

and a good part of the journey would be necessarily after dark. Of all the crowd not one offered to accompany them and assist in the burial of their brother-in-law.[11] When one half mile or more from Graham, Knox Criswell, whose heart was more tender and who had more courage than the rest of the crowd, overtook them.[12] He dismounted, tied his horse behind their hack, and drove over the long and lonely road Boone had traveled in life. When about three miles farther on, a young fellow,[13] who lived with Knox Criswell, overtook them and was sent ahead to communicate the sad tidings to the poor old mother. This young man had the hardest task of all before him. He arrived at the house where the family lived, but found no one at home, so he went to a German's house living near and found them there. The mother and Alfred's wife, not expecting Emma and Lillian back until the next day, were here with the intention of spending the night, little expecting to return so soon to find a third son lying still and cold in the room she had so lately left, and where two of his brothers had lain a week before, robbed of life by the hands of men. If it had been God's work how much easier it could have been borne.

Upon hearing his name, the mother's thoughts instantly flew to George and Charley, thinking Boone far enough away to be out of danger by this time. She rushed to the door, saying:

"Oh, tell me quick, have they killed my boys?"

"They have found Boone," answered the young man evasively.

"What did you say? Found Boone? He is dead then for he would never allow them to take him alive." Then gazing wonderfully and dry-eyed at him, she said:

"Where is my baby boy, can you tell? I must go to him, and bring him home and lay him beside my other darlings. Do you know where he is?"

[11] Ted Johnson remembered that as the women drove out of town with Boone's body "an old Confederate soldier, John Wood, who was watching, said to the younger men who had gathered around, 'My God, men, won't some of you go along and accompany those poor women?'" (Johnson, "Deputy Marshal Johnson," 49). John H. Wood was born in Tennessee in 1840 and moved to Texas at the age of nineteen. He served in Parsons' Brigade in the Confederate Army and went to California for three years after the Civil War. He settled in Young County in 1876 where he became a brickmaker (Crouch, *History of Young County*, 287–88).

[12] This was a surprising volunteer, as Knox was undoubtedly kin, perhaps a brother, to the dead Sam Criswell, but the relationship is unclear.

[13] Ted Johnson identifies this other volunteer as Bill Gilmore (Johnson, "Deputy Marshal Johnson," 49). It was Gilmore, together with Marion Lasater, who had sided with the Marlows against Tom Collier's posse the morning after the fight at Dry Creek.

"I think," he said pityingly, " he is at your house by this time." Then gently taking the half conscious old lady by the arm, he led her in the direction of the house. When a little way on the road, they met Emma coming in the hack to meet them. The weather was so very cold that although he had been dead five days, and hauled very nearly 100 miles in a jolting mail hack, the body was as lifelike as though life had just become extinct.

Lillian had, before the mother came, with the assistance of Mr. Criswell, procured warm water and sponged off the poor hands and face and brushed the soft, wavy hair from the marble brow, where two cruel bullet holes were visible.

When the poor old mother reached the side of the dead boy, she fell across the still, cold form exclaiming:

"Oh! Why did they disfigure your marble brow with those ugly holes? Who did it, my boy? Tell your old mother; whisper in her ear, (laying her ear to the icy lips), my darling, she can hear the tiniest whisper from her baby boy's lips! Can't you hear me, my darling? How did the cowards do it? (Pressing the form of the boy to her bosom.) Oh, my boy, I shall never know the truth; I feel that I shall never, never know how they killed my child. If there is a God, why will he allow such outrages?"

Here the two noble daughters gently forced her from the still form lying so calm and peaceful, and so utterly unconscious of the heartbroken mother and the scalding tears that fell upon him.

After awhile, becoming more quiet, the poor old lady took a position near the corpse of her son, and no persuasion could induce her to leave it till the next morning, when the two men before mentioned, with Jim and Bill Gilmore, did all that could be done for Boone Marlow.

They buried him beside Alfred and Ellie, who were buried in the one grave, and before leaving this place, the mothers and daughters had the spot enclosed by a stone wall, a single headstone marking the place, containing their names, ages, time and cause of death.[14]

When the March term of court came on, the Marlow brothers, with Clift, having so far recovered as to be able to travel, were placed under

[14] Alfred, Ellie, and Boone Marlow are buried together in the remote Finis Cemetery. "A flat ground level stone and the original brown upright stone mark the three graves, A bushy cedar is beside the graves. The inscription on the original stone can be read with great difficulty" (Browning, "Violence Was No Stranger, Volume II," 73).

a heavy guard for protection and returned to Graham, where Clift, who had been confined in the Graham jail for the past two years to answer to the charge of horse stealing, was acquitted without a trial.

The Marlows were placed on trial on the original indictment, charged with stealing horses from Bar-sin-da-Bar, the Caddo Indian. Since the August before, Ed Johnson had made every possible effort to secure witnesses to suit his own interests for this occasion, but hopelessly failed, and as there was no evidence against them, they were acquitted.[15]

The fact was commented on by the judge in his charge to the jury in the trial of the conspirators that no claim was ever set up that any of the horses or mules which George Marlow brought into Young county were stolen property; and further, that before their arrest by Johnson and Sam Criswell, none of the Marlows had ever been charged with crime, arrested or confined in jail.

The conspirators and instigators of the mob were still in possession of the legal machinery of the county, and they used it ingeniously to screen themselves from the consequences of their criminal acts. They procured the indictments of each other in the state court for the murder of the Marlow boys. Their intentions were to go through the forms of trials and secure acquittals, and "Bee" Williams was actually tried and acquitted of this trumped-up indictment.[16]

[15] The *Graham Leader* of March 28, 1889, reported that George and Charles Marlow were found not guilty in the federal court of the charge of larceny. According to Ted Johnson, the federal grand jury that handed down the original horse theft indictment against the Marlows heard testimony from "about fifteen witnesses," including "a few white men and several Comanche Indians," foremost of whom was the celebrated Comanche chieftain, Quanah Parker. But at the trial the charges were "dismissed through sympathy and failure of witnesses to appear, and [a feeling that] really they had been punished enough." Johnson also pointed out that the Marlows were needed as witnesses in the cases pending against the accused conspirators, "and, as we all know, a witness with a felony charge against him is not a desirable witness" (Johnson, "Deputy Marshal Johnson," 6–7, 49).

[16] A newspaper account of the trials tends to support the Marlow brothers' contention that prosecution of the state murder cases against the accused mob members was a farce. When the trials were moved to Jacksboro on a change of venue in January 1890, the *Graham Leader* reported that "much interest is manifested" and "about 40 citizens of this county are in Jacksboro attending court" (January 23, 1890). The state opened with its case against William Williams. After a jury was impaneled, "the first witness called was P. A. Martin for the state, who addressed the Court [and] declined to testify on the ground that there was an indictment pending against him for the same offense. The prosecuting attorney stated that the State could not make out a case without his [Martin's] testimony, and asked the Court to instruct the jury to bring in a verdict of not guilty, which was accordingly done. The case of Verner Wilkinson was next called and dismissed. Tuesday morning the case of Eugene Logan was called and dismissed" (Ibid.).

After the arrest of Logan and others of the mob an indictment was issued against Charley Marlow for the murder of Sheriff Wallace.[17] After being acquitted the three men, Charley, George and Clift, were released under $250 bond each, to appear at the next seating of the United States court as witnesses against the mob.[18]

George returned for the women and children, and they left Dallas soon after for Gainesville, Texas, where they worked at anything they could get to do when their health would admit of it.

Charley's wounds had left him in such a weakened condition that at times he was hardly able to walk. George had the use of only his left hand, and Clift, who was still with them, was quite lame. While in this place, on August 16th, Charley received a letter from Graham which read as follows:

CHAS MARLOW:

The Grand Jury have found a bill against you for the killing of Sheriff Wallace. A Friend.

This was done to frighten him from appearing as a witness at the trial in the United States court. The day he received this note Charley, accompanied by his wife, Alfred [Alpha] and Ellie, the two little namesakes of the murdered brothers, who were but one month old,[19] his mother and Clift, started for Colorado overland.

The bold stand taken by Marion Lasater against Collier and his gang at thc Marlow cabin, on the day after the battle of Dry Creek, had a pronounced effect upon public opinion.

The sober thinking, conservative element of the county applauded his action, and even some who took part in either one or the other of the mobs became convinced that they had been misled, and turned against the conspirators.

The question naturally entered politics, and the people divided. Regardless of party affiliations in national and state affairs, as they

[17] A true bill of indictment charging Charley Marlow with the murder of Sheriff Wallace was brought by the Young County grand jury on August 10, 1889. Appearing as witnesses were Tom Collier, Jeff Short and J. C. Short. The latter two were apparently the J. D. and Charles Short who had posted appearance bond for Epp Marlow back in October; it is not clear what evidence they could offer regarding the Wallace killing (File No. 386, *The State of Texas v. Charley Marlow*).

[18] "George and Charles Marlow are detained in the custody of the Marshal until they give bail in the sum of $250 each to testify as government witnesses in the mob cases" (*Graham Leader*, March 28, 1889).

approved or condemned the acts of the conspirators and of the mobs instigated by them. The county tickets were put in the field known respectively as the Mob and Anti-Mob tickets. On the first were Collier, Eugene Logan, "Bee" Williams and Verna Wilkerson, all of who had taken part in the mob at the jail and the battle of Dry Creek. The Anti-Mob ticket was headed by Marion Lasater.

The campaign was one of long, intense and prolonged excitement. On the day before election Collier, Logan, Williams and Wilkerson, of the Mob ticket, were arrested on indictments found by the United States jury for conspiracy and murder, which created a tremendous sensation. Lasater and the entire Anti-Mob ticket were elected by a round majority. Then followed the arrests of [County] Attorney Martin, Robt. Holman; Sam Waggoner, constable; Ed Johnson, deputy U. S, marshal; John Lewis [*sic*: Leavels], jailer; Marion Wallace, deputy sheriff; Clint Rutherford, stock owner; L. T. Breeks [*sic*: L. P. "Pink" Brooks], land owner; W. C. Hollis; Dink Allan [*sic*: Allen]; W. R. Benedict; Jack Wilkins[20] and Dick Cook—in fact everybody in either mob was indicted and arrested.[21]

Just here it may be well to pause and note the fate of some of these conspirators and mob participants.

Robt. Hill, the son of a wealthy gentleman, came to his death by a blow from Charlie, while trying to enter the cell on the night of the mob at the jail. Sam Criswell, deputy U. S. marshal; Bruce Wheeler, a rich young cattleman, and Frank Harmison, the son of a well-to-do farmer, were left dead on the battle field at Dry Creek. Tom Collier, sheriff, died in the Fort Worth jail, of anxiety and close confinement. "Bee" Williams met with the same fate.[22] His father was the county judge of Young county,

[19] Emma Marlow gave birth to twin girls in July 1889, and she and Charley named them Alpha and Ellie after the brothers killed in the Dry Creek fight. Ted Johnson, confusing the dead brothers with their namesakes, Charley's children, mistakenly believed that Alfred and Llewellyn were twins (Johnson, "Deputy Marshal Johnson," 7).

[20] Wilkins was a cattleman, said Ted Johnson. "Jack was a Texan with a big 'T'—goodhearted and generous at all times" (Ibid., 53).

[21] "In the fall term of the U. S. Court all of the guards [excepting John Girand], including [Deputy Marshal] Johnson and about one-half of the population of Young County, were indicted by a U. S. Grand Jury for acting as participants and conspirators in a mob on Dry Creek and an attempt on the jail, some being indicted on both charges" (Ibid., 49). In addition to those named by Rathmell, Ted Johnson lists several other Young County citizens indicted on the conspiracy charges: Jim Green, Vernon Wilkerson [Verner Wilkinson], Bill Krump and George Mays (Ibid.). Green, Krump and Mays are not named in the newspaper report (*Graham Leader*, November 5, 1890).

[22] See Chapter XIII, n. 10.

and had urged his son to help lynch the Marlows, saying that if the young men had not courage enough to do it the old ones had fire enough left in their veins to go to the front. Ed Johnson's remaining hand had to be amputated on account of a wound received at Dry Creek, and now is perfectly helpless.[23] Eugene Logan, a deputy sheriff, Sam Waggoner and Marion Wallace, constables, are now under sentence of long terms in the penitentiary.

At the time when Boone Marlow's body was first exposed to view it was noticed by the physicians that the wounds did not look as do gunshot wounds inflicted on a live body, and an investigation was afterwards obtained that indicated that Boone Marlow was murdered under peculiar, horrible circumstances. Boone had a sweetheart in one of the white families of the Indian Territory by the name of Harbolt, whom the Marlows had greatly befriended at one time, so when Boone escaped after killing Wallace he went to the part of the country where this family lived. He made his presence known to his sweetheart and kept in hiding, only venturing out to see her and get food that she would leave for him. The girl had a reckless and vicious brother who, in connection with two others, thinking to better their position in life, trailed Boone to this place. Then the three villains put their heads together to think up a way of capturing him. They were afraid to attack him openly, so agreed on the cowardly method of poison. The brutal and ungrateful brother mixed this with food that he knew his sister would soon convey to her lover, and Boone, unsuspectingly, ate of this food and died. The wretches then shot the dead body so as to make it appear that Boone had been killed in a fair fight, as they claimed, at Graham.

[23] The report that Ed Johnson's remaining hand was amputated was "entirely untrue," according to his son. "He never had any part of his left hand removed at that time, but was a bad cripple for life" (Johnson, "Deputy Marshal Johnson," 54). These were tough times for the Ed Johnson family, wrote Ted, the oldest of Johnson's seven children:

> The wounds my father received at the Dry Creek Battle just would not get well. For nearly a year we had to feed him and put his clothes on him. We were almost helpless. My father had saved no money and we were in a desperate condition. Mother taught music at home . . . and we had relatives in the East who helped the best they could. However, I want to say here that God never created a nobler or better class of people than the old-timers of Young County. Many are the ways they helped us until we finally got to where we could make our way.

Johnson said his father moved to California about 1916 where he became a "deputy sheriff in the Civil Department of Los Angeles, being too old for Criminal office" (Ibid., 53). The last time he saw his father was in 1930 (Ibid., 6). Ledbetter asserts that he was killed in Baja, Mexico (Ledbetter, *Ordeal*, 159).

Chapter XVI

ARREST AND TRIAL OF THE CONSPIRATORS

On leaving Gainesville, Charley crossed the Red River at Brown's Ferry, north of Gainesville, crossed the Indian Territory and entered Kansas at Kiowa,[1] took a westerly course here and entered Colorado at Coolidge,[2] and two days later they reached La Junta, where Ellie, one of the twins, became quite ill of pneumonia. Three days later the little one died at this place. Charles was making for the mountains of Colorado, where he thought he would have peace at last.

George left Gainesville, Texas, on the 12th of the following October for Colorado, by rail. He knew Charley was somewhere on the road, but just where he would enter the mountains was a difficult matter to tell, so on reaching Gunnison, Colorado,[3] he left his wife to look for him at this point, while he came on to Dallas,[4] in the same state.

Between La Junta and Gunnison, Charley and Clift were compelled to work three weeks at a saw mill for money to continue their journey on. Charley chose the route by Gunnison, and came across George's

[1] Kiowa is in Barber County, Kansas, some twenty-five miles south of Medicine Lodge.

[2] Coolidge, Kansas, and La Junta, Colorado, are on the line of the Atchison, Topeka & Santa Fe Railroad.

[3] Located in the central Colorado county of the same name, Gunnison was a booming mining camp at this time.

[4] Not to be confused with Dallas, Texas, where the brothers had lately been jailed, Dallas City in Ouray County, Colorado, sprang up as a freight junction point on the site of an abandoned mining camp called Gold City. Named in 1888 for George N. Dallas, vice president under James K. Polk, it lasted only a few years, soon becoming "only a flag stop on the D. & R. G." (Wolle, *Stampede to Timberline*, 381).

wife. She and Clift were sent by rail to Dallas, with directions for George to meet him as soon as possible. Charles had been traveling for the last two hundred miles through snow that ranged from two to three feet in depth, with heavily loaded wagon and only two small mules to drag them. George met him in Blue Canon, and the second day after leaving there they stuck fast in the deep snow, but finally reached Dallas four days later. They remained there, the three men working in a saw mill the rest of the winter.[5]

The following spring George and Charles took up a ranch about two miles further up the mountains from where Ridgway[6] is, a distance of eight miles, for the purpose of conducting one of the icy mountain streams to the new town. They also had a contract to care for a herd of cattle belonging to one Arthur Hyde.[7] In this way they managed to get along all right.

The next July Captain George A. Knight, United States Marshal,[8] inserted an advertisement in the Dallas (Texas) News and the Denver Times to the effect that they were wanted in Texas, and that $500 reward was offered for them, or $250 for any news concerning them.

October found them in Texas again.[9] The trial of the mob leaders and conspirators was an eventful one. It was held at Graham in the United

[5] In 1890 a crew of teamsters under boss Al Cutler were working a tie-hauling contract for the Denver & Rio Grande Railroad then building along the Western Slope. "One night," recalled one of them to an interviewer in the 1930s, "two men with long whiskers, riding bare-back, and each carrying two six-shooters, came to our camp at Coyote Springs, above Ridgway, and asked for grub. We thought they were Blue Mountain country horse thieves. . . . They were the Marlow brothers and had just escaped from Texas." After eating, the Marlows told their story. They had fled Texas into Colorado "and were now camped below us. Cutler gave them flour and other grub to take to their families. Later they settled west of Ridgway and proved to be fine citizens" (Colorado WPA, "Tall Tales and Anecdotes").

[6] When the Denver & Rio Grande chose to bypass Dallas, that camp dried up and was replaced by a new railroad town a couple of miles away. It was named for Superintendent Robert M. Ridgway, a D. & R, G, executive (Brown, *Ghost Towns of the Colorado Rockies*, 121).

[7] Arthur Hyde was a fifty-year-old Canadian who had come to the United States in 1878 (1900 U. S. Census).

[8] Republican Benjamin Harrison was inaugurated in 1889, replacing Democrat Grover Cleveland in the White House, and soon new faces began to appear in federal appointive offices. On April 9, George A. Knight was appointed United States marshal for the Northern District of Texas, replacing W. L. Cabell, and his appointment was confirmed by the U. S. Senate on January 27, 1890. He resigned from office in April 1892 (Robert R. Ernst to Robert K. DeArment, April 12, 1991).

[9] "The Marlow brothers were escorted to the Federal court at Graham by the military infantry of Pueblo, Col. Many anticipate trouble," reported the *Graham Leader*, quoting a October 25 dispatch from Weatherford. "We suppose," added the *Leader*, "the coming of those witnesses will be attended by all the 'pomp and circumstance' of military espionage" (October 29, 1890). The officers responsible for the safety of the Marlow brothers, well aware that the name "Marlow"

States court of the northern district of Texas, sixty miles from a railroad, and lasted thirty days.[10] Judge A. P. McCormick presided, and people flocked in from all the surrounding counties, some coming a hundred miles by wagon or on horse back. Whole families came in covered wagons bringing food with them and camping out at night. Authority was given by the president for the swearing in of all the special deputy marshals required to prevent a rescue of the prisoners, and to protect the chief witnesses, the two surviving Marlows, from attack. Everybody entering the court house was searched for deadly weapons, and an anteroom next to the door was filled with six-shooters, bowie knives and Winchester rifles.

The lawyers of each side were among the leading members of the Texas bar, the government represented by Eugene Marshall, the United States attorney for the district. He drew the indictments which filled

---

still invoked heated passions among the citizens of Young County, took every precaution to prevent a recurrence of mob action against them. The previous February, when the first mob trials were scheduled at Graham, U. S. Marshal George A. Knight wrote to Wilburn H. King, adjutant-general of Texas, requesting the aid of the state rangers in transporting the accused mob members from Dallas to Graham and to maintain order during the court proceedings: "If these cases are tried, there may be an attempt made to rescue [the accused mob members], or to wreak summary vengeance on the Marlowes [*sic*]. Two of whom are still living and are expected to be present to testify" (George A. Knight to W. H. King, February 21, 1890).

[10] The legal history of the prosecution of the accused Young County conspirators is a long and complicated one. In February and March 1889, shortly after the Dry Creek fight, five indictments for conspiracy and murder were brought against Eugene Logan, P. A. Martin and others by the grand jury of the District Court of the Northern District of Texas. In January 1890 four more indictments were returned against Logan, Bee Williams, Verner Wilkinson and Clint Rutherford, charging that they, "together with divers other evil-disposed persons, whose names to the grand jurors aforesaid are unknown, [did] combine, conspire and confederate . . . with force of arms, to injure and oppress [citizens] held in the power, custody and control" of a deputy United States marshal. At the October 1890 session of the court the nine indictments were combined under the title "No. 34 consolidated," and Logan, Wilkinson and Rutherford were tried on the charges. The jury acquitted Rutherford, but could not reach agreement regarding Logan and Wilkinson, who were refused bail by Judge McCormick and committed to the custody of the marshal for return to jail in Dallas (*Logan v. United States*, 264–70).

On October 30, 1890, the federal grand jury brought in indictments against twelve men, charging "conspiracy to deprive citizens of their rights under the Constitution and laws of the United States and murder in the first degree in pursuance of the conspiracy." Arrested that day by deputy U. S. marshals were Sheriff Tom Collier, Deputy Sheriff Marion A. Wallace, Jailer John Y. Leavell, Constable Sam Waggoner, Deputy U. S. Marshal E. W. Johnson, Jailer Dick Cook, Robert Holman, David "Dink" Allen, William R. Benedict, Pink Brooks, Will Hollis and Jack Wilkins (*Graham Leader*, November 5, 1890). The court approved release of citizens Holman, Allen, Benedict, Brooks, Hollis and Wilkins on $5000 bail, but refused applications for bail for law officers Collier, Leavell, Waggoner, Johnson, Cook and Wallace, and they were jailed (Ibid., November 26, 1890).

At the February 1891 term of court, an additional indictment, number 37, was added to "Number 34, consolidated." It charged Collier, Johnson, Leavell, Wallace, Waggoner, Hollis, Cook and five others unnamed with attempted murder on January 17 and murder on January 19 (*Logan v. United States*, 264–70).

175 closely type-written pages and required a whole day to be read to the jury. William L. Crawford[11] of Dallas, was special counsel to assist in the prosecution.

The accused men were ably defended, having ample means at their command, every resource of the law was exhausted in their behalf by their counsel Jerome Kerby [*sic*: Kearby] of Dallas,[12] and R. H. Arnold and Judge Delancy [*sic*: Delaney] of the supreme bench of Texas.[13]

Following are a few extracts from the evidence of some of the most important witnesses:

Mrs. R. C. Lauderdale, the mother-in-law of Sam Criswell, deposed as follows: "I kept a boarding house at Belknap; the house is two stories high and the Masons hold their meetings in the upper story. Between the time of the death of Sheriff Wallace on December 24th, 1888, and the time I heard of the assault on the Graham jail, 'Bee' Williams, Sam Criswell, Wm. Benedict[14] and Eugene Logan were at my house; they were talking about the Marlows killing Wallace; Criswell said he thought they ought to be killed—men, women, children and all; that the old lady had raised them all to be murderers and horse-thieves; Logan said: 'Boys, I think you have got them down meaner than they are. I think you ought to give them a trial; I admit they are bad men, but I would fight for the women and children.' 'Bee' Williams said they had killed our sheriff, one of the best men in the country, and they ought to be hung. There was something said about breaking into the jail, but I don't know who said it; I believe it was Benedict; I think Benedict said they ought to be hung or killed right off. He said if they ever got loose in Graham they would burn the town; Logan argued all the time that they ought to have a trial;

[11] William L. Crawford (1839-1920) was born in Kentucky and taken to Texas in 1843. After service as lieutenant colonel in the Confederate Army he was admitted to the bar in 1866. He served as a member of the Texas Constitutional Convention of 1875, practiced law in Dallas, and was a member of the House of Representatives, 1891–1892 (Tyler, *New Handbook of Texas*, 2:396).

[12] Jerome Claiborne Kearby (1847–1905) came to Texas in 1859 from his native Arkansas. He rose to the rank of major in the Confederate Army, breveted colonel. Admitted to the bar in 1869, he practiced law in Denton (Ibid., 3:1042–43).

[13] William Shelby Delaney (1825-1900) was born and educated in Kentucky. He taught school and was admitted to the bar in that state. He moved to Texas in 1860 and was commissioned as a colonel in the Confederate Army. From 1881 to 1885 he sat on the Texas Commission of Appeals (Ibid., 2:567).

[14] Apparently a relative of Captain Joseph Benedict, a prominent rancher and raiser of fine horses who lived near Fort Belknap (Crouch, *History of Young County*, 177). William R. Benedict was one of those included in the mass indictments and arrests of October 30.

Logan told me that he heard the Marlows when they were cutting off their brothers' feet; that one of them was not quite dead, and he said he heard him moaning when they cut off his feet; he said when he first heard the firing he was up the hill in the lane, beyond where the fight was; heard loud talking, turned and rode back."

Mrs. Dixie Criswell, widow of Sam Criswell,[15] being sworn, deposed: "I have resided in Belknap seven years. My husband was a deputy marshal; I do not remember when Sheriff Wallace was shot; he was buried on Christmas day; I think Mr. Carpenter first informed me of the attack on the jail January 17th; between the burial of Wallace and the time the mob occurred on January 17th, my husband, Eugene Logan, Williams and Benedict were at my mother's house; I saw them there; mother, myself and the gentlemen named were present; it was seven or nine o'clock at night; they were talking about Wallace being killed and the Marlows; I think something was said about a mob; Williams said he knew it was the Marlows who killed Wallace, and that they ought to be punished for it, and that he would tie the rope to hang them; Benedict said he thought they had been mighty bad men; Criswell said they were awful bad men; I do not know whether they had any allusion to their character as fighting men or not; I do not remember all Logan said; he was talking for the Marlows though, and said they ought to give them a fair showing, and let the law take its course; Criswell said they were awful men and would kill him, (Criswell), if they ever got a chance; Bee Williams said the Marlows ought to be punished, that they ought to be mobbed, that Sheriff Wallace had been killed, and he knew it was the Marlows that killed him and that he would tie the rope to hang any of them; I had a conversation with Logan four or five days after the fight at Dry Creek. He told me it was either Alf or Ellie Marlow who killed Criswell; he said the Marlows ought to have been tied in the hack, and that the fight at Dry Creek was a bad job. He said if Johnson had tied the prisoners in the hack, nobody would have been hurt except the Marlows."

O. G. Denson, being sworn, deposed: "In 1888 and 1889 I lived in Young county, fifteen miles from Graham, on what is known as the

15 Sam Criswell, said Ted Johnson, "married a Texas girl by the name of Dixie Lauterdale [*sic*]. They had one daughter and were old-timers of Fort Belknap. Dixie was beautiful and a very popular young lady. The last I heard of her and her one child, they were in Archer City, where they were running a hotel" (Johnson, "Deputy Marshal Johnson," 53).

Denson farm; I knew the Marlow brothers; there were five of them. Two of them, Charley and Alfred, lived on my place. I remember the time Marion Wallace was shot at the house where the Marlows lived, I was in my house when I heard the noise; I was on their bond; I saw Frank Herron in the afternoon who was also on their bond; he asked me if I was going to give them up; I said that I would not give them up till I saw proper cause. I had horses for collateral security; I suppose the horses belonged to them as no one ever claimed them; I heard shots at the Marlow's house when Wallace was wounded and went down with Alfred Marlow. We found Charley, Ellie and Boone Marlow, Sheriff Wallace and Tom Collier there. Just as I walked up, Tom Collier came up from the south of the house and Boone said to him, (pointing to Wallace), 'and you are the cause of that,' Boone said he would not have shot Wallace for the world. Collier made no reply. We moved Wallace into the house; I saw evidence of a wound on Collier. His eye was a little bloodshot, the side of his face a little scratched and the rim of his hat cut. I asked him who did it and he said, 'Boone Marlow.' Boone said to Collier: 'Yes, you just came and shot into me like a dog, and you are the cause of that, for I thought it was you when I shot.' Wallace told me he had a warrant for Boone, and if I did not believe him to look in his pocket and see. I looked and found it in a bundle of papers tied together; there was no indication of the warrant being out of his pocket. I was arrested for the murder of Marion Wallace; Robt. Holman made the affidavit;[16] I was confined in the Graham jail; the Marlows were in jail at that time. Boone Marlow left the house before anybody else came except myself; Tom Collier was thirty or forty steps from the house when I first saw him; he was going toward the house. I heard Charley Marlow talking to Collier; could not tell exactly what he said, but heard him tell Collier to come back, he should not be hurt. I was at home on the morning after the fight at Dry Creek. George, Charley and Clift came to my house that morning. Charley was so muddy and covered with blood, I did not know who he was till he spoke. He had a hole in the breast, another in his neck, another by the side of his nose, and another somewhere on his cheek. He looked

[16] Denson was arrested on December 26, two days after the death of Sheriff Wallace. He was bound over for the grand jury on bail of five hundred dollars. "The case attracted considerable attention," noted the *Graham Leader* of January 3, 1889.

ghastly and weak. George was not so bloody, and unsightly; he had his hand bound up with an old rag. They went down to the house where their wives and mother were. Their mother is about seventy-five years old.[17] I reckon I saw her waiting on Wallace when he was wounded. She was talking to him and rubbing his feet and legs. He was complaining about his feet and legs all the time. I do not know whether Collier was drunk or sober the day that Wallace was killed."[18]

Mrs. M. A. Wallace,[19] government witness, being sworn, testified: "I am the widow of the late Sheriff Wallace, of Young county. In December 1888 and January 1889, I lived in Graham. My husband was wounded on the 17th of December 1888, and died December 24, 1888. From the 15th to the 20th of January 1889, John Leavels, Tom Collier and Marion Wallace boarded with me. Marion Wallace first told me about the fight at Dry Creek, on January 19, 1889. He said a mob had met them there. I asked if any one was hurt. He told me Bruce Wheeler, Frank Harmison, Sam Criswell, and two of the Marlows were killed. Eugene Logan and Ed Johnson were wounded. My husband was wounded on Monday. I went to him. Bob Collier[20] started with me, but he had a scarey horse and I got in the buggy with Dr. Price. We reached the Denson farm where my husband was just before sun down. The old lady Marlow was there. My husband was in the Marlow's house."

T. A. Martin[21] was the next witness examined direct by Colonel Crawford.

"Where are you from to this State?"

"North Carolina, Weber county."

"Were you ever in Iredell county, North Carolina?"

"Yes, sir."

[17] Martha Jane Marlow was sixty-seven years old in 1890.

[18] Within a year O. G. Denson was shot to death at his farmhouse by a man named William Smith, a nephew by marriage. Claiming self defense, Smith said the shooting of Denson on November 21, 1891, resulted from a disagreement over some corn, and that he pulled his pistol and fired after Denson made a move to draw his own weapon (*Graham Leader*, November 25, 1891). Although no evidence surfaced to indicate the killing was an aftermath of the Marlow affair, Denson was known as the strongest supporter of the brothers in Young County and, as a result, had acquired many bitter enemies.

[19] The sheriff's widow was Mrs. M. D. Wallace.

[20] Bob Collier was the brother of Tom Collier (undated clipping from the *Dallas News*).

[21] P. A. Martin.

"Were you ever charged with murder in that county?"

Mr. Crawford, for the government, here objected.—"That is a question of record."[22]

Mr. Kearby—"I suppose we have a right to identify witness with record."

The court—"Submit the record to witness."

The record is handed to witness who, after examination. Answers: "I am the party named in this record of indictment; I am the party named in the verdict and judgment."

Mr. Kearby—"We offer a certified copy of the bill of indictment presented by the Superior court of Iredell county, N. C., charging witness with the murder of Wm. B. Reeves, the arraignment of the jury of twelve men, the charge of the court, and the verdict of the jury."

Colonel Crawford, reading—"The jury, upon rendering their verdict, say that they find the defendant, Phlete A. Martin, is not guilty of the felonious slaying in the manner and form as charged in the full bill of indictment."

After reading the objection of defense is overruled, and the defendants accepted.

Witness continues—"On the 17th of January I filled the office of county attorney of Young county. At that time my office was in the court house, and I slept in a room just over my office. On the night of January 17 Sam Waggoner came to my office to file a complaint before me as county attorney against one Jimmy Vance, charging him with carrying a pistol. I think Jimmy Vance was eighteen years old, judging from his appearance I would consider him rather a youth. I don't remember whether young Vance was arrested on not."

A. T. Gay[23] testified—"I have one case of state against Jimmie Vance. I am the county clerk of Young county and was then. I issued this paper on the day it shows, the 17th of April [*sic:* January]."

By Colonel Crawford—"When did you issue that copias?"

"I did not issue that."

[22] There is much confusion here. Crawford could not object to his own line of questioning. The objection was raised by Attorney Kearby for the defense and Crawford's quotation here is evidently his response to the objection.

[23] Arthur Thomas Gay, born in Tennessee in 1831, was an officer in the Confederate Army, and was county-district clerk of Young County for sixteen years (Crouch, *History of Young County*, 204).

"Who did?"

"My deputy, my son. It is his writing."

"You did not issue that then?"

"No, sir."

"It appears to have been issued by A. T. Gay. Is that your signature?"

"Yes, sir."

"How did you know your son issued that?"

"I know his handwriting."

"Did he have authority to do that?"

"Yes, sir, but he neglected to sign his name as deputy. However, I filled that other complaint."

Mrs. Vance, mother of Jimmy, being sworn, testified that she was a widow, Jimmy was her son, and that he was eighteen years old. "My son left Young county to go west with cattle on the 13th. I knew Tom Collier and Sam Waggoner. If they were ever at my house to arrest my son I never knew it. I never saw Tom Collier or Sam Waggoner anywhere on the night of the 17th. I heard that a warrant was out for my son, and I came to town to see Judge Williams. He said he did not know anything about it, but that he would go and look over the books. He came back after examining the books and said that they did not show that any papers were issued for my son."

(The reader will understand that this warrant for Jimmy Vance was a ruse gotten up by Collier, Martin and Waggoner, for they supposed after a warrant was issued and they had thoroughly circulated the report that they meant to arrest him on the same night—the 17th—they would not be suspected as participants in the mob of the jail of that date, and, to make their scheme more successful, after their attempt to mob the prisoners on the 17th they actually mounted their horses and rode out to the neighborhood where Jimmy Vance's mother lived, but, as the widow testified, did not go near her house but went to one John Luhman, who, being sworn, testified.)

"On the night of January 17, 1889, I was at home. Sam Waggoner and Tom Collier came there that night. They were there at 12 o'clock; I had gone to bed. They said they were looking for Jimmy Vance. When they came they halloed and said that they were cold and wanted to warm. I said, 'Come in, boys,' and then we went into the room and I started up the fire—the clock was setting on the table just beyond us—and they remarked that it was midnight.

"I asked them if they did not intend to unsaddle their horses. They said no, that the horses were too warm. Their horses looked as though they had been ridden hard. They stayed the rest of the night at my house."

S. D. Burns was the next witness sworn, who testified as follows:

"On the 17th of January I was confined in the Graham jail, charged with stealing a saddle. While in jail I knew the Marlow brothers, Lewis Clift, and Burkhart, who were in jail at the same time. I knew Marion Wallace, Jr., Tom Collier, Jno. Leavels, Eugene Logan, Dick Cook, Verner Wilkerson, and Pink Brooks. The five Marlows were in jail when I was put in, and afterwards they were bailed out. I don't know how long they were out when they were recommitted. Ellie was the first recommitted. He was put back on the day that Wallace was shot. Ellie came for a doctor, and told me Wallace was shot. John Leavels put him in jail."

Colonel Crawford—"Who was the turnkey at the jail at that time?"

"I don't know, sir; they all turned the key."

"Who was the jailer?"

"John Leavels, most of the time; he was the jailer that day. When he put him in Ellie asked him if he was going to give him anything to sleep on that night. He said:

"'You don't need anything; go in there, d—n you. We will go down and mob the rest of them.'

"Ellie made no reply that I know of. He was put in the back cage, and we all ran up to the bars to look at him. That night Charley and Alfred were put in and the next day George was put in. I think Collier put them in. The mob assaulted the jail on January 17th, 1889. On the night the attack was made the guards were down below. In the night somebody came to the door and knocked, and some of the guards went to the door and talked a few minutes, then the doors were thrown open and we heard them walking in. I could not then tell how many there were. Then in a little bit they came up stairs, Mr. Leavels in front. He came up and unlocked the door for them, and said, 'Charley, here is a man who wants to talk to you; come out.' Charley and Alf were shackled together. They walked up to the door, one on each side. There were three men coming into the room, and Charley hit one of them. Another one ran down stairs and got a lariat and tried to rope him in there, but couldn't do anything with that. I can not say who it was that tried to rope Charley, but think it was Bruce Wheeler."

Colonel Crawford—"Who in the crowd up stairs did you know?"

"Logan, Dick Cook, and Pink Brooks."

"Who else?"

"Waggoner."

"Who else?"

"Bee Williams."

"Who else?"

"Bob Holman."

"Who else?"

"Frank Harmison."

"Did you know Bruce Wheeler?"

"Yes, he was there."

"And Vernon Wilkerson?"

"He was there, and Marion Wallace was there. Logan had a handkerchief tied over his face, and Wilkerson had on what looked like a night cap. Logan, John Leavels, Marion Wallace and Dick Cook were the guards. Logan had a gun and told Speers to turn around and threatened to shoot him. Speers said he wanted him to shoot him in the face if he was going to shoot. The muzzle of the gun was sticking through the bars. They went down stairs and came back again. While they were down stairs some one screwed off an old bit of water pipe and gave it to Alf Marlow. I do not know which tied up a gallon jug in a handkerchief. They came back then and called us out, that is Speers, Cleft, Burkhart, myself and a little Yankee; I do not recollect his name. They put us in the other cage. When the mob had returned the second time after Charley had struck the man who had started in the cage, I heard Frank Harmison tell Marion Wallace to go in the cage and bring Charley out. Marion Wallace said he would not do it, as they had an old pipe screwed off, and he didn't want to get killed. When Ed Johnson came to the jail the day they took them off the Marlows said: 'Ed, you are taking us out to have us mobbed,' and Johnson replied: 'If they do run on to you I will give you arms.'

"I said to him: 'It is mighty easy to talk, Mr. Johnson, but will you do it?' and he again replied that he would."

P. A. Martin was recalled and detailed the attack on the prisoners on January 19th.

"The party left the jail about moonrise with the four Marlows, Clift and Burkhart. Johnson asked me to drive the hack containing the prisoners for the first few miles, saying they would change about in driving the hack. Johnson and several of the guards were in the second hack, and the buggy with Waggoner and Hollis brought up the rear. Just before reaching Dry Creek, Johnson halted the company and passed around a bottle, then after crossing the creek, and ascending the hill, parties came out of the bushes on each side of the road and ordered me to throw up my hands and to stop. There were a good many of them and they were all disguised. When they first came up Burkhart threw his arms around me and begged my protection. He said: 'For God's sake, Mr. Martin, do not let them kill me.' I tried repeatedly to get out of the hack, but Burkhart held me fast. When the shooting began I saw one man fall who was advancing with a gun. Then a general fusillade took place. By struggling I eventually freed myself from Burkhart and jumped out of the hack. The first man I saw leaving the hack was Marion Wallace. I went into the pasture. A man on horseback, disguised, asked who I was, and when I told him he galloped off. I tied a handkerchief over my face for protection so that the mob would believe I was one of them. I believe the first two I saw were Vernon Wilkerson and Bee Williams. Wilkerson's face was blacked and Williams had a cloth over his face. Williams asked me if I knew who was killed. I told Williams to go to town after a doctor, and he immediately rode off. I saw Logan, who was badly wounded. Logan told me he was shot to pieces and thought he was dying. Wilkerson and I walked down to the battle ground and examined the dead bodies. We found five dead men on the battle ground. Two of the Marlows were dead, with their feet cut off. Alf had a pistol lying on his right hand and a Winchester by his side. The pistol was identified as Ed Johnson's. The gun I gave to Robert Holman. When we arrived I first met Mr. Holman back of the pasture. He was on horse back and had a shot gun. He asked me who I was and who all were hurt, and what had become of the prisoners. I told him that Criswell, Harmison, and Bruce Wheeler and two of the Marlow boys were killed. The other two, with Clift and Burkhart, had gone off in one of the hacks. Holman wanted to go on after them and rearrest them. While the fight was going on I heard one of the Marlows call out that his brother was killed. One of them said: 'Come on, we have got plenty of arms and are not afraid.' Vernon Wilkerson told me the night of the fight that he thought he had got two of them, (Marlows). I did not see Clint Rutherford out there that I know of. When I assisted Logan to lay down he had removed his disguise. I don't think I have been indicted in this case before. I have been indicted in the federal court for the attack on the prisoners on the 19th, and in the state court for murder on the same date. I am under bond now to answer for this indictment."

Kearby—"Have you any agreement with the government authorities by which these prosecutions are to be discharged and dismissed?"

"Yes, sir, that is my understanding."

"In consideration of your testimony in behalf of the government?'

"I do not exactly understand it that way, but that is a consideration in the matter. I understand that the government cannot prosecute me and make a witness of me also. They have promised me I should receive the protection of a witness from prosecution. I was called upon to testify against Williams in the state court at Jacksboro,[24] the grand jury of Young county indicted me for the same offense, for murder, and I told the court that I did not want to testify in the case because I was indicted for the same offense. Logan told me that the leader of the mob was the biggest and tallest man he ever saw, and had a beard like a horse's tail. Leavels said he had a gun which looked big enough for a man to crawl into. Sam Criswell and Marion Wallace told me how they had been tied with ropes and led away to the grave yard. I did not notice any bruises or rope signs on their necks of hands, nor any other evidence of hard treatment. The guards treated the matter as a very light occurrence, they were laughing and talking about it. I saw no evidence of anger in any of the guards."

John Speers deposed as follows:

"On the 19th of January I was in the Graham jail. Burns, Burkhart, Lewis Clift, and the four Marlows were in there with me. I was in jail

[24] Jacksboro was the seat of neighboring Jack County.

when Marion Wallace was sheriff, and after his death when Tom Collier was sheriff. I got acquainted with Eugene Logan about the time I was arrested. I saw Logan every few days. After that he went to guarding the jail. I think he went on guard at the jail just after Wallace was killed or maybe just before. The Marlows broke jail two or three days before the mob of the 17th. When the Marlows were brought back they complained of their feet being sore. Mr. Logan, John Leavels, Wallace, Jr., and Criswell were guards then. After they brought the boys back they chained them two and two. George was chained to Eph, and Charley and Alf were chained together. In the evening before the mob came up I had some knives and gave them to Collier, not having any more need of them. He said: 'I will not iron you, Speers, but I swear to you that those Marlows will catch hell.' He said that I had done nobody any harm in Young county, and he would hate for me to be hurt by a mob, and said, 'You are in no danger.' About the middle of the evening he came back and said the county commissioners had ordered him to iron me and Burkhart, so he chained us. When the mob came to the jail I had been asleep and had just waked up and was lighting my pipe. I heard someone knock at the door below, and someone on the inside asked, 'Who is there?' and I understood the fellow on the outside to say, 'It's me.' They then opened the door and talked awhile; then we heard them coming in. They stayed down stairs about four minutes and then came up. Leavels in the lead. He unlocked the door. They had three lanterns. He came around and unlocked the cell door and told Charley to come out, that someone wanted to see him. I said, 'Don't go, Charley, that is a mob; don't you see they are disguised?' Several of us told them not to go. Charley asked what they wanted, and Leavels said, 'I don't know what they want; come out and see.' They poked their guns in the cracks. I was standing with my back to the cage. Some fellow was cutting down my clothes, another one jabbed me in the side with a gun and as I turned around someone said: 'This is Speers, kill him.' Eugene Logan pointed a gun at me and said, 'I will kill him.' I did not see Charley strike anyone, but I saw a man fall down and say, 'Frank, I am bleeding to death.' Frank Harmison was the man he called Frank. I do not know who the man was that was hit. I recognized Eugene Logan, Clint Rutherford, Verner Wilkerson, Pink Brooks, Marion Wallace, John Leavels, Sam

Criswell, and P. A. Martin. We were talking to them and begging them to let us alone; we said: 'My God, men, don't murder us, the most of us have wives and children.' George Marlow tried to reason with them, but they told us to shut our mouths. We heard none of the guards begging the mob to desist. I told Clift to screw off the water pipe. He got it off, and gave it to Alf Marlow. They took us all out of the north cell the second or third trip up, except the four Marlow boys, and put us in the other cell that the brothers had cut out of a few days before. When the mob had gone down again, Clift crowded out of the hole the Marlows had cut to let the people know how we were being treated, but before he got to the bottom of the steps he saw the guards coming. He ran back and got into the cell again. The guards had off their disguises this time and were telling us about the mob putting ropes around their necks and taking them to the grave-yard. I said: 'You haven't had time to go to the grave-yard yet,' Tom Collier came the next morning and asked me if I knew who was in the mob. I told him I did not know. I knew he knew all about the mob and I was satisfied they would kill me if they thought I knew they were in it themselves. Mr. Adare told me he had heard I had a list of the mob, and told me if I had, I had better destroy it; that it was no use for me to throw my life away for the Marlows. I told him that I did not have it; then Robert Holman came to me and asked about it and wanted to know what I would swear to in regard to those cases. He said he would have me pardoned. On the eve of the 19th Ed Johnson came to the jail and said they were going to start at exactly 9 o'clock. Charley Marlow asked him, 'Don't you think they will mob us?' Johnson said, 'No, I have a guard.' Charley said, 'If the mob runs on us will you give us guns?' Johnson said, 'Yes I will.' Johnson went down stairs and Charley asked me what I thought of it. I told him it was a mob either way and that he would stand better chance outside than he would in jail. They examined their irons, and ironed Clift and Burkhart together."

Charley Marlow deposed as follows:

"I was arrested in the Indian Territory by Ed Johnson, charged with stealing horses from the Indians. On reaching Anadarko we found Boone and Ellie under arrest for the same charge. I had never been arrested before, and had never been inside of a court house or jail up to this time; neither had any of my brothers ever been arrested before. We owned thirty-three head of horses and mules. George brought them down when he came, about two weeks after. Alfred's wife, my wife and my mother came with George and wife. After George had been here something over three weeks he was arrested and sent to jail. I was in jail about two months and a half when I gave bond and was released. I have heard Mr. Johnson say that we were charged with stealing some Indian's horses, but they never told me his name, nor did I ever see any papers. After we got out of jail I went to work for Mr. Denson, rented a house and went to planting wheat. About 12 o'clock on the 17th of December, 1888, Tom Collier came to the house and peeped in at the window. They all said, 'Come in and have some dinner.' We had just sat down to the table and had not begun to eat. He left the window and came around to the door, stepped his right foot in and said: 'Boone Marlow, I am after you,' and just as he said that, he fired. Boone dodged down by the bed and grabbed a gun and fired through the wall or jamb of the door, and fired again almost immediately. Ellie and I jumped up from the table and rushed out. Mr. Wallace lay on the porch where he had fallen. Collier was running towards a little ravine about fifty yards south of the house. We did not know before that Wallace was on the place. We spoke to him and he told me to come and hold his head up. I went out and put his head on my lap. Boone called to Collier to come back. He came back, dropped his pistol and asked me not to let Boone kill him. Collier clung to me, and said to Boone: 'Come up and shake hands, Boone.' Boone came up to Wallace and said: 'I thought it was Tom Collier I shot at when I shot you.' Mr. Denson was there by this time. Wallace was lying with his head in my lap, and Boone had his gun in his hand. He said to Collier: 'You are the cause of that.' Collier replied: 'I know it, but it [is] done so say nothing about it.' Boone raised his gun and said: 'Charley, I want to shoot him between the eyes.' Collier clung to me and begged me not to let Boone kill him. I told Boone to put down his gun. Collier had said nothing to Boone about having a warrant for him; nothing was said about any papers before the fight. We put Ellie on a horse and sent him for a doctor. After Boone had gone Collier got on his horse and rode off. When Mr. Denson came Alfred came with him. When Ellie went for the doctor he did not return, he was put in jail. Alfred and I were put in afterward. I think George was put in the next day. The evening that Wallace was shot Tom

Collier came back to our place with Frank Herrin [*sic*: Herron], and said, 'Charley, your bondsmen have given you up, and you will have to go back to jail.' A short time before the 17th we escaped jail by sawing out of the back of the jail with a pocket knife. We got to the ground by tying blankets together and to some timbers, and swinging to the ground. On the night of the 17th the guards had ordered us to bed about dark, and all of us had lain down and I dropped off to sleep. It might have been fifteen minutes or three or four hours when a noise down stairs caused me to wake up. We heard several voices talking and parties hallooing, and in a few minutes they came up stairs. They came to the cell, Mr. Leavels in the lead. A man stepped in and said: 'I will bring him out' (meaning me). I struck this man with my fist and he fell, and after he had lain there a few minutes, he said: 'Frank, you will have to take me out, I am bleeding to death.' They pulled him out and all went down stairs. I recognized in the party Robert Hill, the man I struck; Frank Harmison, whom Hill had called when down; Logan, Martin, Dick Cooks [*sic*: Cook], Pink Brooks, Sam Waggoner, Wm. Benedict, Marion Wallace, and Leavels. Logan had a handkerchief tied over his face. I recognized him by a slit in the knee of his pants, his voice and eyes. Afterwards the guard came up the stairs and laughed and talked about how they had scared several of the boys. They asked if we had recognized any of the mob. We were afraid, and denied knowing that they were the same parties. When Johnson came on the 19th to take us away, he said: 'Boys, I will take you to Weatherford to-night.' He said that no one except he and the guards knew of the removal. When we got down stairs there were ten or fifteen men on the ground floor, and when we went outside to the hacks there were twenty-five or thirty more standing around. I could not tell the guards from anyone else. Myself and the other five prisoners and the driver climbed into one hack and started. We did not know then who was driving, but afterwards learned that Martin was our driver. Johnson drove up pretty fast and hallooed to Martin to hold up. We stopped, and Johnson said, 'Maybe the boys would like something to drink.' He got out and handed the bottle to us. We all took a little in our mouths and spat it out. While we stood there I said, 'Boys, we will be mobbed in fifteen minutes.' George said, 'Ed, you will stay with us?' and he said, 'Yes, and die with you.' We said, 'You will arm us if it comes to so bad as that?' He said, 'Yes, I will.' I said, 'That mob is lying in the thicket close to us.' We started and had gone about 200 yards when the mob rushed out of the thicket. They hallooed 'Hold up.' We jumped out of the hack and went to the guard hack. When we reached them they were handing their guns and six-shooters to the mob. I got hold of Ed Johnson's six-shooter, Alfred got hold of a gun one of the mob had. I threw the six-shooter down on him. He said: 'Don't shoot, I am a guard.' I said, 'Turn it loose then' and he turned it loose. We than saw George and Ellie scuffling in the road. They had hold of a man trying to take his arms. We next shot into the mob facing us. The mob had then fired twenty-five or thirty shots. No bullets came close to us. I don't think anyone was hit till the second volley began. They were firing all around me. My two brothers were killed and two or three others. The guards made no attempt to assist us. I saw a flash at the buggy, and then I fell, and left only George standing. When he saw me fall, he said, 'Come again, you cowardly dogs, we have plenty of arms and no one is hurt.' After getting loose from our brothers, George started to the hack as a man was coming from the south side to us. George hallooed, 'Halt.' I don't know whether they began firing before or after he hallooed, I saw the man fall. At this time I exchanged several shots with a tall man wearing a slicker, and at the third or fourth shot he dropped his gun and sank down, and crawled away into the edge of some brush, and I saw him no more. George got this man's gun. I think this was Logan. They all had on old looking clothes. One man that fell by the hands of my brother had a red handkerchief tied over his face. When the mob first came to the hack P. A. Martin yelled: 'Here they are, come and take all six of them.' After the fight was over and we had cut off our brothers' ankles, we got back into the hack and drove off to the Denson farm. Clift and Burkhart took no part in the fight. Clift tried to get a gun that the man who wore the slicker had dropped. When he was pulling Burkhart to get there, he was shot in the thigh and Burkhart dragged him to the hack the prisoners had come in. Burkhart crawled under the hack and stayed there till we got ready to drive off. He and Clift were shackled together. Burkhart shook like he was alarmed. I asked him if he could use a gun; he said his arms were not hurt. I thought maybe he was shot through the legs, but he seemed not. Burkhart drove the hack. We went by Finis and wanted to stop with a man there, but he would not let us. We inquired the road to Denson's several times. At Finis we got Clift loose from Burkhart, and Burkhart left us as soon as he got loose and we have never seen or heard of him since. We went by Mr. Denson's and told him what had happened. He told us to go home and he would be down soon. He came in about thirty minutes. William Gilmore, Marion Lasater, and Dr. Price came during the day. Our women folks were pretty well acquainted with Lasater. Lasater and Gilmore stayed with us till we were taken away by Morton and his men. We were brought to Graham at the March term of the federal court, and were acquitted of charges against us for which we were arrested by Deputy Marshal Ed Johnson."

George Marlow was next placed on the witness stand and testified the same as Charles.[25]

[25] At the conclusion of the session of court, Judge McCormick ordered that George and Charles Marlow be held to bail of $1,000 each to insure their appearance at the next trial. "It will be remembered that they jumped their bonds once and were recaptured after a reward of $500 was offered by the U. S. marshal" (*Graham Leader*, November 26, 1890).

Chapter XVII

THE RESULT—EXTRACTS AND OPINIONS

Such a long chapter of testimony may tax the reader's patience somewhat, but as this book is a history as well as a romance, it is necessary to give facts as they occurred. There were many more important witnesses on both sides, whose testimony was but a reiteration of that already gone over, and which is for that reason omitted here.

The trial dragged along through the court with weary monotony for days and weeks. Hundreds of citizens from all parts of the State came and went, and all watched the proceedings with keen interest.

Finally the case was given to the jury, with a long and exhaustive charge by A. P. McCormick, from which the following brief extracts are taken:

"Gentlemen: When a citizen of the United States is committed to the custody of the United States marshal or to a state jail by process issuing from one of the courts of the United States to be held in default of bail to await his trial on a criminal charge, within the exclusive jurisdiction of the national courts, such citizen has a right under the constitution and laws of the United States to a speedy and public trial by an impartial jury, and until tried, has the right to be treated with humanity and to be fully protected against all unlawful violence while he is deprived of the ordinary means of defending and protecting himself.

"The undisputed testimony in this case shows that at the times laid in the indictments Charles Marlow, George Marlow, Alf Marlow, and

Eph Marlow, who were brothers, and citizens of the United States, together with Lewis Clift, and W. D. Burkhart, held in custody by E. W. Johnson, deputy United States marshal of this district, and by Tom Collier, sheriff of Young county, and ex-officio jailer of Young county; and that on the night of Jan. 17, 1889, a body of men, armed and disguised, entered the jail of Young county when and where said prisoners were being held, and without pretense of authority attempted to seize Charles Marlow; and that two days afterward, on the night of January 19, 1889, said deputy United States marshal, acting as such and under the process from the United States court, took actual control of said six prisoners, chained two and two together by irons around one leg of each and an iron chain securely fastened, coupling two of these together; that Lewis Cleft was thus chained to W. D. Burkhart and Charley Marlow and George Marlow were each so ironed and chained, the one to Alf Marlow and the other to Eph Marlow.

"That the six prisoners thus ironed and chained were placed in a hack and P. A. Martin was placed in the hack to drive it; that E. W. Johnson with Sam Criswell, Marion Wallace, and John R. Girand, all well armed, took another hack, and Sam Waggoner and Will Hollis, both armed, too a buggy, and the three vehicles, thus filled and in close order and in the same order given, started after dark toward Weatherford on the regular mail stage road from Graham to Weatherford, and at a point just beyond Dry Creek (from Graham) a large number of men armed and disguised, appeared in the highway and, presenting their guns, commanded 'hold up.'

"That the Marlow brothers immediately dropped out of the hack they were in and ran to the other hack, procured arms, and began to resist the assailants.

"That many shots were fired, Alf and Eph Marlow were killed and George and Charles Marlow and Lewis Clift severely wounded. All the assailants who were able to flee, fled, and George Marlow, Charles Marlow, Lewis Clift and W. D. Burkhart alone remained in sight alive, with the dead bodies of Alf and Eph Marlow and of Sam Criswell, Bruce Wheeler and Frank Harmison.

"That by unjoining an ankle of their dead brothers, George and Charles Marlow freed themselves, and gathered sufficient arms and ammunition, and with Clift and Burkhart, resumed seats in the hack they had left and made their way to Finis, a small town in Jack county, where they unshackled Clift and Burkhart, and where Burkhart left them, and then Clift and the two surviving Marlows, all severely wounded, made their way by early morning to the cabin of the Marlows on the Denson farm, where were the mother of the Marlows, the wives of two of them and their little children.

"That in a very short time after the prisoners left the jail word was brought back to Graham of what had occurred at Dry Creek and as soon as the particulars of the killed and wounded could be gathered from that field of strife, runners were dispatched by Tom Collier, the sheriff, to different parts of Young county to warn people that two of the Marlows had escaped alive and to summon the people to be on the watch that night and as soon as they could and as many as could, to come to Graham to organize for the pursuit of the two surviving Marlows. A deputy sheriff and constable were also dispatched to the sheriff of the neighboring county of Jack to solicit his aid with a posse to pursue and recapture these Marlows.

"As a result of this levy en masse, by noon the next day the sheriff of Jack county reached a point near the Marlows' cabin with twenty-five or thirty men, where he found Tom Collier, the sheriff of Young county, with at least twice as large a posse gathered from this county, and in position just out of rifle range from the cabin of the Marlows.

"That the Marlows refused to surrender to the state officers there present, but expressed their willingness to surrender to the United States marshal, W. L. Cabell, or to his deputy, Capt. Morton.

"That the sheriff of Jack county, as soon as he understood the situation, withdrew his men and went back to Jack county.

"That Tom Collier, sheriff of Young county, kept a guard posse near said Marlow cabin until Tuesday morning or Wednesday morning, 22nd or 23rd of January,[1] when Capt. Morton arrived from Dallas and took charge of the two Marlows and Clift and removed them to Dallas.

"The laws of the United States provide if two or more persons conspire to injure, oppress, threaten or intimidate any citizen in the free

[1] Morton arrived on the morning of Tuesday, January 22 (*San Antonio Daily Express*, January 23, 1889).

exercise or enjoyment of any right or privilege secured to him by the constitution or laws of the United States, they are guilty of the offence of conspiracy to injure or intimidate such citizens in the exercise of such rights and shall be punished, and if in the persecution of any such conspiracy any murder be committed, the offender shall be punished in the United States courts for the same with such punishment as is attached to the offence of murder by the laws of the state in which the offence is committed.

"The rule of law which clothes every person accused of crime with the presumption of innocence, and imposes upon the state the burden of establishing his guilt beyond a reasonable doubt, is not intended to aid anyone who is in fact guilty of crime to escape, but is a humane provision of law, intended so far as human agencies can, to guard against the danger of any innocent person being unjustly punished.

"The court instructs the jury, as a matter of law, that in considering the case the jury are not to go beyond the evidence to hunt up doubts, nor must they entertain such doubts as are merely chimerical or conjecturable. A doubt, to justify any acquittal, must be reasonable, and it must arise from a candid and impartial investigation of all the evidence in the case; and unless it is such that, were the same kind of evidence interposed in the graver transactions of life, it would cause a reasonable and prudent man to hesitate and pause, it is insufficient to authorize a verdict of not guilty. If, after considering all the evidence, you can say you have an abiding conviction of the truth of the charge, you are satisfied beyond a reasonable doubt.

"The court further instructs the jury, as a matter of law, that the doubt which the juror is allowed to retain on his mind and under the influence of which he should frame a verdict of not guilty must always be a reasonable one. A doubt produced by undue sensibility in the mind of any juror, in view of the consequence of his verdict, is not a reasonable doubt and a juror is not allowed to create sources or materials of doubt by resorting to trivial and fanciful suppositions and remote conjectures as to possible states of fact differing from that established by the evidence, you believe as men. Your oath imposes on you no obligation to doubt, where no doubt would exist if no oath had been administered.

"It is entirely immaterial and wholly unnecessary for you to know or find what one or ones of the conspirators fired the fatal shot that killed Alf Marlow and Eph Marlow. Each person shown by the proof beyond a reasonable doubt to have been connected with said conspiracy is guilty of their murder whether such persons were at Dry Creek fight or not."

The jury, after being out a long time, failed to agree, and the prisoners were remanded to jail to await a new trial, bail being refused them, although perfectly able to have given it in almost any amount.

No blame is attached to the jury by the prosecution, as they were twelve men tried and true, but their failing to arrive at a verdict is attributable not to the evidence or lack of evidence, but to the fact that they were afraid for their lives in case they had found the prisoners guilty, as they so richly deserved.

It will be remembered that these men being tried for the serious crimes of conspiracy and murder were all men of high standing in official circles of Texas. They had for years held responsible positions and had naturally acquired influence, financial backing and a host of friends and followers. Therefore, it is not to be wondered at, that intimations should reach a jury that, should they render an adverse verdict, their lives should be the penalty, and neither is it surprising that a jury placed under such trying circumstances, themselves being business men, men of family, and at least human, should think discretion the better part of valor and seek to save themselves from danger and perhaps death by such an casy and plausible loophole as failing to agree.[2]

Days and weeks and months dragged along—dark and gloomy months for the imprisoned wretches. Time and again endeavors were made to get another jury and proceed with another trial, but the same

[2] The inability of the jury to arrive at a verdict in the October 1890 trial of Logan and Wilkinson may have been determined by a reason other than fear. On September 15, 1891, a man named John P. Bennett, one of the jurors in the trial the previous year, was arrested in southern Texas by federal officers and charged with willful perjury. That trial, according to a report in the *San Antonio Daily Express* of September 17, 1891,

> resulted in eleven jurors for conviction and one, Bennett, for acquittal. The jurymen argued themselves hoarse and all out of patience, but Bennett held to his stand for acquittal, until the jury was discharged. The particulars of Bennett's offence are that he swore that he was a freeholder and that he did not know the accused, when the facts in the case were, it is maintained, that he had lived and worked along side of them for years, and that instead of being a freeholder, he was a mere cow boy with no possessions whatever. Although no supporting evidence could be produced, obviously there was a strong suspicion that Juror Bennett had been bought.

reason which caused the first jury to fail on a verdict deterred others from attempting it.

Thus two years passed, and the following extract from the Dallas News will serve the double purpose of showing the status of affairs at that time and of pointing out a verification of the old adage, the "wages of sin is death:"

"Is it fate?"

"Two years ago John Lewell [*sic*: Leavels], Verner Wilkerson, Dick Cook, Thomas Collier, Sam Waggoner, John Williams,[3] and Eugene Logan were arrested by the United States authorities for complicity in the Marlow affray near Graham, in Young county, which occurred on January 17, 1889, and since then they have been prisoners.

"They can not get a trial and are not allowed to make bond although they are amply able to make it.

"A short time ago John [*sic*: "Bee"] Williams died in jail at Belknap of a disease contracted in prison; yesterday Thomas Collier died of typhoid fever at Fort Worth, and now Dick Cook is low with the same malady in the same place.

"The remainder of the party are despondent. They have been in jail so long that they have lost spirit and are inclined to look with dread upon the possibilities of the future, and fear the worst.

"Thomas Collier, who died yesterday morning in the hospital ward of the county jail, was thirty-one years of age. At one time he was the sheriff of Young county. His brother, Robert Collier, who had been telegraphed at Graham, arrived shortly after Thomas died, and was affecting in the lamentation of the death of his brother. The remains were taken in charge by an undertaker to be embalmed. This morning they were shipped to Alabama, where the parents reside.

"John Williams, the other party implicated in the Young county tragedy, who died at Belknap, was not one of the guards at the time of the killing but was at Graham. He was tried in the state court for his share and was acquitted, but was afterwards taken in charge by the Federal authorities, who placed him in the Sherman jail, where he contracted the disease of which he died.

[3] "Bee" Williams' first name is given as William in the local newspaper accounts and court records.

"These prisoners now in the Tarrant county jail were brought here by United States Marshal Knight some eight weeks ago from Dallas, the jail quarters at Dallas being limited.[4]

"The Marlow mob case is one of the most celebrated in the recent history of the State."[5]

Pending the suits against the participants in the mobs, and prior to the time of the last above citation, suits were filed by the Marlows for damages sustained by them in the terrible conflicts they had passed through and hard usage they had been subjected to. These suits were brought against W. L. Cabell and the sureties on his official bond as United States Marshal for the northern district of Texas, and damages were claimed on account of a breach of bond, and appear on the Federal court docket as follows:

"Martha Jane Marlow, mother of the Marlow boys, $10,000 on account of the murder of her son Lewellen [*sic*: Llewellyn].

"Zenia Marlow, widow of Alfred, and her children, on account of his murder, $10,000.

"George Marlow, on account of his wounds, $10,000.

"Charles Marlow, on account of his wounds, $10,000.

"Lewis Clift, a wounded prisoner, on account of his wounds, $10,000.

[4] The accused in the mob cases had been held in the Dallas and Sherman jails. The *Graham Leader* noted in its October 8, 1890, issue that Verner Wilkinson had been confined in the jail at Sherman for eight months. On January 7, 1891, the paper reported: "Federal prisoners at Dallas and Sherman have been removed to the Tarrant county jail at Fort Worth."

[5] At the April 1891 session of the federal court, Eugene Logan, Sam Waggoner, M. A. Wallace, Verner Wilkinson, John Leavell, Dick Cook, and Will Hollis were tried on conspiracy and murder charges. After hearing the evidence and Judge McCormick's charge, the jury on Friday, April 17 brought in a verdict against Logan, Waggoner, and Wallace on the conspiracy counts but acquitted them of murder. The other defendants were acquitted on all charges and released. On Saturday, Judge McCormick announced sentences: the convicted trio were each fined $5,000 and given ten-year prison sentences (Case #263, *The United States v. Eugene Logan, et al.*; *Graham Leader*, April 22, 1891).

Lawyers for Logan, Waggoner and Wallace took the convictions on appeal to the U. S. Supreme Court. Arguing for the defendants before that tribunal on January 26 and 27, 1892, were Jerome C. Kearby, who had represented them at their trial; A. H. Garland, the former United States Attorney General who was reputed to be related to Ed Johnson; and H. J. May. On April 4, 1892, Justice Horace Gray, speaking for the majority, ruled that the trial court "went too far in admitting testimony on the general question of conspiracy," reversed the judgment, and remanded the case to the Circuit Court with directions to set aside the verdict and order a new trial. The Court ruled seven to one, Justice Lucius Lamar dissenting and Justice David Brewer abstaining (*Logan v. United* States, 263–310).

Following the election of Grover Cleveland to the presidency again in 1892 came the usual turnover in federal office holders. The new appointees had little desire to pursue this highly controversial case begun by their predecessors, and in 1893 the cases were quietly dropped. No one ever served penitentiary time for the Marlow affair.

"The same allegation of facts supports each petition."[6]

These suits also dragged wearily along through various terms, public sentiment seeming to figure largely in the ability or disability of the various juries to arrive at a definite conclusion. Finally a compromise verdict was arrived at in favor of the Marlows, awarding them $6,000 and an appeal was taken to a higher court.[7]

George and Charley were summoned to appear as witnesses against the men being tried for mob and murder on an average of twice a year, and on each occasion when they made their appearance near the scenes of their troubles and danger, it was under a heavily armed guard furnished by the government. Had they not been so guarded and protected, their lives would have been forfeit. And their blood would have been spilled to soak the soil made red by their brothers, for although the sentiment and favor of all the law-abiding element had long since turned in their favor, the same old reckless and lawless spirit which served at first to perpetrate, still served to defend the crimes. Crowds flocked to see them, inspired by their morbid curiosity which attracts public notice to all who have passed through great dangers or unusual vicissitudes.

[6] The *Graham Leader* of January 23, 1890, reported that these suits were brought "against the mob who attacked the prisoners on Dry Creek about a year ago." While commenting that "this will no doubt prove a novel case, as the courts are now endeavoring to find out the persons who constituted the mob," the editor added, "While the *Leader* deprecates mob law it has no sympathy with the Marlows, as this move seems to be only another trick of theirs to create further trouble in the county."

[7] Charley Marlow told Charlie Siringo in 1924 that he had "the satisfaction of collecting $6,000 damages from the United States Marshal in Dallas, Tex." (Siringo to Lamborn, February 28, 1925). The Marlow affair triggered acrimonious controversy and litigation, both criminal and civil, in Young County and, according to the county's historian, the

> indictments, and the hundreds of rumors, aroused the citizenry to personal accusations, heated arguments, and never-ending denials. . . . Eventually, everything seemed to have been brought to light, old family skeletons were dug up, the unsanitary condition of the jail was exposed in the report of the Federal Grand Jury. . . . One Vandy West was arrested by United States Deputy Ed Johnson and detained in jail for twenty days before the charges were found to be without basis. For his incarceration, West sued United States Marshal Cabell for $10,000.

The disturbance contributed greatly to the eventual decision in 1896 to move the Federal Court from Graham to Abilene (Crouch, *History of Young County*, 120–21).

Chapter XVIII

RETROSPECTIVE— THE MARLOWS' LIVES, THEIR HAPPINESS AND GRIEFS, PAST AND PRESENT

In reviewing these pages one can not help but consider how true the saying, "truth is stranger than fiction." It seems incredible that men could pass through such hardships, rough usage, danger, and perils untold, and yet survive to tell the tale; and it seems doubly incredible that such atrocious and heinous crimes and outrages against law, society, and human life could be perpetrated in one of the largest states of the Union, in this enlightened day and date of civilization.

The Marlow family was a race of peace-loving and contented people. The wild, free, western life they led was full of happiness for them, peace and contentment, and free from harm of any kind to their fellow men. They hunted the deer in the forest, and trapped the beaver and mink in the streams. They fished in the sparkling lakes and rivers for the speckled beauties of the deep, and roamed over the boundless prairies after the buffalo and elk. They were sons of the great wild west, born beneath its azure skies, reared in its vigorous and healthful influence and bronzed by its sun and winds. They drank into their lungs the fresh breezes which blew over the prairies and stirred the tall blue joint grasses, and bravely battled with the fierce storms which came from the mountain regions. The snows of winter which piled up in great drifts in the sloughs and draws, and the icy blasts which roared through the forests and over the plains were but dreams of wild freedom for them and they loved to resist the elements. The sun-kissed and shower-moistened prairies in summer time were to them an Eden, and not a blade of green bunch grass, tuft of velvety buffalo grass or bright-faced wild flower lifted its head to welcome the smiling warmth of the sunshine or tears of the gentle showers that they loved and felt akin to. No bed so soft and downy to them as one spread beneath the trees along some rippling stream, no roof more sheltering than heaven's own canopy of blue, and no barracks better than the heath. The hooting of the prairie chicken over on the breaking, the call of the quail in the corn field, the babbling brook through the meadow, the lowing of the pasture, the sharp crack of the rifle in the forest and the deep bay of hound in the chase—all this to them was music. The fitful flashes of lightning far over the prairies and the gusts of wind that bent the branches of the trees, telling of the coming storm, the distant rumbling of the thunder and the hurried flight of the rabbit and bird to shelter, to them was poetry. They were of the West a part and parcel, as much as were the rocks and trees.

They cared not for wealth or fame, or glory of any kind, nor yet for money more than enough for their simple needs, which were few. Their food they raised in the fields and herds, hunted in the forests or seined from the streams. Their clothing they made from the soft skins and furs they hunted and trapped. Their horses they lassoed wild upon the prairies, and of cattle they had a plenty. They owed no man a dollar or a grudge, and asked for neither favor or assistance, and only to be treated as one man should treat another.

They belonged to no sect or party, molested no one, went on in an even tenor of their peaceful way, and were God-fearing, law-abiding citizens.

And yet they were hunted down like dogs, wronged, robbed and murdered, and this, too, in the sacred name of the law.

There is no freer, more roving nomadic life than that of the cattle trail, and much of their time was thus spent. They rounded their herds of Texas cattle over the prairies, and made long drives to market, camping out along the way, singing and shouting to each other as they roped some refractory steer or ran races over the trackless stretch of country.

The honorable, upright and ever just spirit which was so deep in the nature of the good old Dr. Marlow had been transmitted to and was mirrored in the sons, and no thought of committing crime or doing what was wrong ever entered their minds.

Their education was limited, and of culture they had none, but of brawn and muscle, courage and daring, honesty and western hospitality and generosity they were bountifully supplied.

When they moved from one clime to another it was always with the West in view. Texas, the Indian Territory, and the prairie countries seemed to be their natural home, and any pilgrimage they made was never toward the East. Mexico, with its wealth of tropical attractions, its fruits and flowers and wild game, was for a brief period their home. California's wild confines also proved a magnet for a time, but caring little for the yellow gold mined there, which enriched, beggared and crazed thousands, they did not tarry long. And now at last they have taken up an abode for the rest of their lives within the shadows of Colorado's lofty mountain peaks, where the deer and elk make a home among the foothills, where the speckled trout leap and play in the noisy streams that dash foaming down the deep canons, where all nature is one grand monument to God's own handiwork, and where untrammeled and unhindered the western man can live a typical life.

Here they now are, but before taking up their life and adventures in Colorado we must go back again to Texas and finish the thread of discourse from that point, though there is not much more to tell.

The following taken from the first book published in 1892:

On the damage suits brought by the Marlow family, $1,000 was awarded to George for injuries received, which sum he got. To Charley was awarded $1,950, and the mother appealed her case to a higher court for another trial. This trial, up to the time of publishing this book, April, 1892, is yet to come off, though there is probably no doubt but what, as her claims are just, a goodly sum will be ordered paid to her by the courts for the wanton murder of her sons by the ruthless mob.[1] A few thousand dollars is but a trifle for a life, but lives are cheap in Texas.

[1]In April 1892, federal awards were granted in a Dallas court as follows: Martha Jane Marlow and Venie Marlow (widow of Alf), $1,500 each; Charley Marlow, $1,950; George Marlow, $1,000 (Ledbetter, *Ordeal*, 157).

At the first trial of the mob conspirators one of them, Clint Weatherford [*sic*: Rutherford], was acquitted, but all the others were remanded to prison for second trial. At the second hearing John Lewell was acquitted, as was also Verner Wilkerson and Dick Cook. Thomas Collier died before the trial and Sam Waggoner and Logan each were sentenced to the penitentiary for a term of ten years and received in addition a fine of $5,000. Seven others applied for a new trial, upon being found guilty, which trial is now pending in the Federal courts of Texas.

The trials were to have taken place in October of '91, but the trouble in getting a jury, already spoken of here, has prevented them coming to an issue as yet. It is only a question of time, however, until heavy fines, long terms of imprisonment at hard labor in the penitentiary, and perhaps execution, will be the harvest reaped by these men who so fearlessly sowed the seeds of death and evil on Texas' fertile soil.

And in the meantime behind the unyielding iron bars of cheerless jails they have had a long and weary time to ponder over the hardness of the ways of the transgressor, and let us hope, that their fate has and will ever prove a warning to evil-doers of whatever nature.

Besides the men incarcerated for the crimes, there are perhaps a hundred who were sympathizers, helpers and connected indirectly more or less with those who perpetrated the outrages, and who are morally as guilty as those who were apprehended. And it is to sincerely be hoped that this awful lesson of retribution finally overtaking the wicked has not been lost to them.

To accuse innocent and inoffensive men of the serious charge of theft, men who would not steal a farthing, much less a horse, is of itself a grave offense against the peace and good name of any honest citizen so accused, but to add in fact every other crime known in the criminal calendar, is of itself criminal.

Then still add to this the prosecutions and persecution; the hounding of not only innocent men but their wives, their little children and their aged mother; the brutal and inhuman treatment; the pain and mortification caused by arrest, imprisonment, false accusations, chained and ironed limbs, curses and blows, and we approach the terrible enormity of the deed of this organized mob.

And now still add to all this the spilling of their loyal blood upon the sacred soil of the state which had for years been their loved home; the bleeding and lacerated wounds inflicted upon them; the taking of their lives; the awful heart-breaking grief of those widowed wives, those orphaned children and that dear old mother, and the curtain is nearly ready to fall upon the last act of the horrid drama of their misdeeds.

Should not the guilty, then, receive the punishment prescribed by the just laws of the land, which they so richly deserve? And should not the others be deterred from evil ways by the contemplation of the awful consequences? If but one man is saved from the path of sin and crime by the perusal of these pages, then this book will not have been written in vain, and the moral it contains will have accomplished a glorious mission.

Let any man or community acquainted with the Marlows step to the front and say if their characters as portrayed in this book are not as represented. Are they not men and women of sterling worth, of tried and true honesty and integrity, unimpeachable characters, and generous almost to a fault? They are possessed of the inborn spirit of generosity and hospitality which is so general and so natural in the West. Go to them if hungry or in need and they will give you freely—not a tract or a sermon, nor yet advice, but half of all their food and goods.

And still, today, with all their freedom, peace and lasting quiet from turmoil and strife, their lot is sad to contemplate in one view which may be taken of it, and that is this: They are, you must remember, western frontiersmen, pure and simple, in all the word implies, and now in their sunset of life their hearts must naturally be sore to contemplate the death and decay of all the scenes so dear to their natures and mode of existence.

From this their mountain home they must sadly contemplate the encroachment of the East and the onward march of the cultured civilization so foreign to the tenets of their inherent faith. The beloved scenes of their youth and vigor are becoming stamped out. Think of yourself, reader.

No one who was not familiar with the vast central region of the continent a quarter of a century ago—a region designated "The Great American Desert," stretching from a few miles beyond the Missouri river to the Rocky Mountains, and then, confidently believed by the majority to be only a race-course for the winds and the arena of the tornado—can by visiting it today form any proper conception of the mighty changes which have been wrought during the period specified. Now, in a palace car surrounded by all the luxuries of modern travel, the tourist is whirled across the once alleged dreary waste, in as many hours as it then required weary months to accomplish. He sees great cities, and all the bustle and energy of a grand civilization—which perhaps he sought refuge from—has followed him even here, two thousand miles from his eastern home.

Gradually as he rushes along the "iron trail," the woods bordering the Missouri lessen, he catches views of beautiful intervales, a bright little stream foams and flashes in the sunlight as the trees seem to separate, and soon he emerges on the great broad sea of prairie shut in only by the great circle of the heavens.

Dotting this motionless ocean everywhere, like whitened sails, are peaceful little homes—true Argosies ventured by the sturdy and hopeful people who have fought their way to that tranquility which surrounds the beautiful pictures.

However strange it may seem to an uninitiated traveler, the rare landscape he looks upon from his polished car window has its tale of blood and dark despair, for only a little more than two decades ago the allied Cheyennes, Kiowa and Arapahoes waged a brutal and relentless warfare upon the frontier of Kansas and Nebraska, and the occupiers of this region were inhumanely butchered all along the line of the savages' raids, from the Platte to the Arkansas.

But that has passed forever—the country is one rapidly developing empire; there is now no longer any frontier; all that is required are granite monuments to mark the dividing line between great states, so wonderful has the change from "Desert" to "Garden" been wrought.

In the almost miraculous metamorphosis—miraculous that it required so few years—great animals that roamed the vast area in countless numbers have nearly become extinct; generations of strange men have vanished, and the Indians themselves, dwindled into insignificance and huddled in reservations, are supported by the bounty of the government.

During the prolonged and bloody wars with the savage races, that marked the end of the early settlement of the country, a class of auxiliaries to the army were evolved from the relatively few white occupiers of the soil, that now, their services no longer demanded, have passed out of sight; and the limited number who survive are gray-headed men bent with age, relics of a generation that has vanished forever.

These were government scouts, and the bones of hundreds lie in as many unmarked graves, from the Yellowstone river to the Canadian far to the south, for their duties called them everywhere—in sunshine and in storm; in daylight or in darkness; in heat or in cold, they were but to go when ordered—though death was almost certain at times.

Rarely riding more than three together, but often single, they were hounded by the Indians, and if for an instant slack or careless in their vigilance, their scalps were the penalty.

Throughout Texas, the Indian Territory and Colorado the Marlow brothers went as deputies and assistants with scouts on many a dangerous mission,[2] and though they are today, the two surviving brothers, Charles and George, deputy sheriffs, it is tame compared with the old-time pioneer days of yore, and represents danger and adventure in name only. They sigh for the days when the wily savages lurked around every water hole, burnt the grass on the trails, and exercised all their wonderful ingenuity to intercept, baffle or to kill, if possible, those carrying dispatches from one remote post to another, between which for more than a hundred miles often, there was nothing but desolate prairie, with perhaps but one running stream, or a single spring in some rocky canon, the whole distance.

Yet for all they are reasonably happy and contented here in Colorado, for it is the West, and always will be. It may not be out of place to note a few of the reasons why they feel at home there and not like exiles in a foreign land.

It is a blessing to live there, in more ways than one, and to the lover of nature's beauties a perfect paradise is spread out to view. There is no wealth of scenery to equal it in all the known world.

Even in mid winter the grandeur passes all imagination and entrances the beholder. The sunlight streaming on the gleaming snow clads the rugged hills and monster overhanging crags in fantastic splendor, that

[2] There is no evidence that any of the Marlow brothers ever were employed as scouts or served as deputies or law officers in Texas or the Indian Territory.

sparkles like ten thousand million crystal jewels. The green pines far up the foothills nod and bend in the chill breezes sweeping over the mountain range, and the emerald-colored cascade or mineral falls pause seemingly in mid air between heaven and earth, and turning into ice await the coming of the summer sun before pursuing their perilous journey and awful leap to moisten the jagged cliffs below.

But the summer season is the time to thoroughly enjoy all of the regal beauty of the Centennial state. Imagine, if you can, a trip through these gigantic mountains with rod and gun. Ascending by circuitous route gradually like a spiral staircase to the summit of the range, perhaps beyond the clouds. One traverses deep the wondrous chasms whose mighty walls tower heavenward for thousands of feet; thence around the brinks of awful gorges and steep precipices whose dizzy heights make the heart faint and the brain reel. Note the mountain stream as it gushes out of solid rock far up toward the sky and dashes down some terrific gorge and becomes mere spray before striking the massive rocks beneath. Stand upon some mountain roadway, hewn from out of solid quartzite, and gaze far upward at the distant snow-clad peaks of the rugged giants of nature as they pierce the clouds and pass upward beyond the storm, and then look down where the river roars and rumbles two thousand feet below, and you can perhaps grasp some faint idea of the grandeur and immensity of the surroundings.

Pursue the fleeing deer and elk through the flowery glens of the mesas, trap the bear in its mountain fatness and land the leaping trout on the rocks behind you on the banks of some gurgling mountain brook, and then go down into a valley and enter some thriving, bustling western city, all ablaze with the electric light, and with street cars, water works, elegant brick buildings and all the modern conveniences and improvements. Can all the world produce the equal? Surely not. The sun as it arises from out its bed of molten flame and casts its effulgent splendor over such scenes, at once awes and entrances the beholder, and holds him spellbound to the spot. All the prismatic hues of the rainbow glint and scintillate and shimmer along the grey boulders, the white peaks, the blood-red rock, the green moss and shrub and tree, and penetrate the shadowed gulch and sparkle on the shining mineral spring that bubbles boiling hot from underneath some frowning cliff, and seem as if some burnished fleck of golden firelight had dropped from out eternal space and made a captive here. Words are inadequate. There is no language which can describe these things, save that of the artist, the poet, the soul.

Chapter XIV[1]

OLD WOUNDS REOPENED—THE COLORADO HOME INVADED

In the summer of '91 the peaceful serenity of the Marlows' cozy mountain home was suddenly invaded by officers who came up from Texas to tear agape the old wounds of their tribulations, to re-arrest them and take them back again as prisoners to the scenes of all their woe.

One bright June day there stepped off the Denver & Rio Grande train upon the depot platform at Ridgway two men. They were large, bronzed, handsome specimens of manhood, wore wide-brimmed hats of the sombrero pattern and were heavily armed with improved Colt's revolvers, which swung in holsters from cartridge belts about their waists. Their dress and manner stamped them for what they were—Texas Rangers.

These were Captain McDonald[2] and A. J. Britton,[3] two of the bravest and most fearless members of the northern division of Texas Rangers

[1]This chapter was misnumbered XIV in the original 1892 edition and the error was not corrected in the later publication. Actually it should have been Chapter XIX.

[2] William Jesse McDonald (1852–1918) was one of the legendary "Four Captains" of the storied Texas Rangers: McDonald, John Reynolds Hughes (1855–1947), John Harris Rogers, (1863–1930), John Abijah Brooks (1855–1944). A generator of legends, he stands high in the pantheon of Ranger heroes. It was said of him that he would "charge hell with a bucket of water." Arriving alone at the scene of a riot, he was asked if he was the only Ranger coming and reportedly replied: "There's only one riot, ain't there?" He had already acquired a wide reputation for fearlessness while acting as deputy sheriff and deputy U. S. marshal prior to his January 1891 appointment to head Company B, Frontier Battalion, Texas Rangers, by his close friend Governor James S. Hogg. He had only held the position a few months when he was sent to Colorado after the Marlows (Paine, *Captain Bill McDonald*, passim; Tyler, *New Handbook of Texas*, 4:391–93; Morris, *A Private in the Texas Rangers*, 273).

[3] James Magruder "Grude" Britton (1863–1910), sergeant of Company B, performed notably during his more than six years service in the Rangers. Glenn Shirley, in his book *The Fighting*

under government employ, and they came armed with a requisition from the governor of Texas for the arrest of George and Charley Marlow, charged with complicity in the killing of Sheriff Wallace by their brother, Boone Marlow, in January of 1888.[4]

They knew the Marlows, these men, and were aware of their dauntless courage. They had known them years ago in Texas and Indian country, and while they admired their courage and abilities, and knew that should they resist arrest there would have to be a desperate fight and perhaps death to face, they had come determined to take them prisoners, let the consequences be what they may, for they were deputized by the law and the court and had a plain duty to perform.

Word was hurriedly dispatched to Ouray, to J. H. Bradley, then sheriff of Ouray county,[5] to come immediately to Ridgway on matters of urgent importance. Sheriff Bradley appeared on the scene a few hours later, and Captain McDonald made known to him the purpose of their errand.

They had warrants for the arrest, besides the requisition from the Texas governor, but under the law it was necessary for the local sheriff to make the arrest and then turn the prisoners over to the Rangers for conveyance and delivery to the Texas authorities. Accordingly Sheriff Bradley, one of the best friends the Marlows have in Colorado, started out from Ridgway, over the foothills and to the broad mesa upon which

---

Marlows, followed Rathmell and incorrectly gave his initials as "A. J." and Albert Paine, McDonald's biographer, misspelled the name "Brittain" (*Captain Bill McDonald*, 143). W. John L. Sullivan, who served with Britton in B Company, recorded the name correctly (*Twelve Years in the Saddle*, 52). After many years service as a peace officer, Britton was shot and killed in a dispute with a Fort Worth police captain in 1910 (Morris, *A Private in the Texas Rangers*, 274–75).

Although Charley Marlow had been indicted in August 1889 for the murder of Sheriff Wallace, it was not until February 3, 1891, that a warrant was issued for his arrest by District Clerk A. T. Gay. Three days later Sheriff William Henry Lewis of Dallas County returned the capias with the notation: "The U. S. Marshal holds Charley Marlow by virtue of a bench warrant and they inform me that they will return him to Graham and when through with him he will be released at that place *if released in the State*." The emphasized words were underlined (File No. 386, *The State of Texas v. Charley Marlow*).

[4] Wallace had of course been killed in December, not January, 1888. Charley alone had been indicted in this case. An application for requisition for his return from Ouray County, Colorado, was filed May 19, 1891, by Joseph W. Akin, county attorney of Young County. It was claimed in the requisition that after Charley's testimony against the conspirators, "in the night time he was slipped out of Young County by Federal officers, and it is a notorious fact that said officers accompanied him to said County." Akin officially nominated "McDonald, Capt. Of Rangers, formerly of Potter County," to receive the fugitive after his apprehension and return him to Young County, Texas. A requisition was issued by the governor's office on May 22 and handed over to Captain McDonald (File No. 561, Application for Requisition; File No. 1903).

[5] J. F. Bradley served as sheriff of Ouray County from 1888 to 1892 (Maiden, *Sheriffs of Colorado*).

was at that date the ranch home of the Marlows, intent upon bringing them into Ridgway and hold a council of war to see what arrangements could be effected regarding this new feature of the case.

There is never a minute, day or night, but what the Marlow boys have close within their reach their trusty Winchesters or revolvers, and their house was so situated, far back on the open mesa, that no one could approach nearer than half a mile without being sighted by the inmates. A Winchester covered Bradley's towering form long before he came within hailing distance, for they, not knowing but what at any time some emissary of the men being held in bondage in Texas might seek to murder them to prevent their appearing as witnesses, were ever on the alert. The rifle was quickly lowered, however, when the sheriff was recognized, and a hearty welcome was tendered him.

Bradley told them what was up, and advised them to go into town with him and have a talk with the Texas Rangers over what was best to be done. This they agreed to, and Charley said:

"Now, Mr. Bradley, we do not propose to be arrested and taken back to Texas by these men, under any circumstances, and if matters cannot be arranged as to prevent this, and an arrest becomes necessary, we want you to stand aside and let the Texas Rangers make the arrest themselves."

Bradley understood what that meant, and agreed to it, after which the three proceeded toward the town, some four miles and a half distant.

"Do you know Captain McDonald and Britton?" asked the sheriff, on the way.

"Yes," replied George, "we know them well. They are good men, brave and fearless, and hard fellows to down when it comes to a battle."

"Will they be apt to make you trouble if you should resist arrest?"

"Yes, undoubtedly, If they make up their minds to take us and we don't go, there will be a fight to the death, for they have no doubt concluded to take us, either dead or alive."

"Why are you so strenuously opposed to going back there? As I understand it, neither of you boys had anything to do with the killing of Wallace. It was Boone that fired that shot, wasn't it?"

"Yes, it was Boone."

"And in absolute and positive self-defense?"

"Yes, in self-defense, and also by accident. Boone fired at a man named Collier, not knowing that Wallace was within twenty miles of there, and the bullet went through the door and killed Wallace, who was outside."

"Why not go back and be tried? You would surely be acquitted."

"Yes, if we are ever tried for being in any way connected with the death of Wallace we will be speedily acquitted and exonerated in any court in the land. That is not what we object to in the least, but we will not be taken, just the same, that is, we will never be taken alive."

"Why?"

"Mr. Bradley," spoke up Charley, "if you knew the circumstances of this matter, all the facts behind it, the desperation of the people and their friends against whom we are witnesses, if you had passed through what we have, you would never ask that question. When we go down there as witnesses we are supplied with a strongly armed guard of fifty brave men by the government, therefore we can give our testimony and return in safety. In this case we would have no protection whatever, and we would no sooner reach the borders of Texas than we would be set upon by the same old mob gang which murdered our brothers and shot us all to pieces years ago, and in short we would be killed, and never live to reach the place of trial. This is true, and if we have to be killed we prefer it should take place here at home, where, at least, our bodies will receive decent burial."

"And I don't blame you," warmly ejaculated Sheriff Bradley. "By Jove, if I wasn't an officer I'd help you in the fight. If it comes to that, and as it is, if they want you they may make the arrest themselves and take the consequences. You boys shall never go back there to be mobbed and murdered by any act of mine."

The Rangers had in the meantime gone up on the train twelve miles to Ouray, and were to return on the next train, so when Sheriff Bradley and the Marlows reached Ridgway, Captain McDonald and Britton were not in town, and some hours were yet to elapse before their arrival.

The people of Ridgway are of the true western stock, and the western spirit so strongly impregnated in their makeup soon began to make itself manifest. They were the friends of the Marlows, who lived among them and had proved themselves to be good citizens, and as soon as it became noised about the little town that two Texas Rangers were on hand to arrest George and Charley and take them dead or alive, little groups of men began to assemble at different places along the streets, and whispered consultations were numerous. Then a murmur became audible, and muttered threats were heard, and finally it was given out "blood raw," as the mountaineers say, that if Texas Rangers wanted to take the Marlows from Colorado, they had better send up 2,000 instead of two men to do it.

Things were looking anything but cheerful for the Texas Rangers when the whistle sounded from up the canon, and the engine came snorting down the mountain grade to the depot. Men were everywhere, and many a hand disappeared toward a back pocket as the two Rangers stepped off on the platform. The baggageman forgot to throw in the trunks, the station agent never thought of carrying out the telegraph orders to the conductor or engineer, and Jack Brown, the best known and best liked conductor in the San Juan country of Colorado, forgot for the first time in twenty years to call out his stentorian, "All aboard!"

Every eye was turned alternately toward the Marlow brothers standing by the side of Sheriff Bradley, their backs up against the station and their right hands out of sight.

The Rangers walked briskly up to where the Marlows and Sheriff Bradley stood, and nodding to them extended their hands. It was noticed, however, that it was the left hand which they put forth, while the right hand disappeared behind them. The Marlow boys also bowed, and took the extended hands of the Rangers in their own left hands. It was a left-handed shake all around.

"Well, boys," said Captain McDonald, "we have come to take you back to Texas. We have a warrant for you for complicity in the killing of Sheriff Wallace, and also a requisition from the governor. We do not want any trouble or hard feelings at all, and trust you will go peaceably."

"Captain McDonald," replied Charley, "we will have to telegraph the governor at Denver about this matter before we can be satisfied. That will take but a short time, and after that we will discuss the question of going back with you as prisoners."

"All right, boys, we are perfectly willing to concede anything that is reasonable. Wire your governor as soon as possible, and in the meantime get ready to go."

To this no reply was made, but the party separated, eyeing each other furtively, the Rangers repairing to a hotel and the Marlows into the telegraph office.[6]

Governor Routt[7] was wired at Denver of the matter, and full particulars given him. It was the opinion of legal talent here that the Marlows, being under the jurisdiction of the United States courts as government witnesses and deputized officials,[8] were not, while that was the case, amenable to civil courts or authorities, and upon consultation with the state's attorney the governor found this to be true, therefore he telegraphed the governor of Texas[9] to ascertain if the Marlows were under federal charge. The Texas governor wired back that such was the state of affairs, whereupon Governor Routt immediately wired the Marlows and the Texas Rangers at Ridgway that under the existing circumstances he would have to deny the requisition issued by the Texas governor and now in possession of Captain McDonald, and refuse to allow the Marlow brothers to be arrested by local authorities of Texas or any other state, so long as they were under government protection.

This settled it. The Rangers were forced to return as they had come, alone. They made the best of a bad bargain and took the situation philosophically, shook hands good naturedly all around and bidding Sheriff McDonald [*sic*: Bradley] good bye and wishing the Marlow boys good luck and prosperity, they boarded the east-bound train and departed for their far away Texas home. On this train the writer of these pages met Capt. McDonald and Mr. Britton and interviewed them relative to the subject in question, and obtained the information herewith given.

[6] "There was an exciting time in 1891 when Texas rangers came after the brothers," recalled an old-timer who claimed to be an eyewitness to this confrontation.

> The news spread through Ridgway and in a short time, several hundred armed men were gathered around the depot. George stepped up and shook hands (left handed) with the rangers. While he was talking to them, the other brother stood slightly to one side and back of George; all parties kept their right hands on their six-shooters. The same positions were held while George's brother shook hands and talked with the rangers. Every one was alert and ready for action. There would have been a big killing that morning if the Texas rangers had attempted to take the Marlow men by force. (Colorado WPA Writers, "Tall Tales and Anecdotes," 2–3)

[7] John Long Routt (1826–1907) was governor of Colorado when it became a state. He served from 1875 to 1879 and again in 1891–1893) (*The National Cyclopedia of American* Biography, 6:449).

[8] George and Charley Marlow had been sworn in as special deputy United States marshals on January 27, 1891.

[9] James Stephen Hogg (1851–1906), the first native governor of Texas, was elected in 1890 and served until 1895 (Tyler, *New Handbook of Texas*, 3:652–53).

INTERESTING SHORT STORIES AND SKETCHES ABOUT THE MARLOW BROTHERS.

The reader will probably remember "Shoat," the little horse referred to in the fore part of this book, who was so full of pranks and almost human intelligence. Well, Shoat is still an honored member of the family, and will be as long as he lives. He has shared their ups and downs, their joys and troubles all through the Indian Territory and Texas, and now enjoys a good, warm stable here at their mountain home in Colorado, with plenty of hay and oats and nothing to do but to enjoy himself.

Shoat is getting well along in years now, but he is as full of his tricks and fun as ever, and often draws a crowd around him when George has him out for exercise. One day while George was showing off his pranks, whispering for him to lie down and be sick, get up and drive the crowd away, and a hundred other things of the like. A tall stranger from over the range ventured the assertion that he could ride him. George smiled knowingly, whispered in Shoat's ear and gave the tall man permission to proceed. Shoat puckered his mouth up into a sort of horse smile and then apparently went fast to sleep standing up. The stranger gathered the bridle reins and sprang with a bound into the saddle. Then he bounded out again in about a second, lit on his head, spun around like a top a few times and then slid down the road on his shoulder blades. He was game, though, and came up smiling and climbed into the saddle again.

Gentle reader, did you ever stand in the gloaming of a summer eve, when the sinking sun cast its blood-red effulgent glory over the distant mountain peaks, and watch an Indian pony enjoy a joke? Shoat's whole life seemed to enter into the spirit of the jest, regardless of expense, and he reached and patted that tall stranger on the back so heartily that he discovered over a hundred new stars and comets then and there. Never in all his life had he received such an enthusiastic demonstration of affection, nor such a malicious, stinging, startling "hist." It rang out on the still evening air like the reverberation of a dying Denver boom and died away in the distance like the whistle of the Denver & Rio Grande coming around a gulch curve. The stranger from over the range lost two of his ribs, his coat tails were very badly frayed out where they had been cracked in the mountain breeze, and the country was visited by a gentle shower of blood. His remarks will not do to print, but he limped home over the beautiful moon-kissed hills and valleys that night in anything but a virtuous frame of mind, while Shoat ate his double measure of oats with a keen relish and as much sang-froid as though nothing unusual had happened.

Inasmuch as a picture of Ouray is given in this book,[10] the principal city where the Marlows live, a few words about the town may not be out of place.

Ouray is not only a city of mining and of business but it is a city of schools, churches and homes. Here is every facility for all the comforts which go to make up life's happiness, and the eastern man who comes out here among the mountains of the great West need have no fear of going through with any of the trials, dangers and hardships of the pioneer, but the rough places in the path of success have been all smoothed over and obliterated.

The early pioneers of this little section suffered and died that we might inherit this glorious and God-given spot on earth. The struggle with them was a nightmare at first, red with blood and dire with woeful want, and they were parched, starving and lonely beyond our pencil's power to tell. But here was nature's great storeroom of mineral and granary of wealth, and man of to-day has but to turn the key to enter and partake.

All these great inducements are open to the world, and a welcome hand is extended to the stranger from every land to come here and help dig the wealth from the hills and garner the harvests from the fertile valleys.

Years and epochs mark but one swath of the relentless scythe of Father Time. For cycles more than you or we can count these mountains with their buried wealth, these valleys and table lands with their untold possibilities of joyous harvest, were owned through the rights of squatter sovereignty by the more or less noble red man and his near relatives, the wolf, the coyote, the bear and mountain lion, and the stone and the pine were used in the rude construction of prehistoric implements.

How different now!

The red man and the wild beast have been subdued and the relentless paleface townsite boomer, the real estate agent, the land investors and

[10] No picture of Ouray appeared in the later edition. The only illustration in the book was a photograph of George and Charley Marlow.

other bunco steerers have usurped their places, and—can you believe it?—right here to-day, among these mountains whose lofty peaks tower far beyond the clouds, and seemingly would shut out all civilization, glares the electric light, plainly the rush of the city water can be heard, while out upon the streets sound the rumble and rush of the traffic belonging to a metropolitan city.

Many will remember the cattle drives made in the early days from Texas and the Indian Territory to Caldwell and Wichita, Kansas, where a market for the great herds was found. The Marlow brothers put in nearly five years at this work, because they were born and bred to an outdoor existence and preferred it to any other. They often refer to it now as the five years they put in on the hurricane deck of a Texas pony.[11] It is great sport to make a cattle drive for those who are toughened to stand it, though to those luxuriously inclined the sleeping out of doors in all kinds of weather and the long continuous life in the saddle would seem hard to bear.

It is a picturesque sight to see them rounding up the cattle, drifting with them in a storm and singing them to sleep when camping time in the evening arrives. A half dozen or more of the cowboys ride round and round the herd, slowly, and chant in a monotone some old religious hymn. In less than twenty minutes every head of cattle in the drove will lie down and complacently chew their cud. Cattle always have to be sung to sleep on the plains.

Wichita was a wild western frontier town and trading post in those days – not much like the elegant city it is to-day—and many were the laughable incidents witnessed by the Marlows.

Texas Jack was marshal there for a time, and it was not at all infrequent for it to be necessary for him to kill a man in the discharge of his duty. He got quite a wide-spread reputation in this way, and started a good-sized private burying ground of his own.[12]

One day the stage brought in a vertiable [*sic*] tenderfoot from the East, who came out for a taste of roughing it, and the usual crowd

[11] Perhaps Rathmell or the Marlows had read Charley Siringo's *A Texas Cowboy; or, Fifteen Years on the Hurricane Deck of a Spanish Pony*, published in 1885.

[12] "Texas Jack" was a popular *nom-de-guerre* on the frontier, but the history of Wichita during its days as major cattle town included no law officer with this sobriquet (Miller and Snell, *Why the West Was Wild*).

gathered at the inn to see who arrived from the "states." Among others were "Curley's" crowd. "Curley" was a noted local tough[13] who was always followed by half a dozen "characters," and who was known far and wide and delighted to have a bit of sport at their expense, in which he was usually successful. So stepping up to the new comer he slapped him on the back with a heartiness which nearly dislocated his spinal column, and said:

"Say, stranger, come and have a drink."

"Beg pardon, sir," replied the young man from the East, as he wiped the tears from his eyes, which "Curley's" whack on the back had caused to accumulate, "but I don't drink."

"You don't drink? D'ye means to insinuate that you're too d—n fine-haired to drink with the likes o' me?"

"Certainly not, sir, certainly not, only I –"

"Look here, stranger, nobody wot's too pert to drink with "Curley" Charley has got to fight, and ye can take yer chance right now between guns and knives."

The gentleman from New York concluded he preferred to take the drink, so all followed "Curley" into the bar room and "irrigated." Then the stranger took a seat as far away from the rest as he could conveniently get, while the others continued to drink. Pretty soon two of them commenced to practice broadsword exercise with a couple of nine-inch bowies over the stranger's head, and his eyes stuck out like door knobs. One of them was "Curley" himself, who roared with laughter every time the eastern man would dodge as one of the knives would shed a shower of sparks in his face, but suddenly paused as a tall and broad shouldered cattle man standing near drew a large Colt's revolver, and cocking it, presented it at "Curley" and said:

"Let up, now, and git."

"What d'ye mean?" growled "Curley."

"Mean just what I say, you git or I'll plug you."

[13] "Curley" was another common frontier nickname which, for some reason, generally attached to brawling outlaw desperadoes. "Curley Bill" Brocius of Arizona is perhaps best remembered. The one mentioned here may have been "Curley" Walker, leader of a gang of toughs who terrorized Wichita in its earliest days. A vigilante committee wiped out most of the gang in the fall of 1870. Walker escaped, only to be shot down and killed at Fort Dodge the following summer by an irate citizen from whom he had stolen cattle (*Abilene* [Kansas] *Chronicle*, July 13, 1871).

Curley looked at the open door to which the cattleman pointed, glanced at the big revolver on a line with his head, and at the eye of the man who held it in his hand, and then without a word walked out and disappeared. His crowd followed him and the cattleman put his gun back in his pocket.

Next day, after taking a wash at the pump and wiping on the long and grimy towel which hung from a roller in the "office," the young tourist remarked to the booted and spurred landlord.

"Say, friend, while I am out here in the West I should like very much to have a real buffalo steak for supper. Could you accommodate me?"

"Buffalo?"

"Yes. It is obtainable, is it not?" I shall be glad to pay any extra charges, don't you know."

The landlord looked the stranger over thoroughly for a moment, and then deliberately squirted about a teacupful of tobacco juice on his highly polished shoe, after which he turned on his heel and strode away. Pausing at the doorway, he turned around, looked hard again at the stranger and remarked:

"Buffalo! Well I'll be damn!"

The fact was that buffalo was so much cheaper than any other meat that there had been nothing else in the house for six months, and the eastern man had been eating it every day, under the impression that it was [a] very tough article of Texas steer.

Next morning the chap from the East was seen booking his name to return on the next stage, and to a real estate agent who was trying to induce him to remain, he said:

"Aw, by Jove, a man's life is not safe here a minute, don't you know."

"Perfectly safe, sir, when you get used to it," replied the real estate man. "Why, there hasn't been a killing here for over a week."

"Yes, bit look at that awful fellow who made me drink that liquor with him."

"Oh, that was Curley Charley. He means well enough."

"Well, that other man would have shot him if he hadn't went away when he told him, wouldn't he?"

"Likely he would, as he's pretty determined when he says anything, but he was taking your part, and didn't want to see you abused. That's

George Marlow, and he's the kindest hearted man in all this country, and he never gets into a muss of any kind, 'less might be the other day when he wouldn't stand by and see one small man picked into by a lot of big ones."

"Well," replied the tourist, "if I was to be killed I'd as soon be killed by the worst man in the world as the best one, and I guess I'll go home."

"All right," said the other, as he turned away. "Next time you come west you better bring along a nursing bottle and some fresh milk."

Every day and almost every hour now, as this is being written, the Marlow brothers are expecting to receive a call to go to Texas again as witnesses for the government against the members of that lawless mob, now imprisoned there.

On the journeys they are met at Trinidad by the following field deputies, who act as their guard: George A. Knight, United States marshal; Hufenton,[14] Lon Burson,[15] D. E. Yokum,[16] R. Yokum,[17] M. C. Gee, F. J. Peland,[18] A. R. Smith, S. M. Huston,[19] Fred Knight, John D. Rodney,[20] T. White, Cap White, John White, John B. Grand[21] and John Kinney, deputies.

In addition to these, thirty-five special deputies are sworn in during the session of court, making in all a guard for them of fifty-two men. They go fifteen to a bunch to meals and are ever on the alert for treachery from the mob sympathizers. A more genial and hearty set of men than this body of guards would be hard to find, and they manage to get a good deal of enjoyment out of their long and somewhat tedious waiting through the lengthy sessions of the Federal court. They get out and run races for exercise, and indulge in all manner of games and pranks, and when evening comes they put in the time smoking and telling yarns of more or less interest relative to life and adventures in the West.

[14] J. M. Huffington (Ledbetter, *Ordeal*, 160).

[15] This was undoubtedly Lon Burrison, the deputy U. S. marshal who had taken appointment with Ed Johnson back in 1885 and had been assigned with Johnson to the court at Graham.

[16] D. E. Yoakum (Ledbetter, *Ordeal*, 160).

[17] R. Yoakum (Ibid.).

[18] F. J. Penland (Ibid.).

[19] S. M. Houston (Ibid.).

[20] James D. Rodney (Ibid.).

[21] This deputy was John Barton Girand, the young guard on the ill-fated prisoner transfer of January 19, 1889, who streaked back to Graham yelling for help and was the only guard not indicted in the conspiracy.

A JOKE AND A FIGHT

"One time," spoke up George Marlow, "when we were helping drive a big bunch of cattle through the Indian Territory, a little band of Indians rode up and asked me for a steer for beef, and said they were hungry and had no meat. My brothers and I had always been kind to the Indians in little matters like that, so they came to us this time the first thing. We told them to go to the boss about it, and likely he would give them a critter, and we also gave them some pointers as to how they should proceed to get a good one. So they struck the boss for a donation, and he picked out the stubbiest, sickliest and most runty yearling there was in the bunch and gave it to them. Charley and I winked at the bucks as they started through the herd with their sickly little yearling, and as soon as they got pretty well toward the middle of the bunch they gave the most blood curdling yells you ever heard and the entire bunch of cattle stampeded in forty different directions. There was upwards of a thousand of 'em and in rounding 'em up again of course us boys had our hands full, and had no time to spare to look after the Indians. Well, sir, those red rascals took advantage of the stampede to drop their little runt of a yearling and cut out the fattest and best four-year-old steer in the bunch, and before we knew it they were two or three miles over the prairie and out of sight. Just like an Indian to be up to such tricks, wasn't it?

"On the same day," continued George, "Charley whipped a man who was big enough to have made a breakfast of him. He was a butcher, and after the drive was over we had contracted and delivered some mutton to him. He would not pay for the last three or four head, and so Charley and I went over to his place to take the sheep back again. To this the butcher objected, and so Charley made the proposition that he would either pay for the mutton or have the price taken out of his hide by a good thrashing. The butcher laughed at the idea of a young fellow like Charley was then bracing up to a big bully like he was, and readily agreed to the proposition, whereupon they both shed their coats and went at it. I felt sure Charley would get badly whipped, but I would not have interfered, no matter how badly he got the worst of it, for we always believe in fair plays to all sides. Well, it didn't seem to be more than five minutes before Charley had that great big double-fisted butcher completely knocked out, he roared for mercy like a stuck pig. In the meantime I had loaded the sheep into our wagon, and we drove off with them without another word of remonstrance from Mr. Butcher, who forever after was among our best friends and supporters. He would fight for us to-day.

TO THE READER:

The following sketches, all duly authenticated, are introduced at this point to throw further light on the life, habits, character and conduct of the Marlow brothers, George and Charley. They were typical frontiersmen, generous to a fault, faithful to a friend, scrupulously honest, and afraid of trouble, but when trouble was forced on them, their conduct under such circumstances was as certain as their acts were scientific. They have been known to take up the quarrel of a defenseless soul and stay until the bulldozer quit, and then walk a quarter of a mile out of their way to avoid meeting a man who had declared he would beat them up on sight. They subscribed $10.00 for the benefit of an injured acquaintance and, within half an hour [had] bitter words with a man who was trying to beat them out of ten cents. They have been known to unhitch from a plow they were using to accommodate a neighbor who wanted to borrow it. As hunters, they had no superiors, and many a neighbor's heart was gladdened to see them coming for they knew it meant a "saddle" of venison or a "quarter" of a fat bear. When a neighbor's crop was ripe, and needed harvesting and the neighbor sick, they just moved over, harvested the crop and presented no bill for services rendered. They gave the best that was in them and for the love of giving. They were insistent for law enforcement as any man in the county and assisted as Deputy Sheriffs in many Ouray County cases, and never abused the power vested in them as officers.

With this introduction to the following sketches, we omit further comment until the close of the book, at which time we will give the reader a short account of their business at the present time.

In the spring of 1886, prior to any trouble of any member of the Marlow family, George Marlow visited the Western Slope of Colorado and remained in Gunnison City a large part of the time. He was then a typical cowboy, ready to capture, saddle and ride a wild bronco, lasso and ride a wild steer, or run a foot race. However much he mixed with that class called frontiersmen, he steadily refused to drink. While in the Gunnison Valley he made the acquaintance of C. W. Shores, better known as "Doc" Shores, who was the sheriff of Gunnison County.[22] Those who are familiar with the early history of Colorado, and especially the Western Slope, remember "Doc" Shores as a man who, if delegated the unpleasant duty of bringing in one of the lawless element, was certain to bring results, and usually without parading his authority or a display of guns. In a short time after George arrived, he and "Doc" became fast friends—friends that knew what friendship means. As they passed the time pleasantly, neither one could have been made to believe that, at a not far distant day, they would be tangled up in a transaction that would lack almost nothing of terminating the life of one of them.

After some weeks of friendly intercourse, George left for the Lone Star State to join his mother, brothers and their families. Soon after he returned to Texas, there began that conspiracy that brought about the death of three of his brothers and left him and Charley so badly wounded as to unfit them for manual labor for some years to come. All was excitement; their friends were more devoted than ever, but their enemies, rich and powerful, were more desperate. Then followed the arrest of the principal conspirators, among them the officers of Young County, Texas, and a Deputy United States Marshal. George and Charley were subpoenaed as witnesses, and the court, fearful that they would leave the state, placed them under bond to appear as witnesses in the trial of

[22] Cyrus Wells Shores acquired his lifelong nickname "Doc" because he was named after the Hicksville, Michigan, doctor who delivered him in 1844. After knocking around the frontier for a number of years, he married in 1877 and three years later settled at Gunnison City, Colorado. In 1884 he was elected sheriff of Gunnison County, a position he held for eight years. He also held a commission most of this period as a deputy U. S. marshal. He remained in law enforcement work after leaving the sheriff's office, putting in twenty-four years as special investigator for Colorado railroad and express companies and chief of police at Salt Lake City. He died at Gunnison in 1934 at the age of 89 (Rockwell, *Memoirs of a Lawman*).

Shores had befriended the Marlows when, practically destitute, they arrived on the Western Slope, and his help is evidenced by a letter received from Charley during this period:

> Mr. Shores, We rescaved you most kind and welcom letter and... glad to get the Christmas Present you Sent us we wernt able to Send you Such a Present Know . . . we will remember that for it helps us out you know we will Stop and See you when we go Down well we all sends our lov to you and family . . . from friends. Charles Marlow, Ridgeway.

This letter, one of several from the Marlows to Shores, was among Shores' papers and is quoted in Look, *Unforgettable Characters of Western Colorado*, 105. Apparently Charley had been schooled by someone since the days in Graham when he could not sign his own name, but his letters still reveal the brothers' rudimentary literary education that would later necessitate the employment of William Rathmell to tell their story.

the conspirators. The bond was $250.00 each. Friends signed the bond and they were at liberty; at liberty to stay in a section where a very few would give them work, if they were able to work; at liberty to face, unarmed, men who had connived with the officers to bring about their destruction. The men that they were to testify against were rich, the cattle barons of that section, with scores of friends as unscrupulous as themselves, who had either taken part in the mob or had aided and abetted those who did take part, and would resort to any means to destroy evidence which might mean a term in prison or the hangman's knot. They applied to the prosecuting attorney for permission to carry guns, but were refused. Here they were under bond to appear as witnesses, in a section hostile to any effort that they might make to gain a living, deprived of the means of defending themselves should such be necessary and without money or means of support. This condition seemed to them intolerable, so, they raised the amount of their bonds, [$500.00] paid it to their bondsmen, and left for parts unknown, firmly believing that by paying their bonds, their bondsmen would be released from liability, they would be free from the order of the court, and no one would suffer.

It was noised around that they had "jumped" their bond and a reward of $500.00 was offered for their return.

In a short time they settled down to what they believed to be a quiet life in Ouray County, Colorado, and filed on or "homesteaded" a piece of government land. They made no attempts to conceal their identity or occupy quarters remote from the busy parts. They just stated their names were George and Charley Marlow.

Now, it just happened that "Doc" Shores read in the newspaper that a reward of $500.00 was offered for their return to Texas, and it was a part of his business to satisfy the demands of justice. He made the trip over to Ridgway, Ouray County, Colorado, with two helpers, one a Mr. Harper and the other, a Mr. Bennett, and appeared at the Marlow ranch early one morning.[23] He, with his helpers, were admitted into the house, but the Marlows were careful not to let the Shores party or any of them get the "drop" on them. Shores stated his business frankly—he was there

[23] Details of this incident as related by Shores in his memoirs agree closely with the Marlow version, but Shores remembered taking only one deputy, Jack Watson, a Texas gunman he liked to have handy in potentially dangerous situations (Rockwell, *Memoirs of a Lawman*, 135–36).

to arrest them and return them to Texas. They quietly informed him that they would not submit to arrest and would not, under any circumstances, lay down their arms, they had been attacked once when they were without arms, and they did not mean to have a recurrence of that experience. Shores argued his case, but not convincingly to them. They were on their guard now and no move was made by Shores or his men that was not viewed with suspicion. Shores insisted that they were making a mistake and reminded them that when a man was wanted by the United States as a witness in a United States Court, the government took means to get him as could insure success. He told them that if the worst came to the worst, soldiers would come and get them, or that a government balloon could come over and destroy or capture; all of this fell on deaf ears. At this time "Mother" Marlow announced dinner; they took their places at the table as follows: George sat at the east end of the table; Charley sat at his left on the south side; Shores and Bennett sat at the west end and Harper on the north side. The argument waxed warm, Shores insisting that they were foolish to take any such position relative to surrender. To show them the utter futility of resisting, he said that he with Bennett's help could tie Charley, and Harper could hold George. It was a tense moment and to make matters worse, Shores, in his excitement, dropped his knife and fork on his plate. An explosion of a stick of dynamite could not have produced greater astonishment. In an instant, George had the muzzle of his gun against Shores' stomach. Shores had both hands in the air. No other one of the party made a move save that Charley had his hand on his gun. George thought that the dropping of the knife and fork was the signal for an attack. With his hands in the air, Shores told George that he always took things wrong and was mistaken this time.

After all had resumed their seats at the table, Shores proposed that George and Charley go with him to Gunnison City; that if they would do this he would make each of them deputy sheriffs, and, in the meantime, they could carry their guns. Shores explained that it was his purpose to have a United States marshal from Texas come, meet them and arrange for their return to Texas under such guard as would insure their safety; he further said that if arrangement could not be made to their satisfaction, he would pay all expenses of the trip to and from Gunnison City and board them while they were away from home. They accepted Shores' proposition, but warned him that any move on his part to effect their arrest, his life would pay the penalty. With this understanding, they took the train for Gunnison City. A few miles out of Gunnison City, they again became suspicious that it was Shores' purpose to have a goodly number of armed deputies waiting at the Gunnison City depot and effect their arrest; accordingly, they called him back to their seat and told him of their fears; he said, "Boys, you are wrong again; this train stops some quarter of a mile from the depot; when it stops, get off and go where you please; come to my office in the morning and I will legally appoint you as deputy sheriffs of Gunnison County." They got off when the train stopped, went out in the country to the home of a friend and stayed all night; next morning they went to the office of Shores who duly and legally appointed them deputy sheriffs. All agreements had been faithfully kept and they were as happy as men could be who had a reward offered for their capture.

Some three days later, Captain George A. Knight, United States marshal from Texas, appeared. Every point upon which Knight and the Marlow boys disagreed was fought out. He made nearly the same argument that Shores had made at the home of the Marlows, but they were determined to take no further chance with the mob element in the section where the conspirators were to be tried. Knight finally yielded to all of their demands, and in addition, agreed that when they had reached his office in Texas, he would make each of them Deputy United States marshals. Knight then said: "I have agreed to every things that you have asked; now I want you to agree to a proposition that I have to make." They told him to state his proposition, to which he replied: "I want to dress you boys for your trip back to Texas." They agreed and he dolled them up as follows: Silk shirts, narrow-brimmed felt hats, toothpick shoes shined to brilliancy, light colored trousers, light colored coats and gray wigs; he then had their mustaches blackened, and they were ready. The contrast between what they always had worn and what they then had on was so marked, that even a close friend would not have known them; they looked like an elderly pair of dudes. With this outfit, they took the train and, at a point agreed upon, Knight went back to Texas by the shortest route, and they went on to Kansas City; here they took a south-bound train for Texas.

In due time Marshal Knight got back to Texas, but alone. He made no explanation. The people were surprised. The friends of the accused rejoiced. Marshal Knight's record was clear; when he located a man or men he wanted, he brought them in. His failure at this time could only be explained on the theory that he had killed the Marlows; anyway, the Marlows were not there for the trial and a possible shooting was averted. When the excitement had subsided, Marshal Knight boarded an east-bound train where he met the Marlows at a point formerly agreed upon and near Dallas, Texas; then they all came back together; proper guards were furnished and the trial, after many delays, came on for hearing. The Marlow boys were each appointed deputy United States marshals in the very section where they had been accused of every crime in the calendar, and testified in the case, and it was due to their testimony that the conspirators were punished—punished for their part in a plot as diabolical as ever disgraced the records of a civilized community.

(Here follows an exact copy of their appointment as Deputy United States marshals):

UNITED STATES OF AMERICA,
Northern District of Texas,

Know all Men by These Presents, That I, George A. Knight, U. S. Marshal, In and for the Northern District of Texas, do hereby constitute and appoint George Marlow of the County of Dallas, State of Texas, my true and lawful Special Deputy.

To hold Chas. Marlow in custody as an attached witness in the U. S. Court at Graham, Texas; hereby authorize him to do and perform any and all things necessary to the execution of the process hereinbefore enumerated and set forth as fully as I myself could do.

Witness my official signature this 27th day of January, 1891.

George A. Knight, U. S. M.

I, GEORGE MARLOW, do solemnly swear that I will faithfully execute all lawful precepts directed to the Marshal of the Northern District of Texas, under the authority of the United States, which may come into my hands, and true returns make; and in all things will truly, and without malice or partiality, perform the duties of the Marshal's

Deputy of the Northern District of Texas, during my continuance in office, and take only my lawful fees. And I do solemnly swear that I will support and defend the Constitution of the United States against all enemies, foreign and domestic; that I will bear true faith and allegiance to the same; that I take this obligation freely, without any mental reservation or purpose of evasion; and that I will well and faithfully discharge the duties of the office on which I am about to enter. So help me God.

GEORGE MARLOW

Subscribed and sworn to before me, this 29th day of January, A. D. 1891.

To the Hon. A. P. McCormick,

U. S. District Judge, Dallas, Texas.

SIR: I, CHAS. H. LEDNUM do hereby certify that GEO. MARLOW, Special Deputy United States Marshal, whose name appears to the oath above, did subscribe and was sworn to the same by me.

CHAS. H. LEDNUM, U. S. Commissioner

CRESTED BUTTE EPISODE

On November 15th, 1891,[24] a telegram came to Ridgway, Colorado, addressed to the Marlow Brothers, inviting them to catch the noon train for Gunnison City, Colorado, and signed by C. W. Shores, Sheriff. At this time the Coal Miners' strike was in full blast at Crested Butte, a coal camp in Gunnison County. Many accounts of atrocities reached the outside, some of which would make an Apache Indian turn green with envy at the refined cruelty practiced by the strikers, but, for the most part, [were] pure fabrications designed to keep strike-breakers and the timid at a respectful distance. When the telegram came, the Marlow brothers speculated on what might be wanted and whether it would be in connection with the Coal Strike. The boys had fought Indians, not voluntarily, but when they were some half mile in advance of the pursuing red-skins, and, with their characteristic handling of a difficult situation, had thrown wide open the throttle valve of the broncho they were riding, and, as they dashed along heedless of criticism, would ever and anon

[24] This would have been on December 15 (*Rocky Mountain News*, December 19, 1891).

lay hold of their crown to see whether the scalplock was yet in place, and be it said to the credit of the "character assassins" of that section, they never started the rumor that the Marlow brothers, in this instance, "throwed the race;" they had induced a well-armed mob to retire from the field when the answer to their challenge of "Come on, you cowards," was the echo of their call, they had forcibly taken passage on the hurricane deck of a fretful and excited broncho and, on many occasions, would have been glad to withdraw and leave the premises, and would have done so except that quitting seemed more dangerous than continuing; so, they journeyed on, the only persons in the wide, wide world that knew that they were scared; they had refused to obey the mandate of a federal court until a sufficient guard was furnished in insure safety; they had accidentally surprised Bruin in his den and killed him before he could stage a demonstration or assert the "right of domicile." They had done all of this, but they had never participated in the recovery of a coal mine that was in possession of striking miners. Every encounter that they had ever had, their adversary knew when he was "licked." Here, however, was new experience. The could anticipate how a man or a half dozen men would act under a fixed condition or circumstance but would this hold good for a force of some 300 men who felt that they had been abused, and were then forcibly holding the property against the owner with a demand to correct the wrongs it had committed? Would the men meekly submit to them when it was almost certain that if they did, all of them that had taken part would be discharged and some of their number receive a jail sentence?

While they were debating just what to do, the noon train pulled out and left them undecided. They were almost glad, and, except for the fact that C. W. Shores was their friend and maybe needed help, they would have been glad. Then, a second telegram came addressed to them and signed by the same man, announcing that a special train would be at the Ridgway depot at 3:00 o'clock P. M., and urging them to come at once. Again, and with added force, it occurred to them that Shores had befriended them when they needed a friend, and was in distress. Now, the Marlow brothers prided themselves on their loyalty; loyalty to a friend was some ninety-odd per cent of their religion, and with the thought uppermost that Shores needed help, they decided to go independent of loss or inconvenience. It was the work of only a few minutes to oil up their "trusties" and make it to the depot, which point they reached ahead of time.

As the one-car special came to a stop, the conductor bounded off and informed the crowd that he was ordered to Ridgway to get two men who would go to Crested Butte, frighten the miners into a condition of subjection and put down the rebellion, to which the Marlow brothers replied: "We are the men," and as they boarded the special, they asked the conductor to make the best time consistent with the laws of the great Commonwealth of Colorado. Aboard the train they saw three nicely dressed, good looking men who, the conductor said, were to go along and drive the strikers off with broom sticks if Shores and his imported deputies failed to restore the property to its owner. These young men had every appearance of being gentleman, out for a lark, but sadly lacking in experience; they seemed to be unarmed, and the contrast between the Marlow brothers and these young men was startling, for the Marlows had two 45s each in scabbards hanging low and strapped to their legs, and also had a sawed-off Winchester each. The conductor, who had never heard of the Marlows and had little faith in their ability, declared that he would lay a wager that any old woman could unbuckle her suit case, get out a gun and disarm them before they could draw their guns; in an instant, the muzzle of two guns pressed against the vest of the conductor who said wonderingly, "Where did those guns come from?" The Marlows staged this demonstration to stop a nagging that might grow irksome, and it had exactly that effect. The three young men who viewed this display of handiness with weapons, pricked up their ears and seemed to wonder if they were not in pretty fast company. The Marlows then engaged the young men in conversation, and partly through jest, partly through desire to test their nerve, partly through a realization that their words might be prophetic, told the boys that there was a chance that none of them would ever see home and friends again, and that it was but the part of wisdom to provide against such contingencies by leaving word with someone where to address their friends or relatives, what disposition to make of their remains and, if they had property, to make such will as would leave it in the hands of those who were most entitled to their bounty; they told the boys that they had done this before leaving

Ridgway because handling a strike situation was a hazardous occupation; they told the boys that if they cared to leave these matters with them, that, if they survived, they would carry out their wishes in detail, and they promised the boys that if they were "bumped off" they would take care of their remains until relatives or the company owning the coal mine at Crested Butte could give them Christian burials; they told the boys that the coal company had promised a "cracking" good funeral, with all of the trimmings for any guard that lost his life in the strike.

The boys were at first amused, then interested and finally scared, and withdrew to the other end of the car for a conference just as the train was entering Montrose. The conductor went into the depot to get his orders and was gone about ten minutes; when he got back and the train was again under headway, it was discovered that the three boys were missing. The brakesman said that they had gotten off the train just as they stopped at Montrose[25] and, when he saw them last, were exceeding the speed limit for pedestrians.

In due time the special reached Gunnison City and the Marlows, now hungry but desirous of observing all of the proprieties of Gunnison City relative to carrying arms, asked the agent at the depot to check their guns until they could get supper. As the agent took the guns, he asked the boys what they were doing, to which they replied, "Just drifting." The agent replied that they had better keep drifting right along, "because, if you don't, Sheriff Shores will get you and lock you up." The Marlows told him that Shores was the very man they would like to see. While the Marlows were at supper, the agent telegraphed Shores at Crested Butte that two toughs, probably bank robbers or desperadoes, were in town looking for him. Shores wired back that a special train must be immediately provided the bank-robbers or desperadoes and they sent to Crested Butte with all haste. When the Marlows got back from supper, the agent gave them their guns and asked them if they were the "hell-roarin'" Marlow brothers that he had been reading about, to which the boys modestly replied, "Our names are Marlow." The special was soon in readiness and away they went as fast as steam and a willing crew could take them, and after many delays on account of snow, reached

[25] Montrose, seat of Montrose County, lies about forty miles north of Ouray. From there the train would head east toward Gunnison, fifty miles further on.

Crested Butte where they met and welcomed C. W. Shores, sheriff of Gunnison County, Colorado.

They found Shores in a large office building with some sixty-five men, "scabs," the miners called them, who were willing to go to work at any time when officers of the coal company could give them protection, but no one of them willing or capable of exercising judgment as an officer in a situation such as confronted Shores at this time. Shores informed the Marlows that the fans were idle, the mine filling up with gas and an explosion possible unless the fans could be started. In less than a week the forces of law had absolute control, the fans going and a good force of men working the mines with most of the men who had been on strike back at their old jobs.[26]

Only one further incident in the coal strike at Crested Butte is worthy of mention. After a considerable force were at work in the mine, Shores proposed to the Marlows that they take a trip down town to see how the business men and others were faring. All agreed and at the first saloon as they rounded the corner of the building they found a man delivering a speech. He reminded his audience, some seventy-five men, that after years of faithful service for the coal company, at a wage wholly inadequate to properly support them and their families, under conditions that dwarfed their intellects and induced premature age, were now to be kicked out, their places filled by "scabs" and, if they complained, they were to be shot down like dogs by imported gun-men. And the last morsel of food taken from their wives and families. At this point Shores interrupted the speech by inquiring of the orator whether he was married, to which he replied that he was not. Shores then asked him what mine he worked at last, and the man replied that he did not work at the mines; that he was there to help the down-trodden miner get his rights. Shores told him that he was under arrest, but he backed away into the saloon with Shores following. George Marlow, fearful of the results if the crowd of men got Shores separated from him, followed at his heels. Charley Marlow saw the crowd close behind Shores and his brother and unable,

[26] Shores got the mine fans running and restored order with a force of twenty-five special deputies, which included, according to the *Rocky Mountain News*, "such well known men as the Marlow boys of Telluride [*sic*], Colo., who are wanted in Texas but whom Governor Routt refused to extradite, John Watson of western Colorado, who has the reputation of having killed several men and of having held up the town of Montrose, and several other well known gentlemen who are very handy with firearms in an emergency" (December 19, 1891).

without force, to follow them, jumped upon the bar and, with a 45 in each hand, remarked: "Boys, I got up here so that I could see just what was going on; I can see every part of the room; I am for peace, but if any man pulls a gun, he will not live long enough to regret his rash act." His vantage point, the two 45s, and his apparent sincerity won a favorable opinion with the men, and Shores and George with power to choose and time to discriminate led seven men captive out of the saloon and over to the improvised Bastille to await free transportation to the Gunnison County jail.[27] After some six weeks, all was quiet in Crested Butte, and the Marlow brothers returned to Ridgway where, within a short time and in addition to the wages, they received a car load of coal for their services in the Crested Butte Coal Strike.[28]

AS A PEACE OFFICER

While George Marlow was serving as deputy under Maurice Corbett, then sheriff of Ouray County, Colorado,[29] he was asked to intercept two men who were charged with stealing dry goods from a firm in Telluride, Colorado.[30] He was given their description and informed that the taller

[27] Shores relates this incident, saying only that "as they closed in around the posse to better see the show, Jack Watson and the Marlow boys raised their guns and ordered the onlookers back. They complied without hesitation" (Rockwell, *Memoirs of a Lawman*, 253).

[28] Although there is no evidence that Shores ever again called on the Marlows for help, their friendship continued as indicated by several undated letters in Shores' files quoted in Look, *Unforgettable Characters*:

> Mr. Shores I got your letter today why didn't you keep them papers I thought you had Read them their was Some partys hear wanted to Read them I was scourry that I written for them well I havent muchNews to write thir was a daygo robd in Ridgeway by five men they got all the men well I wish you would come over and stay a week or to we will treat you as well as we know how, well tell us all the news when you write. Charles Marlow, Ridgeway. (132)
>
> Sir: George wants me to write you we went to Ouray on the 24th to get peper to carry our arms and was refused on the Grounds that we voted the Republican ticket and you air United with all the sheriffs in the country and we want you to get us Special Papers. Just to carry arms for we don't feel like layen off our arms. Marlow Brothers. (136–37)
>
> Sir: . . . Well, Dock. George has had pups again. . . . The finest blood hounds you ever seen, We went back to Missouri for a fine female hound, she is a thurabred, and 6 fine ones. We are going to send you four puppies we want you to train to hunt men and men only, then we want two of them back. . . . Learn the pups to bite men. . . . Marlow Bros. Ridgeway. (137)

[29] Maurice Corbett (1860–1939) served twice as sheriff of Ouray County. He succeeded J. F. Bradley in 1892 and held the office through two terms until 1896. Elected again in 1901, he served three more terms, 1902–1908 (Maiden, *Sheriffs of Colorado; Rocky Mountain News*, July 16, 1939).

[30] San Miguel County was carved out of Ouray County in 1883 and Telluride was made the county seat (Brown, *Ghost Towns*, 355).

of the two men was called "Tallow Face" and the other, "Myrt," and that they were headed for or toward Montrose, Colorado. Accordingly, George went to Montrose by train and started back up the railroad track on foot. Some four miles out of Montrose he met two men that answered the description given him; one had a gun in a holster hanging to his belt. Satisfied that these were the men wanted, he engaged them in conversation about work conditions, the while making a mental estimate of them and, when they were in such position that neither one could beat him drawing a gun, he said: "Tallow Face, give me that gun." Tallow Face made no reply but threw up his hands in token of surrender, and George helped himself to the gun. Myrt as quietly submitted, and after searching the men for other arms and finding none, the three men walked back to Montrose in such manner as would suggest to the ordinary observer that it was merely three acquaintances walking into town. When they arrived, George had all served with dinner, after which he informed them that they must go to jail until train time. They begged to have their suitcase, which request, after search for contraband, was granted. Some two hours afterward, George called for them and found them shaved, cleaned up and dressed like gentlemen. He took them by train to Ridgway, the point where he expected to meet a man from Telluride to take them on, but, instead, he found a telegram for him declaring that they were desperate men and to chain them to a seat in the passenger car bound for Telluride and send them there by the evening train. Now, George had some old-fashioned notions about the way prisoners should be treated, arising partly from a sense of justice and partly from an experience that was yet vivid in his memory. He knew that, under the law, a man is innocent until he is proven guilty and, by this measurement, his men were innocent. To chain an innocent man to a car seat or in any other manner was repugnant to his nature and fraught with consequences not to be ignored. But whether his men were guilty or not guilty, he would not be a party to a transaction that reeked and smelled of the "good old days" when the thumb screw, the rack and the fagot were used to impress the unfortunate of the "majesty of the law." He also knew a prison had just two purposes: one, to reform the criminal, and make a self-supporting and useful member of society of him, and the other was to protect society against the criminal during the period of his reformation. From this he reasoned that even though a man were guilty, reformation could be better accomplished by allowing his every privilege consistent with safety, and, if by so doing, the criminal escaped in the confusion of a railroad wreck and a fire, to have him burned to death. Instead of complying with the request in the telegram he took the two men to his home where his wife prepared a good warm supper for all.

Soon after supper, his brother, Charley Marlow, who was also a deputy sheriff under Maurice Corbett, brought in a prisoner by the name of Ed Best and asked his brother to hold him until morning when Corbett would come down and take him to Ouray. Best declared that friends would rescue him before morning, but George thought otherwise. He had his wife make a bed on the floor wide enough for four men; he then handcuffed Tallow Face, Myrt and Best together, and then handcuffed himself to Tallow Face; the four men thus handcuffed went to bed on the floor and slept—some. Next morning, contrary to the prediction of Best, all prisoners answered to roll call and had breakfast together. Corbett came down early and took Best to Ouray and, in the evening, George took his two prisoners by train to Dallas Divide, where he met the Telluride sheriff[31] who was surprised that George had taken such chances. The Telluride sheriff handcuffed the prisoners and took them to Telluride where they were tried and convicted, Tallow Face receiving a sentence of eighteen months and Myrt a sentence of one year.

After serving hid time, Myrt came back to Ridgway and hunted George up, he was a sorry sight—nearly barefooted, broke and hungry. George fed him and bought him a pair of shoes. A few days later George gave him work in the hayfield where he gave good service for some two weeks, for which George paid him the average wage. Upon leaving, he told George that if there was a thing in the world that would influence a man who had "gone wrong" to change his course, it would be such treatment as he had been given by him, both as a prisoner and as a hired man.

[31]The sheriff of San Miguel County, headquartered in Telluride, was James A. Beattie (Maiden, *Sheriffs of Colorado*).

DEATH

Then there came a day when even the watchful eye of Charley and George and their families had to admit that "Mother" was failing; they noticed that the step that had ever been firm was less secure; that those eyes that had ever been alert lacked some of the sparkle of former times; that the courage that had met every sacrifice that is catalogued and yet pressed on, was not so manifest. For some weeks she had remarked on the weariness that she felt, but at such times she would always conclude speaking of the comfort she had in the new settled affairs of her faithful sons, that, although they had little, they owed no man a penny, and that they could better spare her now than when the clouds were lowering and the machinations of the misguided officers of Young County, Texas, were developing. She gloried, not in the fact that her two surviving sons had compelled the mob that attacked them and their brothers at Dry Creek to retreat to cover, but rather that under the trying circumstances of an attack on unarmed men, unwarranted, un-American, unlawful, and by those sworn duty it was to protect, these boys—her boys had acted the part of men; had remained loyally together then and afterward, and had emerged with a "Clean Bill of Health" from a federal court in the very state and near the scene of their trouble. While the memory of those days would bring a shudder, the triumph of a verdict of "not guilty" to the living and exoneration of the dead, gave high hope to endeavor through the intervening years.

Yes, this bright Sunday morning, they acknowledged that Mother was failing, and so they and each of them redoubled their watchful care hopefully working to defeat the plans of the "Grim Reaper" and again snatch victory from a doubtful chance. It soon became apparent that for once their resourcefulness would not avail, and that try as they would, the end was near.

Then, one sunny day as evening approached, the soul of their Guardian Angel; the mother that had weathered the storms of Border life; who had lost more and won more than any woman of her time; who had passed through the fire of adversity without spoiling a single womanly trait; had passed away, and as they turned from the sad scene and looked through the window facing the west, they saw that the sun, rather than view the departure, had sunk behind Horsefly Peak in a crimson setting.

Alone, except their families, with their dead. They had been alone before with their dead. They had been alone with Albert [*sic*: Alfred] and Lewellen [*sic*: Llewellyn] on that memorable night at Dry Creek, but on that night, they could shout defiance to the destroyer and claim the field. But tonight, there was no monster to engage, no foe to challenge. All was still. On the former occasion, conditions forbade the consolation of grief. Tonight, however, they could indulge their feelings, they could mourn unmolested. The night watch was kept and dawn found their grief unassuaged, but they were resigned and tranquil. They had lost their first fight.

As the day advanced, preparations having been made, they followed all that was mortal of that mother, whose advice had tided them over the rough places, to its last resting place on the farm on Billie Creek, where wintry blast nor summer storm could disturb. The place, a sport on a knoll where the first gleam of the morning and the last ray of the setting sun falls aslant the mound, makes almost cheerful the grave of Martha Jane Marlow, who did life's work well.[32]

A BEAR STORY

Most men of Ouray County considered it a rare piece of good luck to be invited to go hunting with the Marlow brothers or either of them, and would forego the pleasure of an "infare"[33] or a horserace to accept the invitation. They knew that they would, most likely, witness an exhibition of psychology of wild life, for the Marlows held diplomas in the art of stalking game and in marksmanship secured in the school of experience of many years. So when Judge W. R. Kincaid of Ouray and Judge Ira B. Culver of Ridgway were invited to go hunting with George Marlow, they eagerly accepted and prepared for the trip. The two judges were not novices in hunting, and while moderately successful in their annual hunt, they each felt some pyrotechnics would be pulled off on this trip that would amply repay them for any loss they might sustain by temporarily laying aside the judicial ermine. Accordingly, on the day appointed, they joined

[32] Martha Jane Marlow died in October 1907 at the age of eighty-four. Her gravesite on Billy Creek is now part of a federal game preserve (Ledbetter, *Ordeal*, 165).

[33] An infare was a party for a newly married couple.

George Marlow at his ranch, who, with his corps of "bear dogs" and camp fixtures, was waiting for them, and away they went for the mountain fastnesses of the north slop of Mt. Sneffels Peak.[34] They reached the campground in mid-afternoon and after a hasty lunch, left in three directions, each hopeful that he could "bag" a deer, a bear or some game animal and excel any of the others if the party. In the twilight they again met at the campfire; Judge Kincaid had seen nothing; Judge Culver had killed a find buck and George Marlow had seen nothing but a fresh bear track. Over a cup of steaming hot coffee, a big venison steak and baking powder biscuits fresh from the hands of George Marlow, they planned for Bruin's capture or destruction on the morrow. At the first peep-o-day the camp was all life and bustle. Men and dogs were provided with a nourishment calculated to tide them over until late afternoon, then, with high hopes and loaded guns, away. The dogs were put on the trail at the point where George had discovered it the evening before, and the men followed as fast as fallen timber, tangled undergrowth and judicial dignity would permit. About 10:00 o'clock A. M. George told the Judges that the dogs had "jumped" the bear and were running him by sight; by the sound of the cry of the dogs, they must have been, at least, a quarter of a mile away. The Judges exchanged knowing looks over George's statement, each declaring mentally that such evidence as this would not go in his court, but they let the statement go unchallenged and wearily plodded on. It developed that the bear had been surprised by the dogs somcthing over a mile from his home, and persistently refused to seek shelter until he was within his cave, high up on the mountain side. Our heroes toiled up the mountain, arriving at the den, just after noon. They found the den to be a hole behind a big slab of rock that was leaning against the cliff, with, apparently, no entrance or exit other than the one used by the bear to get in. The dogs were ordered to go in and bring the bear out; they declined for reasons that to them seemed sufficient. Then George and the two judges held a council, Judge Kincaid presiding. In stating the case, Judge Kincaid declared that it was a clear case of Contempt of Court, and that the bear should be punished to the limit. Judge Culver disagreed and said that the legal way to get the bear out would be to issue a Writ Ejectment, which he

[34] Mt. Sneffels, lying between Ouray and Telluride, forms the highest peak in the Uncompahgres Mountains (Wolle, *Stampede to Timberline*, 370).

would be glad to do if either of the other fellows would serve it. George Marlow then was recognized and addressed the meeting as follows: "Mr. Chairman and gentlemen: In no other case would I dare oppose the learned gentlemen who have recommended certain action in this case. I am not versed in the usual language of the court and must beg your indulgence while I outline what I believe to [be] the proper procedure. This bear is excited now and would disregard all the Writs your courts could issue in the next century. It is my plan to climb above the den, secure a dry Quaking Aspen pole that stands there, bring it down and prod him with it until, in desperation, he comes out; then the Judge can pronounce judgment." During this parley, which was held almost in the vestibule of the bear's home, the bear became thoroughly aroused and uttered some unprintable remarks and seemed to vow eternal vengeance against the Judiciary of Colorado as well as dogs of every kind and character. There was, at this point, some two feet of snow and climbing difficult, but George, after the assembled judiciary had consented to his plan, made his way up the mountainside to the pole, broke it off and started back to the improvised court room. On his way back and at a point immediately over the center of the bear's den he disappeared—he had fallen through a hole that was covered with snow into the den with the bear. A moment later and the judges heard a report of a revolver in the den, and soon afterward, George came crawling out, a bloody spectacle. His story was that when the dust cleared so he could see, he found the bear advancing open-mouthed; he had no chance to run, so he pulled his "45" and fired into the mouth of the bear; the shot was fatal and with one gasp which covered him with blood, the bear fell dead at his feet. After some difficulty, the bear was pulled from his den, dressed and taken to camp where, again, the thrills of the day were gone over and the events fixed so that the Judges could regale their friends with the excitement of a bear hunt. The next morning Judge Culver killed another deer. All Judge Kincaid got was the exercise, but he felt quite repaid, at that.[35] The next day, all were back to their homes, the Judges expounding the law to the derelicts that came before them, and George arranging for another bear hunt with the uninitiated.

[35] William R. Kincaid (1851–1934), a North Carolinian, came to Colorado in 1881, where he freighted, built homes, and dabbled in politics. He was renowned as a hunter, having one summer supplied the town of Rockwood with all its game. "He was a great sportsman and was considered one of the best shots in the state" (Sarah Platt Decker Chapter, DAR, *Pioneers*, 1:160).

CONCLUSION

"Years have come and passed away,
Golden locks have turned to gray;
Golden ringlets, once so fair,
Time has changed to silvery hair."

But the hearts of Charley and George Marlow beat as warm as when they knew the wild, free life of the plains. The latch-string of their homes hang on the outside as it did in days of yore, and the impulse to do a good turn had not aged with time, nor the feeling that to be poor, is no crime against God or man. No bitterness remains. Of those who sought their destruction, they will say that they were the victims [of] an inordinate and misguided ambition. To friends they talk freely of the past, modestly giving the facts and leaving embellishment to others. They are content with their lot and owe no man a penny.

Charlie[36] Marlow, now 72 years of age and a well-preserved man, lives at 910 1/2 East Adams Street, Glendale, California, where with his wife, they have lived for ten years. Their children, Marguerite, Alpha, Georgia, Charles and Stella, all of whom are married, are scattered, two living in Montrose, Colorado, three in Glendale, California, and one in Oakland, California.[37] He is comfortably fixed, and with his wife who shared with [him] all of the sorrows of earlier days as well as the joys of the present, is travelling down the "Western Slope" hand in hand, "pals" in the truest sense of the word.[38]

George Marlow, now 74 years young, with his wife, Lilly, lives in Ouray, Colorado, and jointly look back over more that half a century of their lives with pride, as man and wife. They saw the "dark" side together and played the game of life clear to the high standards of their ideals. They have little of this world's goods, but enough and some to spare to the "downs and outs" that seem to deserve. No one asked them for help

[36] After spelling the name consistently as "Charley" throughout the book, Rathmell inexplicably spells it "Charlie" on the last two pages.

[37] Rathmell here names five of Charley's children, but gives the homes of six. Actually Charley and Emma Marlow raised seven children: Marguerite (Maggie), Alpha, Charles, Mattie, James, Georgia, and Stella. Ellie, the twin of Alpha, died in infancy (1890 U. S. Census; 1910 U. S. Census; Ledbetter, *Ordeal*, 168).

[38] Charley Marlow, aged eighty-three, died at his son's home near Los Angeles on January 19, 1941, the fifty-second anniversary of that fateful fight at Dry Creek, Young County, Texas. His wife Emma survived him only a few months. They are buried together at Forest Lawn Cemetery, Pasadena, California (Ledbetter, *Ordeal*, 165).

that ever left empty-handed. But above all, they are happy—happy in the thought that although in the past they had enemies, that today they are at peace with the world. Their children, Myrtle, Elisha, Dottie, Barney, Anna and Minnie, all of whom are married,[39] and, as much settled in life as the old folks ever were, with a heritage of honesty, integrity and hospitality to draw from that will never cease while memory lasts.[40]

Everything stated in the foregoing pages is a fact and susceptible of proof at this date. The records of the courts of Young County, Texas, and the records of the federal court from the Northern District of Texas, taken together, will verify every statement made in this book relative to the lives of the Marlow brothers in Texas. The events relating to the lives of the Marlow brothers in Colorado can likewise be verified. C. W. ("Doc") Shores, who figured in some of the Colorado history lives in Denver, Colorado, Post Office Box 868; Judge W. R. Kincaid lives in Ouray, Colorado; the writer of this history, William Rathmell, lives in Ouray, Colorado; any of these men will answer proper questions relative to the life of the Marlow brothers in Colorado. We know of our own knowledge that the Marlow brothers were honest, industrious, hospitable men; that they would do any honorable thing to avoid trouble; we know also that when trouble was forced on them, that they dared to maintain their rights at any hazard necessary to accomplish this end; in short, we know that they were devoted to the law, order and the institutions of our country, and that Ouray County, Colorado, suffered a distinct loss when Charlie Marlow moved away. So, with one accord, we say: "LONG LIVE THE MARLOW BROTHERS."

[39] George and Lillian Marlow had nine children, three of whom died young (1900 U. S. Census).

[40] After his retirement, George and Lillian lived in Denver for a number of years. When she died in 1936 he went to Grand Junction, Colorado, and stayed with his daughter, Anna Jane (Mrs. Clyde V. Hallenbeck). He passed on at the age of ninety on July 5, 1945, and was buried beside his wife at Crown Hill Cemetery, Denver (*Montrose Daily Press*, July 5, 1945; Ledbetter, *Ordeal*, 165).

A few years after the old man's death, his daughter, Mrs. C. V. Hallenbeck, and her contractor husband were interviewed by C. L. Sonnichsen. They said that in his declining years the old man had many friends, including a number of young people to whom he was affectionately known as "Uncle George." With the attack on Pearl Harbor in 1941, many of his young friends went off to war. One, a fighter pilot in the Pacific, kept up a correspondence. "Once he wrote: 'When I see them coming, I just imagine you sitting beside me and I have no fear.' 'Uncle George' carried that letter under the sweat band of his hat for a long time. He couldn't see the words, but he liked to have other people read it to him" (Sonnichsen, *I'll Die Before I'll Run*, 204–5).

Bibliography

Books:

Adams, Ramon F. *Burs Under the Saddle: A Second Look at Books and Histories of the West.* Norman: University of Oklahoma Press, 1964.

———. *More Burs Under the Saddle: Books and Histories of the West.* Norman: University of Oklahoma Press, 1979.

———. *Six-Guns and Saddle Leather: A Bibliography of Books and Pamphlets on Western Outlaws and Gunmen.* Norman: University of Oklahoma Press, 1969.

———. *The Adams One-Fifty: A CheckList of the 150 Most Important Books on Western Outlaws and Lawmen.* Austin, Tex.: Jenkins Publishing Company, 1976.

Blair, Edward. *Leadville: Colorado's Magic City.* Boulder, Colo.: Pruett Publishing Company, 1980.

Brown, Robert L. *An Empire of Silver: A History of the San Juan Silver Rush.* Caldwell, Idaho: Caxton Printers, 1968.

———. *Ghost Towns of the Colorado Rockies.* Caldwell, Idaho: Caxton Printers, 1968.

Browning, James A. *The Western Reader's Guide.* Stillwater, Okla.: Barbed Wire Press, 1992.

Bryan, Howard. *Wildest of the West: True Tales of a Frontier Town on the Santa Fe Trail.* Santa Fe, N.M.: Clear Light Publishers, 1988.

Chrisman, Harry E. *Fifty Years on the Owl Hoot Trail: Jim Herron, the First Sheriff of No Man's Land, Oklahoma Territory.* Chicago: Sage Books, 1969.

Crouch, Carrie J. *A History of Young County, Texas.* Austin, Tex.: Texas State Historical Association, 1956.

DeArment, Robert K. *Bat Masterson: The Man and the Legend.* Norman: University of Oklahoma Press, 1979.

Farber, James. *Texans With Guns.* San Antonio, Tex.: Naylor Company, 1950.

Fehrenbach, T. R. *Fire and Blood: A History of Mexico.* New York: Macmillan Publishing Company, 1973.

Halsell, H. H. *Cowboys and Cattleland: Memories of a Frontier Cowboy.* Nashville, Tenn.: Parthenon Press, 1937.

Hendricks, George D. *The Bad Man of the West.* San Antonio, Tex.: Naylor Company, 1941.

Holloway, Carroll C. *Texas Gun Lore.* San Antonio, Tex.: Naylor Company, 1951.

Horton, Thomas F. *History of Jack County: Being Accounts of Pioneer Times, Excerpts From County Records, Indian Stories, Biographical Sketches, and Interesting Events.* Jacksboro, Tex.: Gazette Print, n.d.

Huffines, Alan C. *A Pilgrim Shadow.* Austin, Tex.: Eakin Press, 2001.

Hunter, J. Marvin, ed. *The Trail Drivers of Texas.* Austin, Tex.: University of Texas Press, 1985.

Jessen, Kenneth. *Colorado Gunsmoke: True Stories of Outlaws and Lawmen on the Colorado Frontier.* Boulder, Colo.: Pruett Publishing Company, 1986.

Ledbetter, Barbara A. Neal. *Fort Belknap Frontier Saga: Indians, Negroes and Anglo-Americans on the Texas Frontier.* Burnet, Tex.: Eakin Press, 1982.

———. *Marlow Brothers Ordeal, 1888–1892: 138 Days of Hell in Graham on the Texas Frontier.* Graham, Tex.: Lavender Books, 1991.

Lockwood, Frank C. *The Apache Indians.* Lincoln: University of Nebraska Press, 1987.

Look, Al. *Unforgettable Characters of Western Colorado.* Boulder, Colo.: Pruett Press, 1966.

Miller, Nyle H. and Joseph W. Snell. *Why the West Was Wild: A Contemporary Look at the Antics of Some Highly Publicized Kansas Cowtown Personalities.* Topeka: Kansas State Historical Society, 1963.

Miller, Rick. *Bounty Hunter.* Austin, Tex.: Creative Publishing Company, 1988.

Morgan, E. Buford. *The Wichita Mountains: Ancient Oasis of the Prairie.* Waco, Tex.: Texian Press, 1973.

Morris, John Miller. *A Private in the Texas Rangers: A. T. Miller of Company B, Frontier Battalion.* College Station, Tex.: Texas A&M University Press, 2001.

National Cyclopedia of American Biography: Being the History of the United States. New York: James T. White & Company, 1896.

Nye, W. S. *Carbine and Lance: The Story of Old Fort Sill*. Norman: University of Oklahoma Press, 1937.

Paine, Albert Bigelow. *Captain Bill McDonald, Texas Ranger: A Story of Frontier Reform*. New York: J. J. Little & Ives Company, 1909.

Pingenot, Ben E. *Siringo*. College Station, Tex.: Texas A & M University Press, 1989.

Raine, William MacLeod. *Famous Sheriffs and Western Outlaws*. Garden City, N.Y.: Doubleday, Doran & Company, 1929.

———, and Will C. Barnes. *Cattle*. Garden City, N.Y.: Doubleday, Doran and Company, Inc., 1930.

Rathmell, Ruth. *Of Record and Reminiscence—Ouray and Silverton*. Ouray, Colo.: Ouray County Plaindealer and Herald, 1976.

Raymond, Dora Neill. *Captain Lee Hall of Texas*. Norman: University of Oklahoma Press, 1940.

Rockwell, Wilson, ed. *Memoirs of a Lawman*. Denver, Colo.: Sage Books, 1962.

Sandoz, Mari. *The Cattlemen, From the Rio Grande Across the Far Marias*. New York: Hastings House, 1958.

Sarah Platt Decker Chapter, D.A.R. *Pioneers of the San Juan Country*. Colorado Springs, Colo.: Out West Printing and Stationery Company, 1942.

Shirk, George H. *Oklahoma Place Names*. Norman: University of Oklahoma Press, 1965.

Shirley, Glenn. *The Fighting Marlows, Men Who Wouldn't Be Lynched*. Fort Worth, Tex.: Texas Christian University Press, 1994.

———. *Toughest of Them All*. Albuquerque, N.M.: University of New Mexico Press, 1953.

Siringo, Charles A. *Riata and Spurs: The Story of a Lifetime Spent in the Saddle as Cowboy and Ranger*. Boston and New York: Houghton Mifflin Company, 1927.

Sonnichsen, C. L. *I'll Die Before I'll Run: The Story of the Great Feuds of Texas*. New York: Harper & Brothers, 1951.

Sullivan, W. J. L. *Twelve Years in the Saddle for Law and Order on the Frontiers of Texas*. Austin, Tex.: Von Boeckmann-Jones Company, Printers, 1909.

Thrapp, Dan L. *Encyclopedia of Frontier Biography*. Glendale, Calif.: Arthur H. Clark, 1988.

Tise, Sammy. *Texas County Sheriffs.* Albuquerque, N.M.: Oakwood Printing, 1989.

Tyler, Ron, ed. *New Handbook of Texas.* Austin: Texas State Historical Association, 1996.

United States Reports, Vol. 144. *Cases Adjudged in the Supreme Court at October Term, 1891.* New York: Banks & Brothers, Law Publishers, 1892.

Webb, Walter Prescott. *The Texas Rangers: A Century of Frontier Defense.* Boston and New York: Houghton Mifflin Company, 1935.

Wolle, Muriel Sibell. *Stampede to Timberline: The Ghost Towns and Mining Camps of Colorado.* Denver, Colo.: Artcraft Press, 1949.

Articles:

Bork, A. W. and Glenn G. Boyer. "The O.K. Corral Fight at Tombstone: A Footnote by Kate Fisher." *Arizona and the West,* Spring 1977.

Hartley, William B. "The Men Who Wouldn't Be Lynched." *True Western Adventures,* August 1959.

Johnson, Edward W. "Ted." "Deputy Marshal Johnson Breaks a Long Silence." *True West,* January–February 1980.

Patten, Josephine. "He Killed a Heap of Men." *Old West,* Winter 1966.

Raine, William MacLeod. "The Fighting Marlows." *Empire Magazine, The Denver Post,* June 14, 1953.

———. "Texas as Was." *Frontier Stories,* January 1928.

Shirley, Glenn. "Hell Riders of the Brazos." *Western Aces,* April 1943.

Stanley, Samuel. "A Desperate Escape." *Real West,* December 1986.

Taylor, Nat M. "Story of the Marlow Boys." *True West,* January-February 1962.

Newspapers and Periodicals:

Abilene (Kansas) *Chronicle*, July 13, 1871.

El Paso Times, May 2, 1896.

Fort Worth Daily Gazette, January 16, 21, 22, 29, 30, 1889.

Galveston Daily News, January 23, 25, 1889.

Graham Leader, July 26, September 6, October 11, December 20, 27, 1888; January 3,17, 24, 31, February 28, March 28, 1889; January 23, October 1, 8, 29, November 5, 26, 1890; April 22, November 25, 1891.

Montrose Daily Press, July 5, 1945; September 15, 1965.

National Detective Review (Wichita, Kansas), April 1889.

Rocky Mountain News, December 19, 1891; July 16, 1939.

San Antonio Daily Express, January 16, 23, February 17, 1889; September 27, 1891.

Unpublished Material:

Browning, James A. "Violence Was No Stranger, Volume II."

Colorado WPA Writers Program. "Tall Tales and Anecdotes." File No. 23, "The Marlow Brothers at Ridgway." Western History Dept., Denver Public Library, Denver, Colorado.

Crouch, Mrs. Carrie J., letter to E. P. Lamborn, October 31, 1927. E. P. Lamborn Collection, Kansas State Historical Society, Topeka, Kansas.

Ernst, Robert R., Research Consultant, U. S. Marshal's Service, letters to R. K. DeArment, January 10, 1991; April 12, 1991.

Kennon, Jan, Wilbarger County, Texas, deputy, letter to R. K. DeArment, March 27, 1991.

Knight, George A., letter to W. H. King, February 21, 1890. C. L. Sonnichsen Papers, Special Collections Department, UTEP Library, The University of Texas at El Paso.

Malden, R. R. "Sheriffs of Colorado Counties, 1858–1958." Colorado Historical Society, Denver, Colorado.

"Memoirs of W. R. Durham, Jr., as given to Aulton Durham. August 18, 1936." Panhandle-Plains Historical Museum, Canyon, Texas.

Rathmell, Mrs. Ruth D. letter to Mrs. Alys Freeze, circa 1967. Western History Dept., Denver Public Library, Denver, Colorado.

Siringo, Charles A., letters to E. P. Lamborn, April 12, 1924; February 28, 1925. E. P. Lamborn Collection, Kansas State Historical Society, Topeka, Kansas.

Smith, Wilene, Genealogy of Clinton Rutherford.

———. Genealogy of Verner Wilkinson.

Sonnichsen, C. L., Papers, Special Collections Department, UTEP Library, The University of Texas at El Paso.

Government Documents:

Application for Requisition of Charles Marlow for murder, dated May 19, 1891 (File No. 561), Adjutant General's Files, Texas State Library and Archives, Austin, Texas.

Criminal Case Files from 1879, U.S. District Court, Northern District of Texas, Abilene Division: Case #234, *The United States v. George*

Marlow; Case #235, *The United States v. Boone Marlow;* Case #236, *The United States v. Epp Marlow;* Case #238, *The United States v. Alf Marlow, et al;* Case #239, *The United States v. Alf Marlow;* Case #246, *The United States v. Charles Marlow;* Case #263, *The United States v. Eugene Logan, et al.*

True Bill of Indictment against Charley Marlow for murder, dated August 10, 1889 (File no. 386). Adjutant General's Files, Texas State Library and Archives, Austin, Texas.

United States Census Reports: 1850, 1860, 1900, 1910.

United States Reports, Vol. 144: Cases Adjudged in the Supreme Court at October Term 1891, *Logan v. United States.*

Index